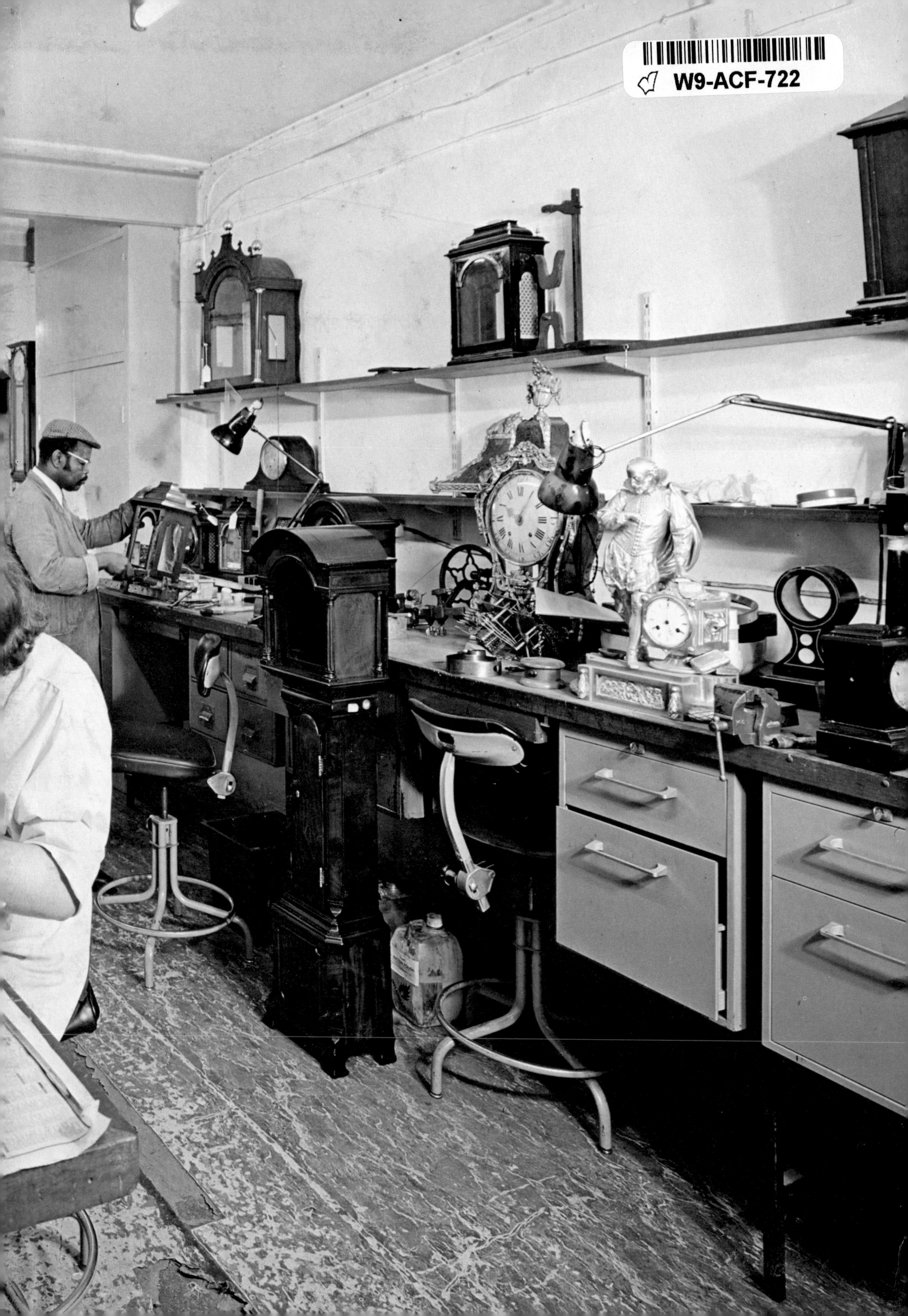

The World's Great
CLOCKS & WATCHES

The World's Great
CLOCKS & WATCHES

Cedric Jagger

Hamlyn

London · New York · Sydney · Toronto

To my wife
CHRISTINE
with my love and gratitude for her skilled
and unstinting help with the preparation of this
book

endpapers
A London dealer's workshop. It is not easy to find a dealer with such expert
facilities of his own. Aubrey Brocklehurst, London.

title pages
See page 106.

Published by
The Hamlyn Publishing Group Limited
London · New York · Sydney · Toronto
Astronaut House, Feltham, Middlesex, England
© Copyright The Hamlyn Publishing Group Limited 1977

ISBN 0 600 34027 9

Printed in England by
Jarrold & Sons Limited, Norwich

Acknowledgments

A.C.L., Brussels 21 top and bottom; Antique Collectors' Club, Woodbridge
241; Ashmolean Museum, Oxford 89 top, 96 top and bottom, 97 right;
Bayerisches Museum, Munich 92 top, 159 top and bottom; Bibliotheque
Nationale, Paris 16; British Museum, London 14, 31, 41, 50, 52, 53, 54, 58,
59, 68, 70, 71, 73, 74, 76 left and right, 78 left, 79 top and bottom, 80 top and
bottom, 81, 82, 83, 84 left, 86, 88, 89 bottom, 91, 101 left and right, 105 top
and bottom, 110, 119, 121, 122, 124, left, 125, 127, 132, 143 right, 147 right,
158 left, 162 left and right, 173, 175, 182, 186 left, 202, 203, 215, 216 left and
right, 217, 218, 219 left and right, 220 top and bottom, 221, 222 top and
bottom, 223 left and right, 224, 225, 227, 230; Eric Bruton, Widmer End 8,
30, 236 bottom; J. Allan Cash, London 17; Copenhagen Town Hall 49 top
and bottom; Glasgow Herald and Evening Times 69; Clockmakers' Company Museum, Guildhall, London 34 right, 65 left, 72 left and right, 75 left
and right, 98 bottom, 144 top and bottom, 170, 171 left and right, 193 top;
Hamlyn Group Picture Library endpapers, 2–3, 102 left, 226, 228 left and
right; Hamlyn Group – John R. Freeman & Co, 13 right, 29 left and right,
46, 57 bottom, 78 right, 93 left and right, 95, 97 left, 98 top, 102 right, 103
bottom, 104 top, 108 left and right, 109 left and right, 111 top and bottom,
112 bottom, 113 top and bottom, 114 left and right, 115, 116 left, 117 left and
right, 120, 123 left, 126, 128 bottom, 129, 120, 131, 147 left, 150 left, 155
bottom, 160, 163, 164 right, 165, 178 top and bottom, 179 top and bottom,
180 top, 181 left and right, 183 right, 184, 185, 187 top and bottom, 188, 189
left and right, 190 top, centre and bottom, 191, 194, 197 left, 199 bottom, 201
top, 205, 209, 210 top, 211, 212 top, 213 left and right, 231 bottom, 235 top,
bottom left and bottom right, 242 right, 248 right, 249 left, 250 bottom;
Hamlyn Group – Hypsos 135 left, 143 left; Hamlyn Group – Marcus Taylor
195; Herzog Anton Ulrich-Museum, Brunswick 92 bottom; Hessisches
Landesmuseum, Kassel 84 right, 85 left and right, 87 left, 90 top; Historisches Uhren-Museum, Wuppertal 12 right; Cedric Jagger 34 left, 37, 51,
55 left and right, 56 top, 100, 124 right, 183 left, 233 bottom; Jurg Stuker
Gallery, Berne 208; A. F. Kersting, London 67; Kunsthistorisches Museum,
Vienna 90 bottom; Edward Leigh, Cambridge 198; Merseyside County
Museums, Liverpool 150 right, 152; Museen der Stadt Vienna 142 left;
Museum of Fine Arts, Boston 10; Museum of the History of Science, Oxford
25 left, 155 top; National Maritime Museum, London 172 top and bottom,
174 left, 177; Nederlands Goud, Zilver en Klokkenmuseum, Utrecht 60;
Partridge, London 156, 157 left and right; Derek de Solla Price Yale University, Newhaven, 26; Rapho, Paris 25 right; Richmond Reference Library,
London 234; Rijksmuseum voor de Geschiedenis der Natuurwetenschap-
pen, Leiden 136; T. R. Robinson, Bristol 66 top; Science Museum, London
11, 12 left, 13 left, 22 left and right, 23 top, 62 right, 63 left, 66 bottom, 135
right, 138, 145, 176; Ronald Sheridan, London 64 left and right, 65 right;
Smithsonian Institution, Washington 62 left; Spectrum, London 23 bottom,
233 top; Strike One, London 142 right, 199 top, 201 bottom; Victoria Art
Gallery, Bath 149 right, Vienna Clock Museum 161 top left and top right;
Wallace Collection, London 137, 139, 140 top and bottom, 141, 146;
Zwinger Museum, Dresden 87 right.

The photographs on pages 123 right, 148, 158 right, 168 top and bottom are
reproduced by Gracious Permission of Her Majesty the Queen.

The remaining photographs were taken for the Hamlyn Group by John
Webb.

Contents

Preface

While naturally I hope that the specialist in anti-quarian horology may find one or two features, at least, to interest him in this book, I have neverthe-less assumed that the majority of its readers will be contemplating the subject, if not for the very first time, then certainly at a very early stage in their developing interest in it. Twenty-five years ago I found myself in precisely that situation and, by the sheerest good fortune, able for a time to indulge my taste for antique timepieces – thanks to the excep-tional kindness of its original owner – with the Ilbert Collection. It seemed to me then, and I still hold to the belief, that it is supremely important to start with a solid diet of the best horological prac-tice, both technically and artistically, and thoroughly to assimilate this before coming to grips with second or third rate work, of which there will always be an abundance in any era. It is of first importance, in other words, not to risk letting the inferior cloud one's judgement before proper stan-dards have been established with which it can be compared.

I have therefore made no attempt – as seems customary in books of this nature – to 'spread' the illustrations over as wide a spectrum of different artisans' work as possible. On the contrary, I have deliberately allotted anything up to half a dozen illustrations to the work of one craftsman, if he happens to be a member of that select group of master horologists of the past who are household names to the initiates of the present day. From David Ramsay, first Master of the Worshipful Company of Clockmakers early in the seventeenth century, to Abraham-Louis Breguet, the French genius almost two centuries later, there are certain illustrious names that will become important to the aspiring antiquarian horologist, whether he shops for his specimens in the world's great auc-tion rooms or its street markets, and whether or not he ever owns an example by any of them.

There is a precedent of a kind for this somewhat arbitrary approach, in that the Master, Wardens and Court of Assistants of the Worshipful Com-pany have, by the terms of their Royal Charter, a traditional power – albeit nowadays no longer exercised – to make periodic inspections of the horological workshops within the geographical limits of the Company's responsibility, for the sole purpose of seeking out and destroying any work not attaining those standards of quality and craftsmanship which the Charter requires it to uphold. Side by side with such harsh discipline, however, the Company for almost the last two hundred years has made a practice of acquiring the best examples of the work of the craft that have come within its reach, whether these were bequeathed, donated, loaned or purchased. It has also assembled the best library that it could find over the years, and this by no means restricted to works in the English language. The original pur-pose both of the collection and the library was to educate members of the craft and show them, by example as well as by theoretical exposition, exactly how the practice of the very best of their contemporaries was developing. That both the col-lection and the library have been continuously available, except in times of national emergency, for the aesthetic and intellectual enjoyment of a much wider audience for more than a century now is due to the public-spirited attitude of the Com-pany and the generosity of the Corporation of London, who have consistently provided suitable accommodation for the purpose adjacent to Guildhall Library; and it is a bonus without which London would be appreciably the poorer.

I have a personal debt of gratitude to the Clockmakers' Company, and this seems an appropriate place to voice it. Although I have been fascinated by old clocks and watches for many years, my formal career, all thirty-odd years of it,

6

centred upon the chemical industry. I could not believe my good fortune when, in 1972, I was offered the option of terminating that career on preferential terms and ten years in advance of normal retirement. Privately I had long held the view that a career which throughout followed the same direction was unduly restrictive of human versatility.

Two years later the Clockmakers' Company invited me to take up a part-time consultancy appointment as its Assistant Curator, specifically to look after the collection and to deal with enquiries, requests for photography, the displays, conservation and so forth. I shall always be grateful to the Company for placing such a very fulfilling occupation in my hands. It is partly as a result of having worked with the collection for more than two years now that has led me to the conclusion that it has been under-illustrated in horological books by comparison with other well-known specialist collections in the same field. To some extent I have tried to rectify this omission here.

As a result of this same appointment I have had both the pleasure and the privilege of working closely with a library staff who must rank among the most expert in the world. Guildhall Library specialises, as one would expect, in London – its history, topography, business life, inhabitants and so on. It also has custody of a number of unrelated specialist collections which have been deposited with it over the years and which are, in themselves, of substantial value and interest. The Clockmakers' Company library is but one among many. It follows that there is among the library staff a fund of knowledge on a wide spectrum of subjects, all of which they will willingly share with the multitude of researchers using the Reading Room each day. They are quite unstinting in dealing with questions ranging from the trivial to the most erudite, unfailing in their good humour and, in my own experience, quite without parallel anywhere else in the world of books. To them all, from the Librarian – who is, incidentally, my nominal Curator since he is responsible for the building, services and general staffing – to the most junior attendant, I offer my thanks for all the help I have so consistently received at their hands, and especially while compiling this book.

Although professionally engaged in the museum field for such a short time, I have for years past admired the competence and enjoyed the help, and often enough the friendship, of those in our national museums concerned with the collections relating to timekeeping. In preparing this book I have had inevitably to rely upon their close cooperation over photographs, and they have been meticulous in double-checking whenever there has been any doubt as to exactly what was required. I would particularly thank, in this connection, the staff concerned at the British Museum, the National Maritime Museum, the Science Museum, and the Victoria and Albert Museum, as well as the many helpful people in the overseas museums from which I have also drawn material for the book.

The Antiquarian Horological Society, which is devoted to the needs of students and collectors of old timekeepers, is mentioned elsewhere in this book. Here I would simply express my thanks for its permission to make use, quite freely, of its large photographic library, known as the Lloyd Collection after the late H. Alan Lloyd who assembled it. This is a wonderful horological archive.

I have tried to avoid identifying individuals by name when expressing my thanks because it is so easy to omit someone by mistake, thereby quite inadvertently giving offence. That I omit the names of private collectors is for the additional reason of security. There is a sprinkling of treasures from such sources in these pages, and I am duly grateful that I have been permitted to include them.

Finally, however, there is one person whom I can and will identify. My wife's secretarial and editorial skills, intelligently, devotedly and unstintingly applied to the manuscript of this book over a period of months have been of incalculable worth. I wish I could find words to express my gratitude.

In the Beginning

Evolution is generally associated with living creatures, and though it is not usually thought of in connection with such familiar everyday objects as clocks and watches, it is by no means a new concept. As far back as 1931 the collector and enthusiast J. Drummond Robertson wrote what has come to be regarded as a classic work, *The Evolution of Clockwork*. It broke much new ground at the time, including revelations about the principles and practice of time-measurement in Japan which underlined how very much they differed from those current in the West.

Just as evolution in nature affects not only the animals themselves but also their habitat, so in the human world it touches man's most sophisticated possessions. But while natural evolution is infinitely, laboriously, imperceptibly slow, where machines are concerned change is often almost instantaneous. It was Ralph Waldo Emerson who remarked that 'if a man . . . make a better mousetrap than his neighbour, though he build his house in the woods, the world will make a beaten path to his door.' In the case of time-measurement, certainly, innovation has usually led to fairly rapid change.

It is as well to recognise that time-measurement is both an art and a science, and for a proper understanding, it is best to appreciate them side by side. They seem so far to have passed through two main phases of development, and there are clear signs that they may be on the verge of entering a third. The first and earliest phase is still only imperfectly understood; it might be said to extend from the dimmest recesses of ancient history almost to the end of the Middle Ages. During this period, the time-measuring instruments in use were wholly non-mechanical although at some point within the same span of time some unknown genius conceived the fundamental elements of the mechanical clock. This, when it appeared, seems

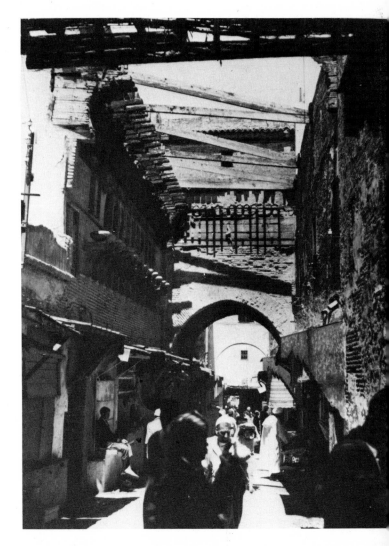

This monumental Arab water clock dates from 1357, when it was built by the Emir Abou Inane at Fez in Morocco. All that remains are the thirteen great bronze bells resting on carved wood brackets below the twelve windows through which formerly automata would have appeared. Of the mechanism nothing but part of the transmission has survived.

8

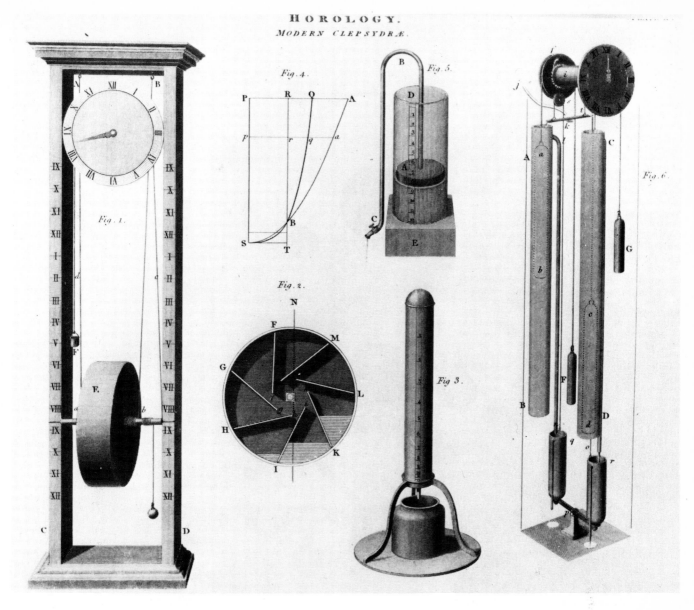

Rees's *Cyclopaedia* published in 1819–20 was the finest reference work to early nineteenth-century technology ever produced in English. This Plate from it demonstrates the continuing preoccupation up to quite recent times with the concept of the clepsydra.

to have burst upon the scene suddenly; but whether this is indeed what happened, or whether some links in the chain of events have not yet been uncovered, is still not certain.

For at least the ensuing six centuries the continuing process of invention, stimulated by evolving human needs, refined and improved the techniques of mechanical timekeeping. Most of the basic inventions in the field had been made by the end of the eighteenth century; and the peak of precision craftsmanship was certainly reached in Victorian times. As early as 1800 it was possible to acquire a pocket watch with a far greater built-in accuracy than the average modern wristwatch, and the principles of self-winding had been used in the pedometer. The ordinary domestic clock had been all but perfected a century earlier.

It may be argued that electrical horology, springing from the inventions of Alexander Bain in the 1840s, really constitutes a third phase of evolution. On the other hand, however, while electrical systems have run alongside mechanical ones for decades now, they have never superseded them. Again, in many cases electricity has been used simply as a power source to drive a pendulum or a balance, and the main transmission remains mechanical. Finally, of course, it would have been little short of miraculous if the Industrial Revolution, affecting virtually every aspect of people's lives, had not produced at least one viable alternative to the mechanical methods for regulating their day-to-day activities which had existed for so long.

The development of time-measuring methods has broadly paralleled man's own evolution. Coarser, non-mechanical means coincided with a life-style largely governed by natural phenomena – the rotation of crops and seasons, day and night, and so forth – where there can have been no particular sense of urgency or immediacy and where errors of an hour or more in twenty-four were of no

great moment. Even when mechanical systems were at last introduced, to aid the proper observance of religious offices, their initial accuracy, which was subject to then unknown forces such as friction, was not at all impressive, even though it was far better than anything that had gone before.

Necessity, it is said, is the mother of invention. As the process of civilisation gathered momentum so also did the efficiency of man's time-measuring. Two examples of this will illustrate the principle. By the beginning of the eighteenth century, losses at sea from shipwreck and other natural hazards, not to mention avoidable diseases such as scurvy, had become so great that the British Parliament was stung into offering a considerable cash prize for a solution to the problem of exact navigation. In essence the difficulty was that, to calculate with any precision a ship's position when out of sight of land, the captain had to have at his disposal a timekeeper which would function not only despite the motion of the vessel – and technically this was not then possible – but also with predictable accuracy, maintaining its performance throughout what, in those days, might well be a lengthy voyage. It took half a century to find answers to the complex questions this provoked; but it gave Britain a lead in chronometry which, when based on mechanical systems, has never been surpassed.

For a second example, it is only necessary to turn, once again, to the Industrial Revolution. The advent of railways in Britain rendered obsolete, almost overnight, the grid of local times throughout the country which had sufficed during the coaching era. Occupancy of the permanent way in accordance with pre-published timetables, and the absolute necessity of avoiding accidents caused by misplaced trains, enforced upon the country a universal time system, as well as the means to measure it accurately. Also, the industrialisation of a hitherto agricultural work-force, more or less at the farmer's beck and call at any hour and governed only by the needs of crop or livestock, brought in its wake the concept of hours of work at the office or factory, and the need to arrive and depart to time. There was also, of course, a resulting rise in the wealth and independence of the worker, and this certainly provided much of the impetus towards mass-production, not least of clocks and watches. Where previously it was necessary to be fairly well-to-do to possess a clock, let alone a watch, such gradually became essentials and within the reach of all.

So we come to the present century, now in its final quarter. Mechanical time-measurement is still generally preferred, but for how much longer?

Arabian water clocks, like this medieval example by Al-Jazari, not only told the time but were entertaining on account of their theatrical complications and complex automata. Museum of Fine Arts, Boston.

This working reconstruction by P. N. Haward, D. R. Hill and C. Melling demonstrates clearly that complicated feats of hydraulic engineering – of which usually only remnants of the originals survive – were nonetheless thoroughly feasible. Science Museum, London.

The system is by no means perfect – not, certainly, in its everyday manifestations – so that error is still measured in seconds per day for the average clock or watch. Yet the techniques involved have probably reached their peak of perfection, certainly in economic terms. To make further demonstrable improvements in mechanical time-measurement would be so costly as to nullify the effort involved, since any resulting instruments would certainly be beyond the reach of the great mass of consumers. What happens next?

The twentieth-century equivalent of the earlier Industrial Revolution may well appear, when assessed by future historians, to be the enormous investment, mainly by the United States and the Soviet Union but also, in a smaller way, by many other nations, in aerospace research and exploration. Present indications are that, in the course of

The 'merkhet' (*top*) enabled early Egyptians to tell the time at night, and was also used in surveying. This example has an inscription attributing its ownership to Bes, who was an astronomer priest in Upper Egypt about 600 BC. It is of bronze inlaid with a gold-silver alloy. Science Museum, London.

above
'Destructive' timekeepers depending on the consumption of one or another commodity are found in a number of countries, and this Chinese dragon vessel measures the time passing by burning incense. The Japanese had a timekeeper working on the same principle but of different design. Historisches Uhren-Museum, Wuppertal.

time, it will bring as many beneficial changes in its wake, as a direct 'spin-off' from the highly specialised technologies developed over a wide range of fields, as did its predecessor. One of these, and invaluable in its original context, has been the extremely accurate guidance systems springing from succeeding generations of ever more sophisticated computers and, of course, from the ancillary time-measuring equipment. In all of these the basis has been electronics.

Electronic timekeepers for domestic use have been on the market for about a decade now, and manufacturers continue to develop newer and more attractive modules as each year passes. Consumers are rapidly becoming accustomed to the very functional illuminated display which is a recent feature of such equipment – the same applies to the pocket calculator, for instance – and there is much to be said for the direct readings thus obtained, by contrast with the need to interpret two hands against a dial whose legibility can vary greatly from one style to another, not to mention the problem of reading it in the dark.

But possibly the principal factor to be taken into consideration, as always, is the economic one. The manufacture of mechanical timekeepers is a labour-intensive industry; that of electronic timekeepers is not, or at least not to anything like the same extent. While there may remain, for a very few with both the money and the inclination, a top-price market for the best in mechanical timekeepers, it would be strange indeed if we were not at this moment witnessing the start of a third phase in the evolution of time-measuring systems, based on electronics, and a true system in the sense that it will completely supplant its predecessors.

The old adage that 'beauty is in the eye of the beholder' is nowhere more clearly demonstrated than among those enthusiasts who collect the instruments of time-measurement – and especially among those who have narrowed their enthusiasm to some small corner of what is indeed a wide field. It probably was not always so. While it was still possible, three or four decades ago, to acquire a fine seventeenth-century longcase clock for a modest outlay, it is inconceivable that anyone could have preferred, say, one of the early manifestations of mass-production. Now, of course, the most beautiful pieces judged by any conventional standard have priced themselves out of reach of any but the really rich; and today's enthusiasts have perforce to confer the accolade of beauty on what are often some of the ugliest machines imaginable. They do it with great gusto!

This is just one of the considerations that needs to be taken into account in trying to arrive at a definition of what constitutes a 'great' clock or watch. There are all sorts of standards which may be applied. Domestic clocks, for example, have always tended to follow, or at least to merge happily with, contemporary furniture design which in its turn, often enough, has clear associations with the architectural fashions of the period. It must follow then that the finest architectural periods have inevitably given rise to the best clocks; but is the reverse also true? The reader may contemplate, perhaps, the present-day enthusiasm for Art Nouveau and Art Deco in arriving at a conclusion.

Again there are those who insist that beauty and greatness together can be found in mechanical design – for example, in the relationships of the numbers of teeth on wheels and the leaves of pinions with which they engage; in the way wheels are 'crossed out', i.e. the care with which the spokes have been cut as well as their number; in the symmetry with which a clock or watch movement has been laid out and its various elements 'planted', i.e. positioned. There are many criteria which can be brought into play when judging clocks and watches from this viewpoint; the enthusiast-mechanic will extol the 'proportions' of, say, an escapement with all the verve and spirit of an admirer of classical sculpture.

So it is probably important for anybody taking an active acquisitive interest in time-measuring paraphernalia to decide for themselves, before get-

Sand glasses came in all sizes. Standing over thirteen inches high, this one measures a period of four hours, and was probably made in France before 1750 for use at sea. The frame is oak. Museum of the Worshipful Company of Clockmakers, Guildhall, London.

Another form of 'destructive' timekeeper, this eighteenth-century pewter oil clock from north Germany incorporates a glass reservoir equally graduated in hours from 8 p.m. to 7 a.m., the level of unburnt oil indicating the time. Such clocks, useful though they may have been at night, could hardly have been other than inaccurate, in view of the irregular shape of the reservoir. Science Museum, London.

ting too immersed in the study, the particular keystone of taste with which they are in sympathy, always accepting, of course, that their tastes will change over the years. This is inevitable since there are no hard-and-fast standards; but at least it is not without purpose to decide upon some such propositions as 'the Vienna Regulator of the late nineteenth century is the finest clock ever made' – or not, as the case may be – if only in order to set one's personal parameters, against which those objects that will be encountered in the course of pursuing the subject may be measured.

Earlier, the concept of evolution was considered in relation to living things and to the inanimate objects associated with them. There are also, of course, evolutionary tendencies in ideas, and, not least, in ideas about taste. The definition of the word 'great' as it appears in the title of this book, therefore, may be taken to be more relative to those particular developments in practical horology that have influenced subsequent mechanical and stylistic trends than to any catalogue of individual masterpieces which might, under one heading or another, qualify for that same overworked adjective. If in so doing, the book helps the reader to arrive at a personal, as well as satisfying,

determination of the meaning of 'great' in the context of horology, then its principal purpose will have been fulfilled.

There can be little doubt that the pace of modern civilisation continues to accelerate. As good an example of this as one could wish for is to be found in the realisation that, until not much more than two centuries ago, the clock was by far the most sophisticated machine invented by man. His achievements in technology during that period have been immense and, if you broaden the perspective – simply in the field of time-measurement – to encompass the dawn of civilisation, little short of miraculous.

But how did it all start? Life on this planet has always revolved round repetitive sequences of events based entirely upon natural phenomena by which, in a rough and ready manner, time can be measured. Admittedly the units were large: twelve hours (and subject to considerable variation) in the case of day and night, much longer if you consider the passage of the seasons (as well as much more liable to inaccuracy on the grand scale). The human stomach requires to be fuelled at relatively shorter intervals and must certainly have been used by primitive man as a rough and ready guide; it is in any case a more feasible, not to say reliable, method.

Nevertheless all this is reasoned supposition; supporting evidence is hard to find. The situation does not greatly improve when we move on from the earliest manifestations of civilisation – when, apart from the needs of agriculture and the

impulse of superstition, there was really little necessity to mark events in time anyway – to some point, probably centuries later, when man's innate intelligence enabled him to conceive of more artificial but, at the same time, more consistent methods of measuring off time. There is no clear-cut starting-point for the introduction of such techniques and certainly no finishing point; indeed, in some cases – for example, sundials and sand glasses – it is easy to find examples of their usage right to the present time, if only, in the latter instance, to boil the breakfast egg. This blurring of the edges between one style and another, between any particular type of time-measuring instrument and another, in general between the entry and exit of any stylistic or technical innovation, is typical of the whole history of horology. Thus at a much later period it is not uncommon to find an interval of several decades before the best usage of a metropolitan centre of clockmaking drawing upon a rich clientèle or substantial patronage, filtered down to the individual craftsmen working in the provinces of the same country. Certainly so far as man's first attempts to construct and use time-measuring apparatus are concerned, it is well-nigh impossible to encompass them within any chronological parameters.

If man was capable of utilising the regular recurrence of sunrise and sunset as a makeshift clock, then it can only have been a matter of course before he refined, by observation, his employment of the motions of heavenly bodies for timekeeping. The single most important instrument originating

left
Mary Queen of Scots' sand glass is probably the most famous instrument of its kind in the world. It is described on page 18. British Museum, London.

right
Portable sundials come in a variety of attractive designs, one of the less common being a cube with faces on all five exposed sides. National Maritime Museum, Greenwich.

below right
Michael Butterfield, who worked in Paris during the last quarter of the seventeenth century, designed a form of pocket dial which was much copied by other makers and is always described by his name. The adjustable gnomon carries a scale which is read against the bird's beak and must be set to the latitude of the place where the dial is being used. The back of a Butterfield dial always carries a list of principal cities with their relevant latitudes. National Maritime Museum, Greenwich.

below
Back of the Butterfield dial.

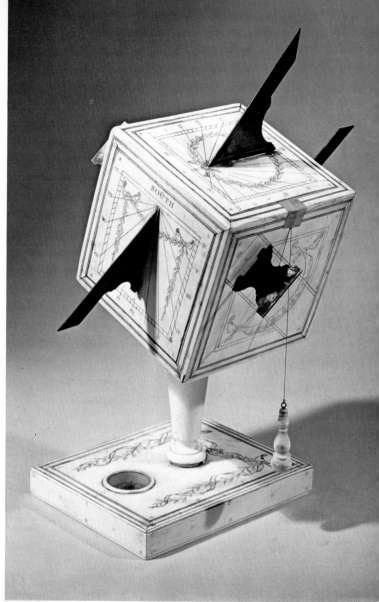

Islamic scientists are generally considered to have provided the link in scholarship between the classical and medieval worlds. In Islam, the sundial aided Muslims not only in determining times for prayer, but also in finding the direction of the Holy City of Mecca which must be faced at such times. This earliest known portable Islamic sundial is dated 1159 AD. Bibliothèque Nationale, Paris.

from this development was, of course, the sundial; but it may be helpful first to mention other forms of apparatus for marking the passage of time which were neither so long-lasting nor so scientifically well founded, even though they were still in use long after the introduction of this most important of the non-mechanical timekeepers.

The rate at which a flame will burn down a candle or smoulder along a knotted rope can obviously be related to the passage of time. Techniques like this – so called 'destructive' timekeepers – certainly existed in the borient, and there are quite elaborate examples from China, often based on the rate of consumption of joss sticks or incense. In one arrangement, the Chinese 'dragon boat', this system can even be made to sound an alarm at predetermined intervals. At a later period, lamps burning oil from a graduated glass reservoir became fashionable.

Equally ingenious was man's utilisation of fire's opposing element – water. The water clock – called by the Greeks the clepsydra, and sometimes known by this name in other countries – occurs in several versions based either on the concept that water can escape at a predetermined rate from a perforated container, or that a similar container, placed upon the surface of a body of water, will fill up at a predetermined rate and eventually sink. Elaborated versions of these principles, enabling time to be read off by a moving pointer against a dial, or by such means as the sounding of gongs, are also on record. Water clocks probably first appeared in Egypt, from where they were introduced into Greece and used extensively during the times of the Greek and Roman Empires; and there are quite a number of references to them in classical literature.

In considering clepsydrae, however, a few cautionary words are not out of context. Nobody would be so foolish as to dispute their existence in antiquity, but no less an authority than Courtenay Ilbert – the world's leading collector of clocks, watches and the like until his death in 1956, when his enormous collection was acquired by the British Museum – used to say that, throughout a lifetime of collecting his treasures all over the world, he was never offered a water clock of whose genuineness he was convinced. It is also a fact that for years a firm in Birmingham was quite openly manufacturing 'water clocks', each bearing a spurious date, and catalogued by the maker as reproductions, but that subsequently these have not infrequently been passed off as genuine by unscrupulous antique dealers. Even if a genuine clepsydra was encountered, it might not be recognised by the uninitiated. There is, for example, one in the collection belonging to the Worshipful Company of Clockmakers, of London, which is simply an unmarked copper bowl with a small hole in the base. The all-revealing detail is that this tiny hole is bushed in gold, to prevent the water acting upon the copper so as eventually to restrict the inflow. The bowl comes from Ceylon, and in use was certainly floated upon a surface of water, into which it sinks after about twenty-five minutes. It is impossible to date on the basis of presentday knowledge.

Another 'elemental' device which measured flow – in this case, of sand – probably arrived on the scene rather later than the water clock, but survives in use to this day. Sand glasses – sometimes called hour glasses, but incorrectly, because they can be constructed to measure any interval of time – were used in the Royal Navy to time the duty watch right up to 1839, as well as in the House of Commons to time divisions. The 'sermon glass' in church was used by preachers in the sixteenth century and later, and there still exist sets of glasses – usually four in number, all in one frame –

A general view of the astronomical observatory at Jaipur
constructed by the Maharaja Sawai Jai Singh II
(1686–1743).

This seventeenth-century treatise by a French monk went through five editions between 1641 and 1701, and treated the subject of dialling with considerable erudition.

each measuring a different interval, sometimes compounds of fifteen minutes, which must have had numerous domestic uses.

Of this latter version there exists a particularly elegant example in the same Ilbert Collection in the British Museum to which reference has already been made. The four glasses are arranged between circular ebony plates with moulded borders, separated by turned baluster pillars, the whole contained within a cylindrical leather case with cover. The top and base have recessed panels painted with the arms of Scotland and France. Ilbert purchased this beautiful object unseen: it had been hidden for years in a jeweller's safe that was bombed during the Second World War, and for the contents of which he offered a lump sum. At the time, the significance of the very individual monogram – 'M' for Mary entwined with the Greek 'ϕ' or 'phi', representing King Francis II of France, the Queen's first husband – escaped him, and it was not until some months later that he woke in the early hours of the morning, suddenly

recollecting where he had seen the same monogram previously. Waiting only to put on his dressing gown, it is said, he stumbled out of his house, found a taxi and drove straight to the private home of a very celebrated museum director, whom he unceremoniously awoke. They both then, taking the waiting taxi, drove to the museum, to which they managed to obtain access. Their researches there, at about 3 a.m., are said to have confirmed the provenance of the sand glass. The monogram, in fact, appears on a small cannon, reputedly the property of the Scottish Queen.

The contrivances which have so far been described, at least in their most sophisticated forms, appear to have been current in those parts of the world which we now call the Near and Middle East, and in China. The Egyptians certainly were most advanced in such matters – there is even a hieroglyph which is believed to represent a water clock – while the Christian world was largely starved of such useful appliances except in their most simple form. They were reputedly current during a total span of some two thousand years – excluding freak survivals to the present time such as the sand glass egg-timer, of course!

Of the more scientifically based non-mechanical timekeepers, however, rather more information is available. It is reasonable to suppose that, certainly in all those areas mentioned above where sunshine is a fairly continuous feature of the climate, it cannot have been long after the dawn of civilisation that the movement of cast shadows – of trees, perhaps – was noticed. Trees, however, were not always sited in the most convenient locations, so that it was probably necessary at first to erect poles in public places, where the movements of their shadows across the ground could indicate to all concerned the passage of the daylight hours. These in turn were replaced by large stone 'needles' or obelisks, of which plenty of examples remain. There are something like twenty of these in Rome, carried there by the early Emperors; one in Paris, which came originally from Luxor; and the famous Cleopatra's Needle, which was first erected at Heliopolis, outside Cairo, in 1500 BC, removed to Alexandria in 23 BC, and finally brought to London in 1878. It weighs 166 tons, stands 70 feet high, and is otherwise celebrated for the great variety of its Egyptian inscriptions, in one of which, for the first known time, is found the phrase 'King of Kings'. It was, incidentally, one of a pair of such obelisks, of which the other was erected in Central Park, New York, in 1881.

The first documentary reference to a sundial would appear to be in chapter twenty of the Second Book of Kings, where Isaiah the prophet miraculously retarded the shadow of the sun by ten degrees or steps. This particular dial belonged to King Ahaz and may well have been of the monumental kind; fine examples of this sort from the

This magnificent equinoctial ('equal hours') dial was made by William Dean of London about 1690. A number of different craft skills have been combined to make this both a scientific instrument and a work of art. National Maritime Museum, Greenwich.

The seventeenth and eighteenth centuries saw the design of sundials reach a peak. This spherical dial of French origin was made in 1767. National Maritime Museum, Greenwich.

early Islamic observatories in Persia still exist, in which the shadow of a wall or similar projecting object falls upon an ascending flight of steps.

Ruins of other massive sundials are scattered throughout a number of countries. In Britain, the rings of megalithic stones on Salisbury Plain, known as Stonehenge, fall into this category; estimates of their age suggest about 2000 BC. At Jaipur, in India, some vast curved stones serve a similar purpose; the Aztecs in Peru constructed rock pillars as their sun clocks. Such instruments were, of course, the equivalent of public clocks or for the use of astronomers; personal sundials, as used in India and Tibet, were in the form of a simple time-stick with a peg inserted in it at right-angles. The side of the stick was calibrated, and the shadow of the peg falling upon these gradations gave a reading of the time.

Clearly the sundial could only be used by day, but other systems, particularly the clepsydra, were available for night use. In addition, however, the Egyptians had the merkhet, which was in essence a plumb-line; its use was to observe the transit of known fixed stars across the meridian. At later periods various types of 'nocturnals' were designed, often being built into a compendium with a conventional sundial, for portable use.

Sundials come in an enormous variety of designs: cubes on a carved stand, with each of the five available faces showing a different time system; so-called diptych or tablet dials, which open like books; dials with built-in compasses to ensure that they were set up on the correct bearing, facing south, and plumb-bobs to verify their level. There were also, of course, horizontal dials on baluster pillars for public use, as well as vertical dials often set upon church walls.

In use, the only snag with such a seemingly simple and efficient tool as the sundial, is that day and night are not the same length all the year round, certainly in northern Europe where winter nights can be twice as long as those in summer. In the Mediterranean basin, though, the variation is very much smaller, so that for the early civilisations in that region such an instrument was certainly a practical proposition.

The problem, whether it be more or less acute, can be resolved into two parts: how to divide into convenient quantities the periods of day and night, remembering that except at the equinoxes (Lat., 'equal nights') these vary in length; and, having done that, how to compensate for such variables on a sundial.

A lunar month of thirty days, adapted to a solar year of 365 days to suit their religious celebrations, was in use more than 3,000 years ago by the Egyptians, although probably not originated by them. An even older system, adopted by the ancient Sumerians, divided the period between one sunset and the next into twelve, and each of these 'hours'

Another common form of sundial in the eighteenth century was the folding ring dial. In addition to finding solar time, such dials generally had a subsidiary use of obtaining the altitude of the sun. Musées Royaux d'Art et d'Histoire, Brussels.

below
The nocturnal dial was intended to show the hours during the night by observing the position of the Pole star in relation to certain other stars. This fine specimen, although unsigned, can be dated from other evidence as about 1582, and is possibly French. Musées Royaux d'Art et d'Histoire, Brussels.

left and above
A beautiful silver gilt chalice sundial dated 1596, this example was probably made either in Italy or southern Germany. It is designed for use on the latitude of Rome and shows the time in Italian hours. The gnomon extends vertically from the bottom of the cup around which are engraved appropriate time scales. It is upon these that the shadow of the gnomon is cast by the sun. Science Museum, London.

was subdivided into thirty. This system seems to have found its way across to China and thence to Japan, where time was reckoned on a similar basis. Why it should have been determined to assign twelve 'hours' to a day is not known, although it has been suggested that there was thought to be a magical significance in that number. The concept of twenty-four equal hours – i.e. two periods of twelve, for day and night – did not enter into common use until the beginning of the fourteenth century; and it is interesting to note that there is no exact term in the English language to differentiate a daylight from a night-time hour, nor any separate term to denote a complete twenty-four hour period. It also is simply a 'day'.

Before leaving the pre-mechanical era, there is one other scientific instrument that should be mentioned – the astrolabe. In its simplest form it was an altitude dial, consisting of a round engraved plate with a sighting bar pivoted at the centre to measure the sun's altitude and thus calculate the time. As such, its provenance dates back to Greece,

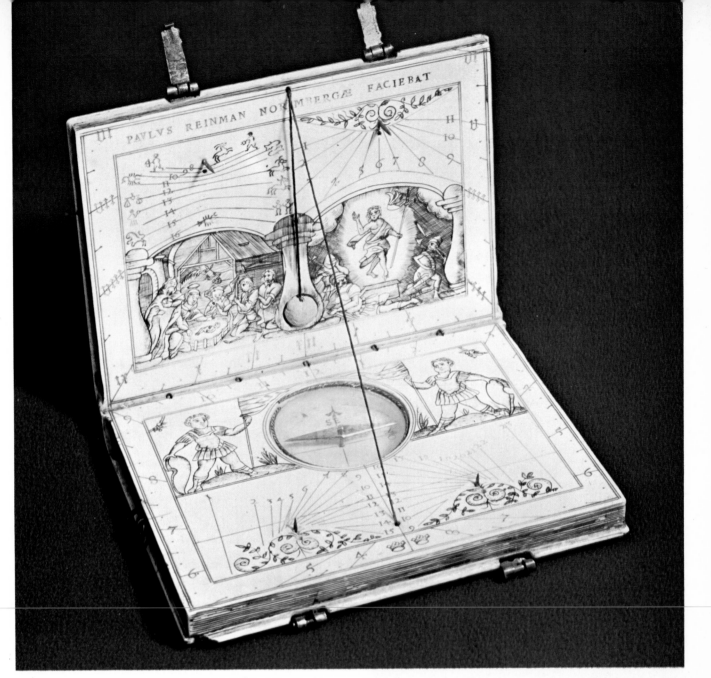

Diptych or tablet sundials were generally made of ivory although examples are known in gilt brass and other materials. This one by Paul Reinman of Nuremberg was made in 1599 and, when closed, is in the form of a book. Tablet dials were a particularly popular design over a long period in the sixteenth and seventeenth centuries. Science Museum, London.

The commonest type of astrolabe – a scientific compendium used for determining the time by day or night, for fixing the times when Muslims must pray, for elementary surveying and navigation and for teaching astronomy – is called 'planispheric' because it functions on a flat surface as opposed to a spherical one.

Sundials have remained sources of fascination and interest into modern times. A so-called 'Patent Pantochronometer', this pocket device, according to instructions printed on the bottom, gives a reading of the time, not only where it is used, but also in a range of principal cities throughout the world, and can also be used as a compass. Internal evidence points to its having been made for use in Australia, probably at the turn of the nineteenth century.

somewhere about 150 BC. Also pivoting upon the disc was a star map which, when rotated, reproduced the appearance of the sky at any moment, past, present or future. From this could be deduced the rising or setting of a star, the length of day or night, the time of ritual prayers, as in Islamic practice, and it even performed certain functions related to predictions by astrology, to which, formerly, so many cultures subscribed. The astrolabe has been described as combining all other astronomical instruments in one; certainly it has had a long history, for the earliest surviving specimens are Islamic, of the late ninth century. It first came to Christian Europe about two centuries later. In the seventeenth century it was improved for more accurate navigational use at sea. Astrolabes were in use in the mosques of Morocco within the last fifty years; and to this day there is still one workshop in Isfahan which manufactures them.

The sundial also, of course, survived as a very functional tool long after the appearance of the mechanical timekeeper. The earliest mechanisms were so very haphazard in their performance that the easiest – indeed the only – means of keeping a check on them was to compare their readings with those obtained with a sundial. The latter, of course, only displayed solar time, and a conversion factor had to be applied to such readings in order to calculate mean time such as should be shown on a clock or watch. The calculation was described as the Equation of Time, and tables giving the appropriate conversion according to the time of year were produced, in particular in the seventeenth and eighteenth centuries when pocket sundials in a variety of attractive designs, and principally intended for checking clocks and watches, were produced in quantity. Several of the makers of these became famous in their own right, notably such French craftsmen as Michael Butterfield and Nicholas Bion in Paris, and Charles Bloud in Dieppe, while in Germany there was Johann Willebrand of Augsburg and a number of others. Such dials were often sufficiently sophisticated as to have a gnomon – the projection whose shadow falls on the calibrated dial plate – that could be adjusted, so that the angle it formed with the plate could be made to conform with the latitude of the locality where the dial was being used; they also had several concentric time scales, each relating to a different span of latitudes. This was essential in order to obtain a correct reading, and the reverse of such dials often is inscribed with a list of capital cities and their latitudes. Where a sundial is fitted with a fixed gnomon, it can only be used in places on the one latitude to which it is matched.

The Islamic concept of the astrolabe requires it to be both a scientific instrument and a work of art. Although in Western eyes this remarkable combination instrument – really a form of early computer – has long since been superseded, a few astrolabists continue to this day to pursue their ancient craft.

Made of brass with damascening and laminated silver, this Eastern Islamic spherical astrolabe, a great rarity, is signed 'Work of Musa, year 885'. This corresponds to AD 1480. Museum of the History of Science, Oxford.

The Rudiments of Clockwork

For the amateur, even if only a dilettante, some knowledge and appreciation of the mechanics of clocks and watches is necessary, not only because it helps to round out data obtained about, say, the historical and decorative aspects but, even more essentially, because it will enable him to communicate much more fully with others of like tastes. Nobody who is active in this field can afford to be so narrowly specialised as to ignore completely any of the complementary disciplines of which it is comprised.

Having said that, the importance which he attaches to his technical knowledge and the extent to which he cultivates it are matters entirely for his own judgement and will largely result from his particular tastes, inclinations and experience. Let it be said straight away that there is nothing so obscure and abstruse about the subject as to render it impossible for even the most unmechanically minded to grasp sufficient of the essentials for all ordinary purposes. The purpose of this chapter will therefore be to explain, in simple terms and avoiding as far as possible the 'private language' of the technologist, the systems of clock- and watchwork which are most likely to be encountered and the salient features by which they can be recognised. The most important developments and inventions over the centuries will be pointed out, and fundamental principles explained. Anything more than this, however, is clearly beyond the scope of this book, and if the reader intends, for instance, to practise as a restorer of antique mechanisms he will need very much more practical information. He is therefore referred to the 'Further Reading' list (page 254); and he is also advised to seek first-hand practical training either by apprenticeship or, if this is inappropriate, by means of a course of instruction. Some information in this regard will be found on page 254, where organisations that cater for both modern industry and the antiquarian horologist are described.

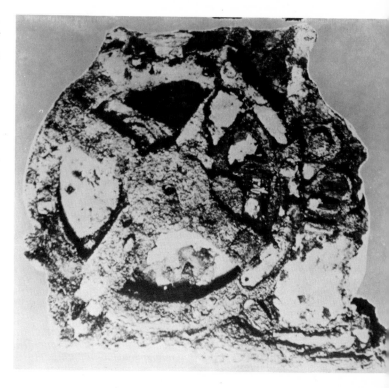

The corroded, almost fossilised, fragments of what is believed to have been some kind of planetary machine were found among the remnants of a treasure ship which sank off the coast of Antikythera in AD 250 (see page 27).

opposite page, left
This plate from Rees's *Cyclopaedia* of 1820 illustrates the principle of the thirty-hour 'endless line' weight-driven clock. Winding the large driving weight is accomplished by pulling on the loop carrying the small counterpoise ring.

opposite page, right
Rees's *Cyclopaedia* contains an admirable diagram of the layout of a common two-train spring-driven clock. The left-hand (striking) train shows the spring coiled in its spring barrel – the cover being momentarily removed – while the assembled driving gear can be seen on the right-hand (going) train.

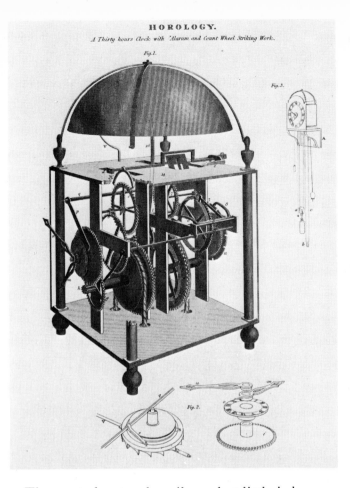

The next chapter describes what little is known – and it is very little indeed – about the birth of the clock, and here it is simply necessary to point out that primitive machinery involving the meshing together of toothed wheels existed long before the clock came upon the scene. Hero of Alexandria, who lived during the first century AD although his exact dates have not been ascertained, describes two examples of the use of wooden wheels with widely spaced teeth, but in a context which suggests that even in his lifetime this was nothing new; so it is quite conceivable that such devices extended back to the birth of Christ. There is also some material evidence of much more recent discovery. Seventy-five years ago there was salvaged from a Greek treasure-ship, thought to have sunk off the island of Antikythera about 250 AD, the remains of a machine which consisted of metal wheels having finely cut teeth which meshed with one another to form a kind of gearing. From considerations of the mechanics of the machine, so far as the remaining fragments reveal them, and also of the inscriptions, of which there are some traces, it seems most probable that in its original state the device was some kind of manually operated planetarium which was used to illustrate the motions of certain heavenly bodies.

When one is examining such archaeological remains, how can one be so certain that they were not once part of a clock? The answer is that early clock mechanisms have one element peculiar to themselves alone, which does not figure in any kind of machinery that is not devoted wholly or partially to measuring intervals of time. This single element is the escapement, which is dealt with in some detail on page 34; suffice it to say at this point that unless there is clear evidence of the existence of an escapement, even if no longer *in situ,* then there is a strong presumption that a machine is not a clock.

Like any other machine, a clock or watch needs stored up energy – a power source – to drive it, and when we wind up our longcase clock once a week or our wristwatch every day, we are simply regenerating this supply. The use of a particular power source is governed by the type and size of timekeeper concerned, its age, the purpose for which it was designed and similar considerations.

Everybody has encountered a clock driven by a falling weight which is periodically hauled up again, either as a result of being wound up with a key fitting on to a winding 'square' which can be seen through a hole in the clock dial, or, especially with clocks of thirty-hours 'duration of going', by pulling directly upon the 'line' hanging down inside the clock case. In the latter instance, the clock weight is simply threaded on an endless rope or chain, a loop, in fact; this loop passes through the clock movement and hangs down below it on either side, the driving side containing the main weight on its pulley, the slack side simply held reasonably taut with a small counterpoise, either

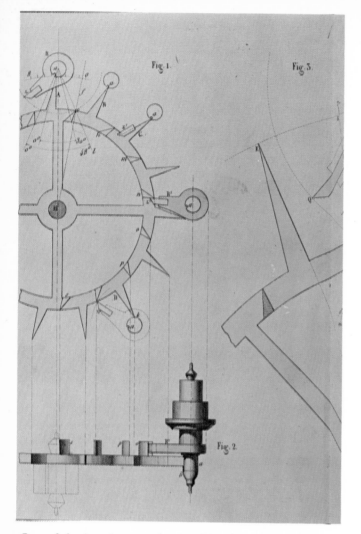

One of the best-known nineteenth-century French horological textbooks is Claude Saunier's *Treatise on Modern Horology* which first appeared in 1869 in Paris. The best English edition which has the technical drawings in colour to demonstrate the use of the two principal metals, brass and steel, and ruby jewelling, appeared in 1880. This is part of Plate 2 which shows the duplex escapement with its characteristic escape wheel employing two sets of teeth cut in planes at right angles to one another.

just a ring of lead like a weight for a fishing line, or sometimes a smaller version of the driving weight and also on a pulley. Pulling down the counter-poised side of the line pulls up the main driving weight and thus winds up the clock. In either case, the weight is pulling upon a line wound round a drum, called a 'barrel', with which is associated the main driving wheel of the machine – the 'great' wheel, as it is called.

The falling-weight type of power source is probably the most efficient that could have been contrived, since the weight is acting under the force of gravity, which is constant; thus, at whatever height the weight may be in its passage from fully wound up to fully 'run out', the driving force it applies to the clock remains the same. Its only disadvantage as a system is that, while the weight is being wound up, the power supply to drive the

clock is interrupted, since the two motions cannot coexist except in the case of the loop-drive of thirty-hour clocks, where it does not apply. To overcome this, especially in the finest clocks, 'maintaining power' is provided. This takes the form of a small ancillary spring, so arranged that the clock cannot be wound at all without activating it; this gives sufficient additional power to keep the clock running while the winding-up procedure takes place. When a clock has the type known as 'bolt and shutter' maintaining power, it is necessary first to operate a lever, sometimes projecting through the dial but on other clocks at the side of the movement, in order to lift shutters that normally obstruct access to the winding squares in the dial. Not only weight-driven but also the finest quality spring-driven clocks, as well as many watches, are fitted with maintaining power, on much the same principle.

The falling weight was the earliest source of power, apart from the very rare, almost freak, use of hydraulics in clocks that were anyway only partially mechanical; these will be considered in the next chapter. The other main mechanical power source was the coiled spring, contained within a cylindrical drum also called a 'barrel'. It was a long time after the first use of falling weights to drive a clock that iron and steel technology became sufficiently advanced to allow a spring to be made successfully. The metal had first to be beaten into a ribbon by hand; and it must have been extremely difficult to obtain uniformity in all dimensions throughout its whole length. Then it had to be heat-treated to obtain the correct 'temper'. It seems likely that when, probably in Italy during the fifteenth century, the first springs were made – possibly by a swordsmith or locksmith rather than a clockmaker – the reject rate must have been inordinately high.

The disadvantages of the coiled spring as a power source are, first, its liability to break without warning, and second the uneven 'pull' which it exerts to drive the timekeeper. The first of these has been largely overcome – but only in the present century – by the perfection of various alloys that are nearly, if not completely, unbreakable. The second has required a great deal more mechanical ingenuity to cure.

When a spring is fully wound up, it exerts a much stronger force – in its efforts to unwind – than when it is partially or nearly run down. Clearly this inconsistency of energy supply must affect the going of the clock, so that it would run fast when fully wound up, its rate falling away as the spring uncoils. Among early attempts to correct this fault was a device called the stackfreed. Developed in Germany, it was a far from satisfactory remedy and did not survive long into the seventeenth century. In essence, it used a cam to turn with the mainspring, its rotation being helped

When used with the fusee, the central arbor is held fast and the barrel revolved by pulling upon a fine chain or, in the case of spring clocks, a gut or wire line, coiled around the outside of the barrel and fixed at the far end to it. The other end of this line is attached to the fusee, which is a cone-shaped pulley around which is cut a spiral groove in which the line runs.

To wind up the spring, a key is placed on the squared end of the fusee arbor and turned. This action pulls the line on to the fusee and off the spring barrel, thus rotating it; and since the barrel arbor is held tight, the spring is thereby coiled up. The reverse of this action – that is, as the spring runs down – sees the coiled spring rotating the barrel, and pulling the line back off the fusee again. But the fusee is essentially a cone, and the arrangement provides that when the spring is fully wound it is pulling, via the line to the fusee, against the smallest diameter of the latter, which will therefore be exercising the least leverage – called 'torque' – to the system. Maximum torque, on the other hand, comes into play when the mainspring is nearly run out, by which time the line is then pulling upon the largest diameter of the fusee. The

Watches are susceptible to positional error, and this is mainly felt in the escapement. To compensate for this, two similar devices, called respectively the tourbillon and the karrusel, have been used. The former was invented by Breguet, and the latter by Bonniksen. Both involve mounting the escapement in a slowly rotating carriage – the average time for one revolution can be about forty minutes. This illustration shows the tourbillon of a watch by Girard Perregaux. Museum of the Worshipful Company of Clockmakers, Guildhall, London.

or impeded by a spring-loaded roller acting along its edge, the intention being thus to cancel out the natural irregularity of the mainspring's action.

The first and still the commonest device to correct this fault, both on clocks and watches of any quality, is called the fusee. It provides a most elegant solution, not only practical as well as satisfactory in operation, but also theoretically perfect. In essentials, the ends of the mainspring coiled in its barrel are both fixed, the outer end hooked on to the inside of the barrel wall, and the inner to a spindle – or 'arbor' – which passes through the centre of the barrel. To wind up the mainspring – that is, to coil it up under maximum tension – clearly either the central spindle can be held static and the barrel revolved, or the barrel held static and the central arbor revolved.

So called 'triple-complicated' watches are well illustrated by this example made by S. Smith & Son in 1899. The dial shows not only the time, but also the phases of the moon, and has a perpetual calendar. Apart from this, the watch is a minute repeater and has split-seconds chronograph action. Museum of the Worshipful Company of Clockmakers, Guildhall, London.

arrangement completely compensates, therefore, for the innate defects of the spring; and since the main driving wheel to the mechanism, the great wheel, shares the same arbor as the fusee but is connected with it only by a ratchet arrangement – so that, in one direction only, the fusee can be rotated separately from the great wheel, this being necessary when winding up – the source of power must be delivered evenly to the mechanism throughout the duration of its going, and right at the start of the transmission.

arrangement completely compensates, therefore, for the innate defects of the spring; and since the main driving wheel to the mechanism, the great wheel, shares the same arbor as the fusee but is connected with it only by a ratchet arrangement – so that, in one direction only, the fusee can be rotated separately from the great wheel, this being necessary when winding up – the source of power must be delivered evenly to the mechanism throughout the duration of its going, and right at the start of the transmission.

With the fusee, it will be remembered that the barrel arbor is fixed tight and the barrel itself turned to wind up the spring. There is, however, another arrangement – of rather more modern usage and, to some extent, associated with the decline in the market for the finest quality clocks and watches – which goes by the name of a 'going barrel'. In this, the fusee is dispensed with altogether, and the concept depends upon eliminating the worst effects of uneven drive from the mainspring by utilising only a certain portion – effectively the middle coils of the spring – as a power source. It is true that the worst manifestations of unevenness occur when the spring is either fully wound or almost run out; so if you can ensure – by a device called 'stop work' – that even when the spring stops driving the clock it is still under some residual tension in the barrel, and similarly that when it is effectively wound it would still coil up further, were it not for the stop work, then you are principally using the middle coils of the spring, which in practice give a fairly even pull throughout their length. In a going barrel, the great wheel is integral with it; and the system requires that the spring be wound by turning the barrel arbor itself, the barrel being unable to rotate except as it drives the mechanism through the great wheel.

A short-lived device for equalising the pull of the mainspring was tried out in Germany during the last half of the sixteenth century. Called the stackfreed (see page 28), this consisted essentially of a spring-loaded roller abutting against a snail-shaped cam both of which can be clearly seen in this picture. Also visible is the dumb-bell foliot and hog's bristle which regulated it. Basingstoke Museum.

right
One of the finest examples of a clock showing the equation of time, this one by George Graham is dated about 1740. In addition to the equation dial in the break-arch, there is a gilt minute hand which always points to solar time, while the steel hand points to mean time. See also page 162. British Museum, London.

Before leaving the question of residual tension, it is just worth mentioning that, whereas in the going barrel the residual tension is achieved by using stop work, with the fusee also some residual tension must remain in the spring even when the system is effectively run out, in order that the device shall operate most efficiently and so as to keep the line from barrel to fusee taut. To achieve this, the mainspring has to be 'set up', and this is normally done by a ratchet and click applied to the end of the barrel arbor, or by an endless screw. There is a special tool, called a fusee testing rod, by which watch- and clockmakers have to test such pretensioning of the mainspring to ensure that it is compatible with the proportions of the barrel and fusee actually in use, and thus that the system provides an even power supply throughout its cycle of operation.

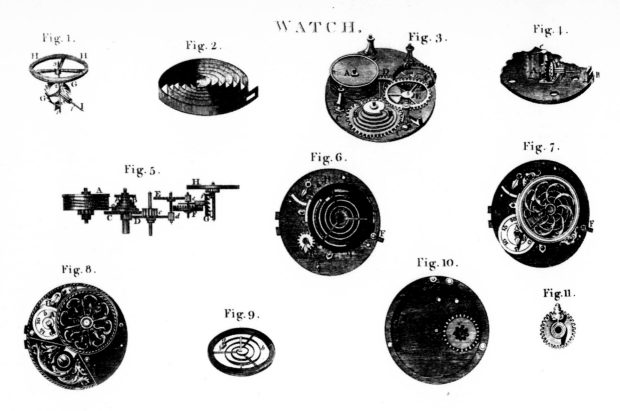

Fig. 1. Fig. 2. Fig. 3. Fig. 4. Fig. 5. Fig. 6. Fig. 7. Fig. 8. Fig. 9. Fig. 10. Fig. 11.

The nineteenth century was remarkable for the plethora of well-produced technical encyclopedias that appeared, and this is the plate dealing with 'watch' taken from *The English Encyclopaedia* of 1802. Self-evident among the various figures can be seen the verge escapement as applied to a watch, an unhoused mainspring and the layout of spring barrel, fusee and train in a watch whose back plate has not yet been placed in position. Figure 5 shows the relationship of wheels and pinions in the same train, starting from the spring barrel at left and extending to the escapement – a verge – at right. Figures 7 and 8 show the typical continental and English watch movements of the period as seen from the back.

Once given an efficient power source, it is clearly necessary to have some means of passing it through the machine, dividing it up into the right proportions to fit the eventual needs of each particular part to which it travels. This is done by a 'train' of engaging gears; and any clock or watch may have more than one train. Thus, a big clock is likely to have a going train, a striking train (to strike the required number of times at each hour) and a chiming train (to chime at each quarter), the two last-named being interdependent and triggered off by the going train, which, of necessity, provides the basic control of the machine.

A train of gears consists of a sequence of wheels meshing with pinions; usually the wheels are of brass, mounted upon steel arbors out of which are also formed the pinions, and it is customary to speak of the wheels as having teeth but pinions as having leaves. In early clockwork, wheels were made of iron by smithing techniques, and the teeth were cut out by hand; at that time, too, lantern pinions were the usual design, that is, instead of being formed from solid metal, they were in the form of a cage, made up of two end-discs separated by pins which constituted the leaves. For some centuries past, however, it has been possible to produce wheels on a wheel-cutting 'engine', which utilises a 'dividing plate' to direct the cutter, somewhat in the manner of a pantograph.

In most going trains – that is, the gear train that leads from the power source eventually to show the time by hands on a dial – the starting point, as has been shown, is the great wheel. Except where the train has an unusually long duration of going – more than eight days, at any rate – the usual arrangement is for the great wheel to drive the pinion of the centre wheel; that wheel drives the third wheel pinion, the third wheel drives the fourth wheel pinion and so on. The fourth or fifth wheel is generally the escape wheel – an integral part of the escapement, which will be described shortly.

Arbors carrying wheels and pinions are shaped at their ends into 'pivots' running in pivot holes in the main frame of the clock or watch. Such a frame will usually consist of front and back 'plates' separated by turned or otherwise ornamental 'pillars', and between which the movement is supported. These pivot holes may simply be drilled in the metal, or they may be 'jewel holes', that is to say, bushed with hardstone to make a hard-wearing bearing: While nowadays synthetic stones are used, formerly ruby, sapphire or garnet were the customary material. Jewelled surfaces were also used elsewhere in both clocks and watches where much wear was likely as, for instance, on the bearing faces of the pallets in the escapement.

The centre wheel arbor extends through the dial, in most arrangements, the projecting part

being called the centre post. Friction tight upon this post is carried the 'cannon pinion', which drives the 'motion work', as it is called. Its sole purpose is to divide the rotation of the centre post between the requirements of the hour and minute hands – the latter, of course, rotating twelve times as fast as the former. The motion work is a mini-train all of its own, consisting of the cannon pinion which drives the minute wheel, which rides free upon a stud fixed to the main frame of the clock or watch. The minute wheel pinion drives the hour wheel, which is mounted upon a pipe that fits freely over the cannon pinion. On this pipe is mounted the hour hand. The end of the cannon pinion is squared off and projects through and beyond the pipe of the hour wheel carrying the hour hand; and upon this squared end is mounted the minute hand. If there is a 'supplementary' seconds hand – frequently sited just above six on the dial – it is usually carried upon the extended arbor of the fourth wheel, or, in the case of the conventional seconds-beating pendulum clock, upon the escape wheel arbor.

If the mechanism, as it has been described so far, were wound up and allowed free rein, it would race to unwind itself in a totally uncontrolled way and most probably cause itself irretrievable damage in so doing: teeth would be stripped from wheels, and the whole machine might even disintegrate. Clearly this would serve no useful purpose whatever.

The element that is lacking is that single device which, as we said earlier, is peculiar to early time-measuring instruments and features in no other sort of machinery – the escapement. This is, in effect, the governor that slows down the rate at

above left
A beautifully engraved plate from Rees's *Cyclopaedia* shows a conventional three-train spring-driven rack striking and chiming clock, the chime being on eight bells.

above
The principle of a wheel-cutting engine is based on the precise graduating of a circular plate – called the dividing plate – so that a range of concentric circles engraved thereon are each marked out in a different number of equal arcs. It is necessary then only to select that circle which is divided into the same number of sections as a wheel-blank is to have teeth cut into it, and then to line up the cutter point by point around that circle on a system something like a pantograph. This small wheel-cutting engine, which is Swiss, of about 1850, is specially designed to cut the teeth of verge escape wheels which, because of their shape, are usually called crown wheels. The number of teeth in such a wheel is limited, and the dividing plate of this engine ranges from seven to twenty-one teeth only.

which the power supply is used up to one that is commensurate with the passage of time; in other words, it allows power to 'escape' at carefully controlled intervals which, within limits, can be slowed down or speeded up to make the clock run 'to time'.

In understanding the fundamentals of an escapement, it is necessary to bear in mind, firstly, that the escape wheel is always the last wheel in the going train – right at the end of the line, as it were – and secondly that its natural inclination is to rotate freely under the influence of the power being applied to it through the rest of the train, starting from the power source. It is necessary, therefore, to impede that natural motion, but this can only be done to a wheel that is not meshing with yet another pinion – hence the need for it to be the last one in the train.

The wheel can be impeded from rotating freely by first locking, and then releasing it, one tooth at a time; and if some kind of regularly swinging or vibrating component be used for the purpose, the wheel can be made to give that component 'impulse' – that is, give it a push – each time it is frustrated in its endeavour to run free. Imagine, therefore, a pendulum on a free suspension with, attached to it, a pair of jaws designed to embrace a number of teeth of the escape wheel; set the pendulum swinging, so that at each extreme of its swing it locks – or intercepts – a tooth on one side of the wheel but releases one on the other, and there is the simplest form of escapement. Providing the shape of the escape wheel teeth and the 'pallets' – the contacting surfaces of the jaws – are properly designed, the pendulum, once set in motion, will continue swinging until the spring or weight runs out, obtaining all the impulse it needs through the system.

above left
Although this three-train clock is weight-driven, there are clear points of resemblance with the plate from Rees's *Cyclopaedia*. The hands – including seconds hand above centre – have been replaced to aid orientation, and the system of striking and chiming by rack and snail is clearly demonstrated.

above
This end-on view of the same clock shows the chiming barrel, pinned as in a musical box, and in this case it can be altered at will to chime on four or eight bells. The change is effected by raising or lowering the lever in the foreground which shifts the pin-barrel slightly sideways to bring a different set of pins into action.

The theory of pendulums is complex. An ideal length exists for pendulums 'beating' certain intervals of time, and probably that most commonly encountered is the seconds pendulum, the theoretically perfect length of which is approximately one metre. This is the pendulum used in most longcase – familiarly called grandfather – clocks. To obtain a perfect pendulum that will beat longer intervals than one second, however, it is not enough simply to multiply up – a two-seconds pendulum, for instance, should measure four metres in length, and these are sometimes found on church clocks. Short 'bob' pendulums are also found on small domestic clocks, and one beating three times per second has a length of only 10.6cm.

This extraordinary clock movement – how it was originally cased is now not known – is a short-period timer which might possibly have been used for horseracing. It was made at the end of the eighteenth century by Justin Vulliamy, and its nine dials can be activated by levers to work in various combinations. The escapement, unusually for a clock, is a very large cylinder of which it seems to be the only known weight-driven example.

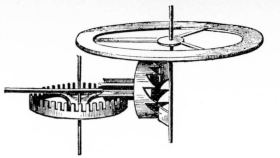

The verge escapement, when applied to watches, is arranged as in this illustration, also from *Clocks and Watches and Bells*. The wheel in a horizontal plane with teeth sticking upwards is usually called the contrate wheel, and this drives the pinion of the escape – or crown – wheel. The pallets, which look like two small flags on the upright arbor of the balance wheel, are clearly visible.

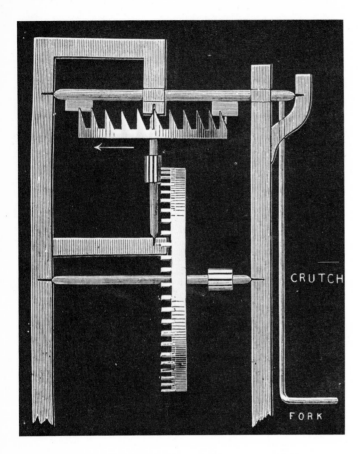

CRUTCH

FORK

This illustration – which shows the verge escapement as applied to a clock – comes from the seventh edition which appeared in 1883 of a celebrated nineteenth-century treatise on horology entitled *Clocks and Watches and Bells* by Sir Edmund Beckett, Q.C. The author of this book, afterwards Lord Grimthorpe, designed the mechanism for 'Big Ben'. In the illustration, the pendulum hangs on the right, passing between the right-angled forked end of the crutch.

A fine drawing, again from Sir Edmund Beckett, of the action of the cylinder or horizontal escapement. Identifying features of this assembly include the curiously shaped escape wheel teeth with their small platforms on top, so formed in order to pass through the cylinder seen in action with the escape wheel, and also, on extreme left, by itself. The swinging balance wheel would be attached to the latter.

For any timekeeper that is going to remain reasonably static, a pendulum is probably the best form of controller for the escapement that can be devised; it is also true, that the longer the pendulum the more perfectly it will perform in a clock, since it is desirable that, whatever type of controlling device is used, the interval between the impulses it receives from the escape wheel should be as long as possible, to allow it to remain 'detached' from the machine and able to 'vibrate' – or swing – freely for as much of the time as can be contrived.

But for smaller clocks as well as for portable timekeepers, especially watches, the alternative to the pendulum is the balance wheel; and the balance spring was invented to recreate, often in a horizontal rather than a vertical plane, the backwards and forwards effect which, in the pendulum, is a combination of impulse from the mainspring pushing it outwards and gravity bringing it back to the zero point again.

To put this in correct historical perspective, the very first type of controller, on the earliest monastic clocks, was a flat bar, pivoting at the centre and oscillating in a horizontal plane. Called a 'foliot', this had movable weights suspended from each half of the bar by which some adjustment could be effected. It can be argued that the balance wheel, which simply added a rim to the foliot to turn it into a kind of flywheel, was a logical progression from it rather than a separate invention; in any event, neither can be attributed to any particular person in the present state of our knowledge. The pendulum, however, was certainly recognised by Leonardo da Vinci even though he never applied it to a clock, so far as is known. Galileo wrote about the pendulum as a philosophical instrument; and it was left to Christiaan Huygens, the eminent

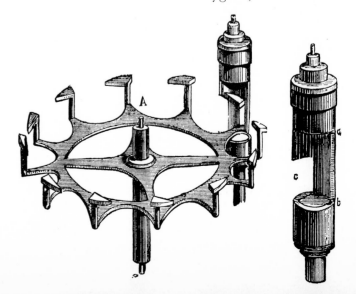

Dutch physicist, to apply the pendulum to a timekeeper. As for that other component, the balance spring – often called the hairspring, although such is not a correct horological term – this was originated by Robert Hooke for application to watches, and later perfected and marketed by Huygens.

It is probably not an exaggeration to say that dozens upon dozens, if not indeed several hundred, designs of escapement have been drawn up over the centuries – although far fewer than that were ever actually made; and it is possible to say with certainty that many of those which exist only as figments on paper could never have worked anyway. There are perhaps nearly a dozen types of escapement with which anybody taking an interest in horology should familiarise themselves, and these can be summarised as follows.

The verge is the oldest of all escapements. Found in the first clocks, where it was controlled by a foliot, it was quickly adapted for watches, when the technology permitted of these being made. Provincial craftsmen in Britain were still using it as late as 1900. It is robust and relatively trouble-free in use, and will run for long periods with minimal attention, but its timekeeping properties are not remarkable.

The cylinder, which was perfected by Thomas Tompion's partner George Graham and used in virtually all his watches after 1725, became the preferred escapement for the well-to-do, although it never completely supplanted the verge. The escape wheel works in a horizontal plane, hence it is sometimes called the 'horizontal' escapement. The cylinder is an extremely difficult escapement to make, and – except in that variant known as the ruby cylinder, in which the acting surfaces are made of precious hardstone – subject to wear. It is also much more fragile than the verge, and these disadvantages tend to cancel out any slight timekeeping edge it may possess over the best verge watches.

Incidentally, the cylinder was reincarnated by the Swiss in the latter half of the last century, in the enormous quantities of fairly low-grade export watches which they manufactured, and also as a platform escapement in the poorer carriage clocks.

The duplex was originally invented and perfected in Paris during the first half of the eighteenth century by J. B. Dutertre and Pierre Le Roy. It appeared in England in 1782 under a patent taken out by Thomas Tyrer, and became the heart of the English high-quality watch – apart from the pocket chronometer – for at least the first three decades of the nineteenth century. It was still being made until at least 1845. The individual characteristic of the duplex is that its escape wheel

These two escape wheels, both for use with the duplex escapement, show the difference between English and continental practice. The English preferred to cut their two sets of teeth on the same wheel, whereas elsewhere it was commonplace to cut two separate wheels and mount them on the same arbor.

requires two sets of teeth in planes at right angles to one another. In the English version, this is usually accomplished by cutting the two sets of teeth on the same wheel, but on the Continent the preferred arrangement is usually to have two separate wheels mounted upon the same common arbor.

Like the cylinder, the duplex was also resuscitated, but this time in cheap machine-made American watches towards the end of the nineteenth century. Its inherent disadvantage is difficulty of lubrication.

The detent or chronometer escapement existed in several designs, based mainly upon the inventions of John Arnold and Thomas Earnshaw in this country, and of Pierre Le Roy and Ferdinand Berthoud in France, during the second half of the eighteenth and the earliest years of the nineteenth centuries. The two forms most usually encountered are the spring detent and the pivoted detent, with sub-forms of the former according to Arnold's or Earnshaw's patterns. This escapement is the one most suitable for marine chronometers and deck watches – that is to say, for navigational use – and might be thought a little too fragile for everyday wear, although plenty of examples were carried on the person.

The split-second chronograph is so named because in its original form it consisted of two seconds hands, one above the other, which normally rotated together. By pressing a push-piece, it was possible to halt one of the seconds hands while the other continued. When the end of the interval to be measured was reached – and for convenience it had to be less than a minute – the difference between the two seconds hands could be read off. A further pressure on the push-piece caused the hand that was stationary to catch up with the other one. This particular specimen by Barraud & Lund of London was made in 1859.

In this simplified sketch of the English lever escapement, which is also taken from Sir Edmund Beckett's book, the plain flat balance wheel swings backwards and forwards taking with it the pin P. This engages and disengages with the notch at the end of the lever which is pivoted at C, causing this to rock backwards and forwards, alternately engaging with and releasing a tooth of the escape wheel.

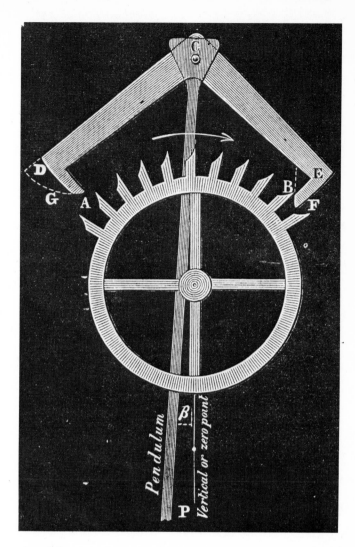

The lever, the principal escapement used today in mechanical wristwatches and in many small clocks, was invented in its original form by Thomas Mudge in the mid eighteenth century, but discarded by him as too complicated for ordinary purposes. Towards the end of the same century a handful of the finest craftsmen made a few special watches incorporating versions of this escapement, which are numbered among the great rarities by collectors today. The lever escapement then died a second death, only to re-emerge eventually, in a simplified form known as the table-roller lever, about 1825. There were intermediate develop¹ments, examples of which are still to be found: these include Peter Litherland's rack lever, patented in 1791, Edward Massey's crank-roller lever of 1814, and George Savage's two-pin lever of only two or three years later. Quite independently, one or two French craftsmen had tried their hand at a similar device; both the great A.-L. Breguet and Robert Robin, for instance, made some interesting lever watches in the last decade of the eighteenth century. By about 1860, the lever watch had swept all before it; gone were the duplex and chronometer watches and, apart from the cheap Swiss version, the cylinder had long since disappeared.

With the exception of the verge, nearly all the escapements listed so far have had their main application in watches – and there were a number of others, too, which are more rarely encountered even among advanced circles of collectors today. Such were the virgule – and that exceptional rarity, the double virgule – and the Debaufre-type escapements, of which no two ever seem to be quite the same. The chance of the average collector coming face to face with one of these is becoming increasingly less likely as each year succeeds the last.

39

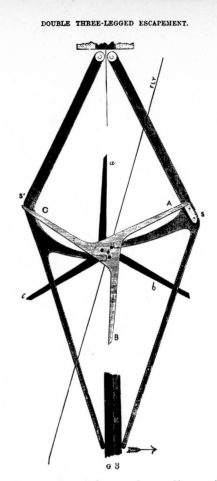

But what about clock escapements? Apart from the solid long-lasting verge, the commonest antique clock escapement is:

The anchor or recoil escapement. Variously attributed to Robert Hooke and William Clement, it seems to have appeared about 1671 and for the first time made really accurate clocks possible. It supplanted the verge escapement in clocks, and many originally fitted with verges were subsequently converted to this more accurate form. When, on page 34, a basic escapement was described as a swinging pendulum fitted with jaws that embraced a number of teeth of the escape wheel, this was an oversimplified description of the anchor escapement.

The dead-beat escapement is a recoilless version of the anchor, invented in 1715 by George Graham and especially used in regulator clocks, that is to say, clocks built to observatory standards of accuracy. Such clocks are frequently fitted with the most sophisticated means of improving and maintaining performance, so that it is not unusual to find bearings running in jewels – in the same manner as so many watches boast of nowadays, although not all their jewelling is necessarily quite what it may appear to be. The pallets, too, may be surfaced in the same material.

There are other forms of clock escapement – the pin-pallet, for example, much loved by the Victorians, and not to be confused with the pin-wheel escapement found in many good-quality French clocks – including, from the collector's point of view, several great rarities. The grasshopper is one of these. The invention of John Harrison for his great wooden regulator clocks, its great advantage is that it needs no oil. It was modified and used later by Vulliamy and rarely by one or two other makers.

The gravity escapement will be the last one to be mentioned here, and this because, in one or another version, it is to be found on some of the finest turret clocks. Towards the end of the third

above left
There are several versions of the pin-wheel escapement for clocks, even though the principle is the same. This example is Sir Edmund Beckett's design, the difference being that for technical reasons he has flattened the underside of the pins on the escape wheel, which are generally left rounded, as shown on the left of the illustration.

above
Sir Edmund Beckett's greatest contribution to horology was probably his design of the double three-legged gravity escapement for large public clocks. It was originally intended for the Westminster clock 'Big Ben' and the performance of that timekeeper is world-famous.

right
Automata in clocks have a very long history. This example of the Heralds and Electors paying homage to the Emperor is a detail from the ship-clock or *nef* attributed to Hans Schlottheim, and which was made for Emperor Rudolf II, probably in Prague about 1580. British Museum, London.

quarter of the eighteenth century, two famous London makers, Thomas Mudge and Alexander Cumming seem independently of one another to have devised escapements of this kind. The essential principle of them is that impulse is imparted by the mainspring not directly to the pendulum or balance but through an intermediary system which the mainspring activates. Thus the pendulum is never in direct contact with the power source, and variations in power will not affect it, providing there is always sufficient energy to activate the intermediary system. This principle is usually called a remontoire. One of the most spectacular gravity escapements to be found in turret clocks – and especially in its prototype, London's 'Big Ben' on the Houses of Parliament – is the double three-legged gravity escapement especially invented by Lord Grimthorpe as part of his design for this famous clock.

The final word on escapements should perhaps be to reiterate something implied earlier on, in postulating the amateur's approach to clockwork. The technical complexities of escapements, studied in depth, are immense. Proponents of the early forms of lever, for example, will argue for hours on whether they incorporate 'draw', which is a stage in the cycle of operation of this escapement. Arguments will embrace mathematical and mechanical concepts calling for specialised knowledge, not to say aptitude. Yet, for the amateur, an escapement need not really mean any more than a system that twists or swings, back and forth, letting the escape wheel revolve one tooth at a time in a manner compatible with its main function which is to measure time!

Any clockwork mechanism is a comedy – or perhaps tragedy would be more appropriate – of errors; and at least part of the art of persuading it to run to time is to find means of getting these errors to compensate for one another, or cancel each other out. Some of the errors are due to friction which, for example, acts differently upon such parts as the pivots, depending upon the position of the timekeeper; that is to say, whether it is upright, upon its back, front or whatever. This applies only to watches, and their position is designated 'dial up' or 'down', 'pendant up', 'down', 'left' or 'right' when they are tested 'in positions'.

Yet other errors are due to changes in the temperature of the timekeeper's surroundings. It is a well-known phenomenon that metals tend to expand in heat and contract in cold, and obviously any compensation for this effect needs to act automatically upon the regulating component, adjusting it to make the machine run fast when the temperature change would cause it to slow down, and vice versa.

A number of devices have been tried, in attempts to correct for positional error in watches. The most successful have been directed towards

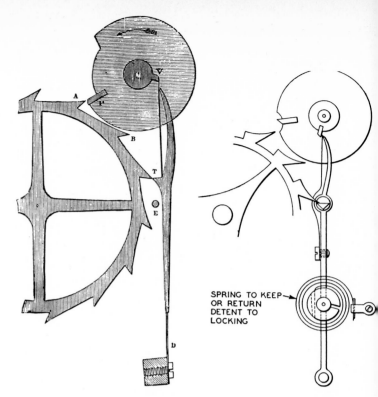

SPRING TO KEEP
OR RETURN
DETENT TO
LOCKING

mounting the entire escapement in a revolving carriage. Of two similar designs of this kind, the best-known is probably the tourbillon, one of Breguet's brilliant inventions and dating from 1801. Generally, in his arrangement, the carriage revolves once a minute. The other one, called a karrusel and originated by Aarne Bonniksen of Coventry in 1894, revolves in 52½ minutes.

While of course temperature error acts on all metal parts, its most serious effects are upon the pendulum rod of a clock, and, separately, upon the balance wheel and balance spring of a watch.

There are several well-established temperature compensation systems for metal pendulum rods. In the mercurial pendulum, which was designed by George Graham in 1721 and applied by him to his regulator clocks, the pendulum bob takes the form of a reservoir of mercury. As the pendulum rod lengthens in heat, the mercury expands upwards, thus keeping the effective length the same.

In Harrison's gridiron pendulum, of 1726, the same objective – maintaining the effective length constant – is achieved by using a grid of brass and steel rods, their ends fixed to cross-members alternately top and bottom so that the expansion upwards of the one metal cancels out the corresponding expansion downwards of the other. Yet again, in 1752, John Ellicott published details of a device he had perfected twenty years before, by which the downward expansion of a pendulum rod pressed upon levers located inside the pendulum bob, raising it and thus preserving its effective length.

Temperature compensation devices for watches and chronometers mostly depend upon the principle that a bi-metallic strip of brass and steel, riveted together, bends under the influence of heat

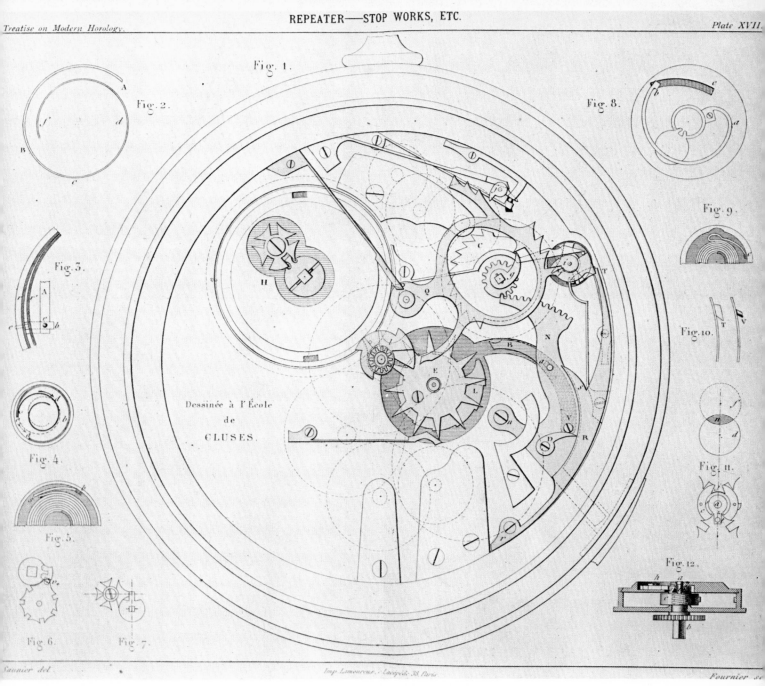

Fig. 1.

Fig. 2.

Fig. 8.

Fig. 9.

Fig. 3.

Fig. 10.

Dessinée à l'École de CLUSES.

Fig. 4.

Fig. 5.

Fig. 11.

Fig. 6.

Fig. 7.

Fig. 12.

opposite page, left

After the initial pioneering efforts of John Harrison, complemented by experimental work from a small number of makers such as Thomas Mudge and Josiah Emery, the final form of marine chronometer escapement followed two superficially similar patterns devised respectively by John Arnold and Thomas Earnshaw. Modern chronometers have settled upon the latter arrangement, and this is shown in this drawing from *Clocks and Watches and Bells*. The most significant feature is the tooth V which, when it is moving anti-clockwise – it being on the same arbor as the balance wheel – displaces the detent DTV. When, however, it returns in the opposite direction, it simply pushes aside a weak spring TV, set on the end of the detent, which is called the passing spring.

opposite page, right

Another form of chronometer escapement defined as the pivoted detent was originally developed in France and has been favoured by continental manufacturers. The main difference between this form and the spring detent previously described is the necessity to incorporate a spiral spring similar to a balance spring.

above

Plate 17 from Saunier's *Treatise on Modern Horology* of 1880 (see also page 28) illustrates very well the high standard of technical drawing reached in the late nineteenth century. This particular diagram represents a typical continental design for a quarter-repeating watch.

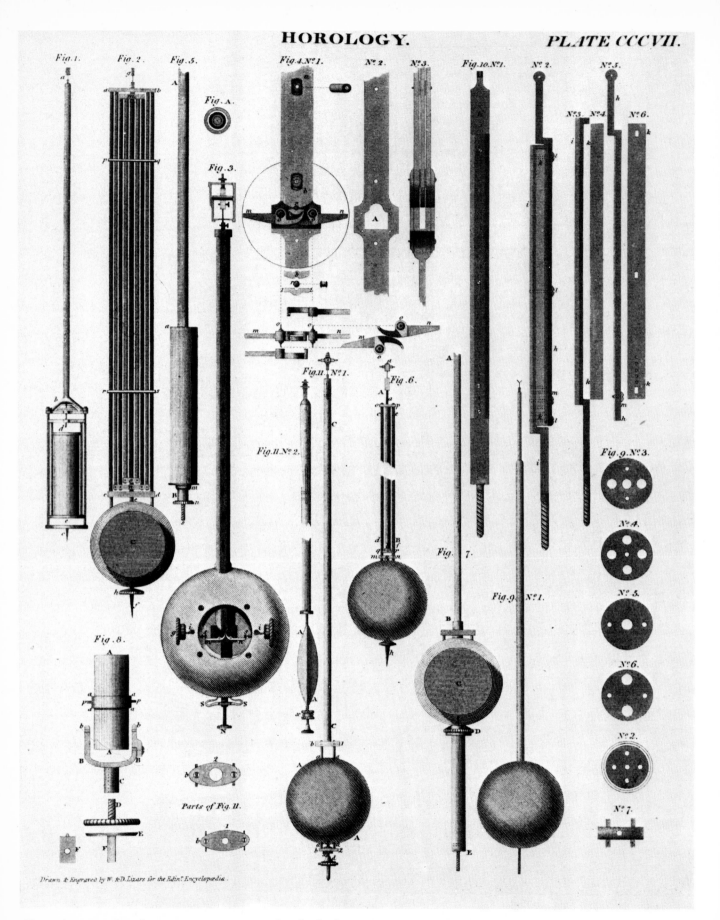

Once the necessity of temperature compensation for both clocks and watches had been accepted, a great deal of experimentation was applied to the problem as this plate taken from *The Edinburgh Encyclopaedia* shows. This work, which was edited by David Brewster LL.D., F.R.S., appeared in 1816, and some of the designs include: Figure 1, Graham's mercury pendulum as improved by Thomas Reid; Figure 2, Harrison's gridiron pendulum; Figure 3, Ellicott's pendulum.

44

or cold. The compensation curb, usually a U-shaped bi-metallic strip, is so arranged that the ends of the 'U' close up in heat; if one of these is fixed and the other grasps the outermost coil of the balance spring, it will, under these conditions, pull on the spring, effectively shortening it and thus causing the watch to gain when it would otherwise lose. This system has certain defects and was eventually abandoned in British watches, although elsewhere in Europe it survived in use even on the more expensive products providing that no exceptional degree of accuracy was required.

A better system was possible once the laminating of the brass and steel strips had been perfected; riveting was insufficiently rigid, so that soldering, and eventually fusing, the strips together was infinitely preferable. The improved arrangement, which survives in use today, depended upon forming the rim of the balance wheel out of two semi-circular bi-metallic strips, one end of each being fixed to the arm of the balance wheel, the other, unattached end carrying a small weight. The free ends of the strips move towards or away from the the centre of the balance with changes in temperature. Balances of this kind are sometimes called 'cut balances', to distinguish them from those with a solid rim. For most practical uses they give an adequate performance, but they do introduce an added complexity called 'middle temperature error' which, when affecting marine chronometers used in navigation, can be significant. To correct this, many different methods of so called 'auxiliary compensation' have been tried.

There are other factors – barometric pressure, for instance – that can affect the accuracy of timekeeping of a clock, but none of such significance as those mentioned at length. Positional errors nowadays are averaged out; that is to say, a good wristwatch is tried in the six principal positions and the best average performance obtained in each. An inexpensive wristwatch will only be tried in two positions, while in a pocket watch positional errors have a relatively small effect anyway. As for temperature compensation, the situation was revolutionised by the inventions earlier this century of the alloys 'Invar' and 'Elinvar'. The inventor, Dr Guillaume of Paris, won the Nobel Prize in 1920 for these improved alloys, which undergo negligible change as a result of differences in temperature. 'Invar' was used for pendulum rods, while 'Elinvar', used for balance springs, eliminated middle temperature error as well as rendering both balance wheel and spring non-magnetic.

'Complications', as applied to clocks and watches, is almost a self-explanatory term. A 'complicated' clock or watch is, at least in theory, any that does more than simply tell the time. Nowadays many so-called complications have become so commonplace as to make the term inappropriate.

Edinburgh was the home not only of the *Encyclopaedia*, but also of a very fine early nineteenth-century horologist and technical writer, Thomas Reid. This clock of his presents some curious contradictions. Its massive chronometer escapement, beating two seconds, and therefore essentially a precision controller, is nevertheless allied to a solid uncompensated balance wheel. The back plate of the movement is signed 'Thos. Reid, Edinburgh. 1803', and it is possible that it was intended mainly for demonstration purposes.

riate. Nevertheless, for the sake of completeness, it may be convenient to review the various kinds of 'attachments', as they are also sometimes called, which may be superimposed upon the basic 'going' train, that is, the mechanism that just tells the time.

The indicators of any clock or watch are, of course, the dial and hands; the first is usually fixed, with the second moving against it. There is a whole range of complications that extend these visible indications, of which a number derive from the calendar. A simple calendar mechanism, which is just pushed forward once every twenty-four hours by the going train, can still give both day of the week and day of the month indications, as well as the month itself and sometimes the year. Such a mechanism has, of course, to be adjusted manually for leap years, as well as for months of less than thirty-one days. In the most complicated clocks and watches, however, it is possible for this to be done automatically, and then the mechanism is described as a 'perpetual calendar'.

The need to compensate a balance wheel against temperature changes is most marked when it is applied to chronometers, and many chronometermakers of the eighteenth and nineteenth centuries designed special balances to this end. A selection of these is shown. Museum of the Worshipful Company of Clockmakers, Guildhall, London.

An extension of simple calendarwork is the moon dial. The lunar cycle is 29½ days, and 'age of the moon' or 'moon phases', as it is variously called, was a popular adjunct in both clocks and watches, even until quite recent times. Essentially it consists of a disc with, usually, two representations of the moon thereon; this disc revolves behind a cut-away aperture in the dial. Generally the moon disc has fifty-nine teeth cut upon its outer edge – twice 29½, that is – and these are nudged forward one at a time every twelve or twenty-four hours, depending upon the particular arrangement. Before the time when street lighting became universal, it was quite important to know whether or not the moon would be up; and lunar work on clocks is a well-recognised feature from about 1750.

Associated with a moon dial is, rather more rarely, a tidal dial which purports to give an approximation of high tide at a designated place. Found on some eighteenth-century longcase and spring clocks, they must have been useful in tidal waters where the river or coast provided a means of transport.

Another visible indication of value in earlier times, but even then rarely provided, was an 'equation' dial. The equation referred to is the so-called equation of time, that is to say, the relationship between mean time and solar time. Given this relationship, it is possible, whenever the sun shines, to check one's clock or watch by a sundial; and before the advent of the time signal by telephone or radio, and unless one lived within easy reach either of an observatory or of a watch- or clockmaker possessing a regulator clock, this was the only way to do it, except by setting up a telescope and carrying out an observation of 'a transit of a specified star across a meridian' – which no layman in his right mind would be inclined to

undertake! Having said this, tables setting out the equation of time were printed year by year – they will sometimes be discovered fixed inside the long-case clocks – so that a separate equation dial was something of a luxury. Technically, too, it was not without its difficulties of accomplishment. Mean time and solar time only agree on four days during any year, and at other times the difference between them varies between extremes of about +16½ minutes and −14½. The principal component of the motion work by which this reading is given continuously on a clock is an ingeniously designed cam, which, because of its shape, is called the 'kidney piece'.

Remembering that mechanical clocks can be designed to go for as long as a year at one winding, any information at all which is based on time-measurement, whether the interval concerned be long or short, can be shown on a clock dial – and probably has been, at some time or another. Thus times of sunrise and sunset for the farmer, Saints' days for the religious community, or just a ship rocking on painted waves to show that time passes – or that the clock is still going – are all to be found in varying degrees of rarity. In some early clocks, certainly in the monumental astronomical clocks of the sixteenth century, much more information was provided, since these catered not only for the astronomer but for the astrologer as well. To appreciate that there was formerly a most intimate relationship between astronomy and astrology, it is only necessary to know that, in the latter, it was firmly held that the five planets which had up to that time been located, together with the sun and the moon, influenced the lives of all on earth, successively each hour according to their distances from it, starting with the most distant and working inwards. Hence the appearance on such clocks of the Zodiac, which was thought to be a belt, about 18° wide, in the heavens, outside which the sun, moon and planets do not pass. There was also a certain amount of other miscellaneous information, probably of use both to laity and to clergy, such as the Dominical Letter, from which was ascertained the date of Easter Sunday; the Golden Number, which is related to the nineteen-year cycle regulating the repetition of the days of the full moon; the Epact, which is the age of the moon on each 1st January; and the Solar Cycle, a period of twenty-eight years after which the days of the month fall on the same days of the week once again. It is really not too long a step from clocks of this kind, to those much more modern ones with a multiplicity of dials, which each show the time in some stated capital city of the world. Anyone who may wish to see a modern example of a hyper-complicated clock, embracing a number of those indications listed above as well as many more, has only to visit the Jens Olsen World Clock in Copenhagen, completed as recently as 1945.

Another whole class of visible complications, of which mention must be made, is that which would nowadays be called 'timers'. These are devices drawing upon the main timekeeping property of the clock or watch mechanism to measure off smaller intervals for special purposes. The 'stop watch' is, strictly speaking, simply a watch with a seconds hand and a means of halting the escapement – that is to say, the entire watch – usually by the simple expedient of a lever that pushes a pin in between the teeth of the escape wheel. Many watches were so equipped during the nineteenth century and earlier, and they are sometimes called 'doctor's watches' although whether they served any useful purpose when measuring the pulse it is hard to say. The chronograph, in horology, is associated with the kind of watch that has a separate seconds hand, capable of being stopped, started and returned to zero, although its literal meaning – a writer of time – does have some foundation in the so-called 'inking chronograph', patented by F. L. Fatton in 1822. In his design, there was a dial on both sides of the watch. That on the back revolved, but there was a fixed arm terminating in an ink reservoir and nib which, by pressing a button on the outside of the case, could be brought momentarily in contact with it, leaving a tiny mark. At the end of the

This under-dial view shows a particularly complicated Swiss watch by Nicholas Monnier, of the early nineteenth century. Not only does it strike the hours – properly, it is called a clock-watch – but it repeats the quarters; furthermore, by operating a slide on the band, Grande Sonnerie is obtainable. If that was not enough, this clock-watch possesses the rare virgule escapement.

The most common form of musical watch movement is that introduced by the Swiss, early in the nineteenth century in which a disc, pinned on both sides, revolves between individually tuned steel teeth. This example by Piguet et Meylan illustrates the arrangement. Such watches are generally based on the cylinder escapement and often also have a quarter-repeating motion.

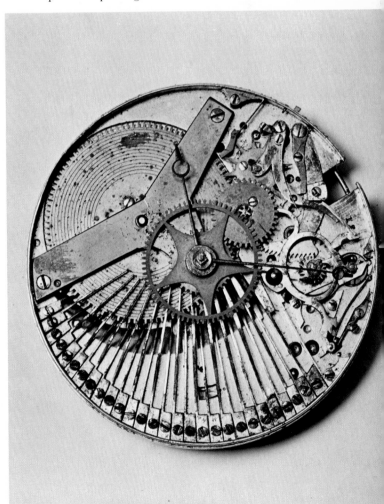

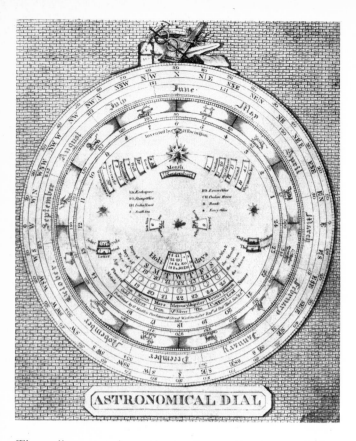

ASTRONOMICAL DIAL

The ordinary man's continuing interest in astronomical – and, in view of the inclusion of the zodiac, presumably also astrological – phenomena is well demonstrated by this cardboard 'Astronomical Dial'. Apparently 'invented by H. Ewington' and 'Published by G. Medley, Parliament Street, Westminster, entered at Stationers' Hall, November 25th, 1802', it consists essentially of a printed dial with a number of cut-out sectors behind which volvelles can be moved by hand to give a variety of interrelated information.

interval being timed, a second mark could be made upon the dial and the time between the two marks computed. Afterwards, the marks were simply erased and the procedure could start again. Another form of this type of instrument is called a 'split seconds chronograph'. In this, two seconds hands, mounted on the same axis one above the other, revolve together continuously in normal use. However, one of them can be stopped at will, for instance at the start of a period to be timed, the end of the period being noted on the other hand as it continues to revolve. The stopped hand can then be zeroed back to the revolving hand. In yet another form, of long usage throughout the eighteenth and nineteenth centuries, subsidiary hands, often driven by an independent train with its own mainspring, 'jumped' various fractions of a second, usually fifths or quarters, and could be stopped and started by a lever or push-piece. It is difficult, at this distance of time, to say with certainty what some of them may have been used for; they are generally beautifully made, yet their actions sometimes have an air of novelty about them. Present-day chronographs, of course, not only measure

seconds, but also have dials recording minutes and even hours.

So far we have been concerned with visible complications, and before we leave them to deal with audible ones mention should be made of another sort of visual effect, which, although generally not intended to be of an informative nature, occurs in various forms at virtually all horological periods. This is the automation, defined as 'a machine which moves by concealed machinery'. In clocks and watches, the word is applied to any image of man or beast of which part, or the whole, moves.

There were certainly some simple automata incorporated in various early water clocks, but the first application to a mechanical clock was probably the monumental cock which surmounted the first Strasbourg cathedral clock, constructed about 1355. This remarkable automaton is dealt with at length in the next chapter.

Other automata were regularly associated with huge astronomical clocks of similar type. Usually these took the form of processions – either of religious figures or of royal ones – which passed through a cycle of movements at set times, returning to their original state at the end in readiness for their next appearance. The sixteenth and early seventeenth centuries were renowned for the great heights to which the finest mechanics had developed clockwork, and many examples of their skill remain. The great gilt ship-clock or *nef* attributed to Hans Schlottheim, and made for Emperor Rudolph II about 1580, almost incidentally incorporates a clock; far more spectacular was its capacity to run up and down the banqueting table under its own power, swaying to imaginary waves and firing its guns as it went, while an organ played and the Heralds and Electors processed past the enthroned Emperor. Then again, the clocks of Isaac Harbrecht – who made the second Strasbourg cathedral clock between about 1571 and 1574 – tend to combine a fine show of astronomical information with automata. The lineal descendants of such clocks as these are to be seen in the succession of Guinness exhibition clocks which were such a feature of life in Britain in quite recent years, and also the Liberty's clock, set above the entrance to that department store just off Regent Street in London.

So far, examples given have been on the grand scale – public clocks, in the main. This prolific early period surprisingly also provided many examples of domestic clocks incorporating automata, the great majority coming from centres such as Augsburg, renowned for its highly skilled mechanics. There is such a huge variety of these clocks that it is only possible to summarise them briefly. Their themes were either religious – the Crucifix clock is a well-known type – or else animals were the basis of the design, and in these cases it was customary for their eyes to roll in time with the escapement, wings to flap or beaks to open at the hour, and so on.

There was, from earliest times, a much simpler automaton than any of the rather sophisticated mechanisms so far described. This was the clock 'jack' – contracted by the English from '*jaquemart*', which is said to mean 'Jack o' the clock' in reference to the fourteenth-century clock in Dijon, in France. A 'jack' is simply a figure holding a hammer, with which it strikes the hour on a bell. One of the best-known examples is Jack Blandifer, the figure that performs this duty in Wells cathedral; he also kicks the quarters with his heels on two other bells.

Watches were not without their automata, too, although generally this was a much later development than in clocks, and often somewhat less reputable. The Swiss, by the beginning of the nineteenth century, had perfected watches which, on depressing the pendant, set in motion complete scenes of moving people and animals – stonemasons or woodcutters at work, smithy work of all kinds, often accompanied by swans feeding on a millpond, goats browsing and so forth. In another version, *jaquemart* figures were placed either side of a dial made smaller to accommodate them; these appeared to strike the hours on tiny bells when activated by the pendant, although such striking was actually carried out inside the watch, upon curved tuned wire gongs sited around the edge of the case. It was not long, however, before this penchant for mechanical invention degenerated, resulting in a spate of so-called erotic watches, often incorporating secret panels above the dial or in the back of the case which had first to be opened before the scene could be viewed. Some of these were well executed, but the great majority were of coarse workmanship, and have been correctly compared to the other phenomenon, of more recent provenance, which is so aptly summed up in the opening gambit of the trader in such objects: 'Filthy postcards for nice English gentleman?' Such products do not bear comparison, either, with another type of erotic watch, usually of the late eighteenth century, in which a static scene is painted in enamels behind a secret double back of the case. Many watches of this variety are of genuinely high quality, incorporating painting of exceptional standard so that despite their content, they will frequently be acceptable as works of art in their own right.

The final variant, as well as the commonest, in this catalogue of the complications that can be associated with simple time-measurement is the audible effect. The first device to sound the time was the alarm; it preceded any arrangement for striking the hours or even for showing the time. Indeed, the first clocks in monastic usage were nothing other than what nowadays would be called 'timers'. They simply sounded a bell at pre-

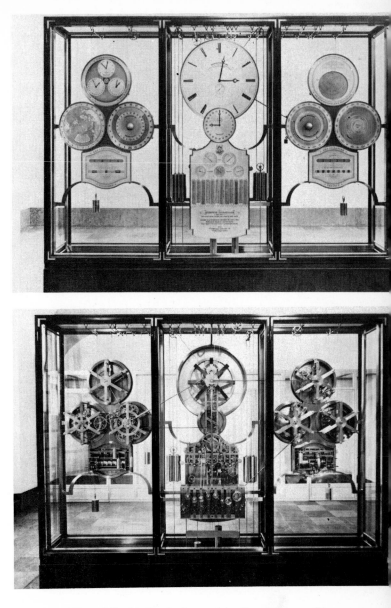

The Jens Olsen World Clock, housed in Copenhagen City Hall, was completed in 1945 and is probably the most complicated modern mechanical clock in existence. It is a worthy successor to the tradition of great complicated clocks elsewhere in Europe.

determined intervals, to warn the clock-keeper that some particular office was due. In effect, the going train unlocked the alarm train when the correct point in time was reached, and the latter continued ringing until it ran down. Alarms have been commonplace ever since those early days, in both clocks and watches, with no great variation in the principle involved, except perhaps that the alarm action can usually be curtailed at will.

The ability to strike hours upon a bell has been known from very early times, and the first, and simplest, method of doing it, which was applied to both clocks and watches, is known as 'count wheel' or 'locking plate' striking. The count wheel, which effectually 'counts' the strokes of the hour being struck, is a toothless wheel, the edge of which has been divided into unequal sections, running

Another variant of the musical watch exactly copies the principle of a musical box in that the tunes are pinned out – the horological term is 'pricked' – on to a revolving cylinder which abuts upon the ends of the tuned teeth of a steel comb. This model also generally dates from the early nineteenth century. British Museum, London.

from the shortest to the longest in relation to striking the hours of one through to twelve. A notch divides each section from its neighbour, and, at rest, the striking detent, which is a kind of lever used for locking and unlocking parts of a machine, lies in one of the notches. When the going train reaches the hour, it lifts the detent out of its notch, and the count wheel starts to rotate, at the same time as the hammer sounds the hour at a controlled rate on the hour-bell. The detent rides over the slowly turning edge of the count wheel until the hour corresponding to that segment of the wheel has been struck, when it reaches the next notch along the edge, into which it drops, locking up the striking train until the next time.

The system works quite well although it is more susceptible to derangement than the one which succeeded it; but its major drawback is its capacity for getting out of synchronisation with the going train, more often than not due to resetting the hands without allowing the striking train to strike in full every intervening hour between the old setting and the new, a time-consuming operation. It is quite easy to correct this fault if it arises: it is simply necessary to leave the clock hands as they are, but keep on releasing the striking train by hand until eventually it strikes the hour shown on the dial; but the system is not foolproof, and misuse can possibly damage it. Even so, in some countries and in clocks where there were no complications, locking plate striking found considerable popularity; it appears in many French and American clocks throughout the nineteenth century.

A better system, invented by the Rev. Edward Barlow in 1676, is called 'rack and snail' striking. A rack, in horological parlance, is a segment of a toothed wheel, while a snail is a cam cut in steps. At the hour, the rack drops, its tail resting against the snail. This component revolves with the hour hand, exhibiting to the tail of the rack a different step for each hour, and leaving to be gathered up only the related number of teeth on the rack. When the train is released, a 'gathering pallet' rotates, collecting up the rack one tooth at a time until the hour striking is completed. The train is then locked up once more. The great advantage of this system is that, since the hour snail is directly connected to the hour hand, the two can never get out of synchronisation, and the hands can always be reset in a continuous manoeuvre, without any need to strike out each intervening hour in full. The system catches up by itself.

In passing, it is worth noting that there have been other forms of striking than that with which most of us today are familiar. Joseph Knibb, a celebrated seventeenth-century clockmaker, devised 'Roman striking', in which two bells of different pitch were used, the one representing the Roman 'I', the other the Roman 'V'. Using this method, and regarding 'X' as twice 'V', no more than four strokes need ever be heard, whatever the hour; and this was particularly important at a time when most domestic clocks went for eight days, throughout which duration it would require an inordinately long spring to drive the striking train, with only one winding. Another method of striking, known as Dutch striking, was directed towards clarifying the half-hour stroke of a clock which, if heard from so far away that the hands could not be read against the dial, was of little practical use. In this system, again, two bells were used. The hour was struck on the larger, deeper bell; but when the half-hour arrived, the next succeeding hour was struck on the smaller, higher-pitched bell. This system eventually led to that

Although this particular watch, which is unsigned, dates from about 1860 and is apparently of Swiss manufacture, it is not clear, as with so many early timers, what it was intended to do. The escapement beats quarter-seconds, and both the large hand and the small hand below the centre of the dial, measure off quarters. The small hand was probably intended to confirm to the nearest quarter second the movement of the larger second hand, and it is possible that the watch was associated with gunnery. This type of watch – although previously key wound, rather than keyless – was made from the end of the eighteenth century onwards, beating either quarters or fifths of a second, and usually based on a cylinder escapement.

known as full Grande Sonnerie striking, during the last quarter of the seventeenth century. In this latter arrangement, after each quarter is sounded, it is followed by the last preceding hour.

It was a simple step from hour striking by rack and snail to chiming the quarters by a similar system. Dr Barlow further modified his system to produce the first 'repeater', that is to say, a clock or watch that one can cause to sound the time at will, either by pulling a cord at the side of the case or, for a watch, depressing the pendant or pushing a sliding piece set into the band of the case. His application for a patent for this invention was opposed by the celebrated London clockmaker Daniel Quare, supported by the Worshipful Company of Clockmakers. In the end, the matter was referred to the monarch, who gave preference to Quare only because in his arrangement one process activated both hours and quarters, whereas in Barlow's two actions were necessary to achieve the same result.

In case it may be thought that hour-striking has always been a facility confined to clocks, it may perhaps be mentioned at this point that hour-

This large clock by George Lindsay was a favourite of the late Courtenay Ilbert when it was in his collection. Lindsay, who frequently signed himself 'Servant to the Prince of Wales' or 'Watchmaker to His Majesty', enjoyed a Royal Warrant from George III and seems to have specialised in elaborate musical clocks; both organ clocks and clocks incorporating a musical train on bells are recorded. British Museum, London.

This rear view of the previous illustration shows the small organ operating automatically. It plays a choice of eight tunes every three hours. British Museum, London.

Isaac Habrecht's famous clock of 1589 has four levels of automata above the clock mechanism proper. These show, starting from the bottom, the planetary deities representing the days of the week, next a seated Madonna and Child in silver accepting the homage of angels. The third floor up has four silver figures representing the four Ages of Man, and on the topmost floor is the figure of Death who strikes the hours, whilst from the left and through a door the figure of the resurrected Christ appears. British Museum, London.

striking watches have been known for centuries, certainly from early in the seventeenth century to the present time. Correctly, they are called 'clock-watches' – or, a more recent usage, 'striking watches' – and some of the finest early watches combined striking and alarm facilities.

Repetition work, in general, utilises the rack and snail system used for hour striking and quarter chiming, but allows them to be activated at will. The first repeating systems gave the time only to the nearest quarter, usually on two bells – 'ting-tang quarters', as they were sometimes called – the usual arrangement being first to sound the last hour struck, followed by double strokes, one on each of two bells, for each quarter-hour completed since that last full hour. Thus, say, at a quarter to ten, the repeater would sound nine strokes for the last full hour, followed by three double strokes, one for each subsequent quarter.

During the eighteenth century, repetition work was greatly refined, so that the hour became divided by half-quarters – that is, eight periods of seven and a half minutes each – and then into twelve periods of five minutes. Half-quarter and five-minute repeaters operate upon the same system as quarter repeaters, only that, after the last complete quarter sounded, there may be a further 'tang' if more than seven and a half minutes of the

The Swiss have been supreme in devising automata for watches, and this particular example by Piguet et Meylan and dating from the early nineteenth century was formerly in the collection of King Farouk of Egypt which was sold up in 1954. Not only has the watch a musical train, but below the dial is a figure of a boy playing a triangle and a girl playing a hurdygurdy, both in vari-coloured gold.

above right
In this remarkable creation, the automaton is not in the image of a human being, but in the coloured revolving spiral supported by swans which surmounts the whole. In the base is a carillon musical movement, while the timekeeping is by Staplin of London and dates from the late eighteenth century. Formerly the property of King Farouk of Egypt.

succeeding quarter has passed; or, if it is a five-minute repeater, conceivably up to two 'tangs' indicating ten minutes of the next quarter has been measured off. Inevitably, of course, the final refinement, the minute repeater, appeared upon the scene; there are eighteenth-century examples of this, although it was not until the nineteenth century that it was made in any quantity, particularly in the case of watches. In the minute repeater, the last hour is struck upon the lower-pitched of two bells or gongs; the last quarter is represented as double strokes, exactly as previously; then the number of minutes completed after the last quarter struck is sounded with single strokes upon the higher-pitched bell.

Although not frequently encountered, it might make a fitting finish to this examination of the rudiments of clockwork to mention the part played in it by music of various kinds. It has always been only a short step, technically, from a clock that chimes quarters upon eight bells to one that plays a selection from several different tunes on, perhaps, fourteen. The principle is simply that of the commonplace musical box, but with the rotating barrel and the strategically placed pins protruding from it actuating the tails of bell hammers, rather than the steel teeth of the tuned musical 'comb' with which everyone is familiar.

Of the two methods of controlling the striking used on both clocks and watches, the later and more efficient was that known as the rack and snail, which can be seen on page 33. The earlier system was known as count wheel striking and depended upon dividing the circumference of a wheel into sectors proportional to the number of hours to be struck from 1 to 12. This photograph shows the count wheel of a tower clock on a large country house: the clock dates from Queen Anne's time and has recently been thoroughly restored.

It was not long after quarter-repeating work had been perfected that this was further refined to give half quarters – i.e. seven and a half minutes – and then five-minute repeaters. This early eighteenth-century movement by John Bushman is an example of the latter.

The ultimate refinement of a repeating watch had to be striking the time to the nearest minute. It is possible that this was perfected before the end of the eighteenth century, but it did not come into common usage until the nineteenth. This example is by Dent, watchmakers to the Queen and the firm that built Big Ben. The unique characteristic of a minute repeating mechanism is clearly visible: this is the four-armed snail, each arm having fourteen teeth cut into it, which can be seen in the centre of the movement.

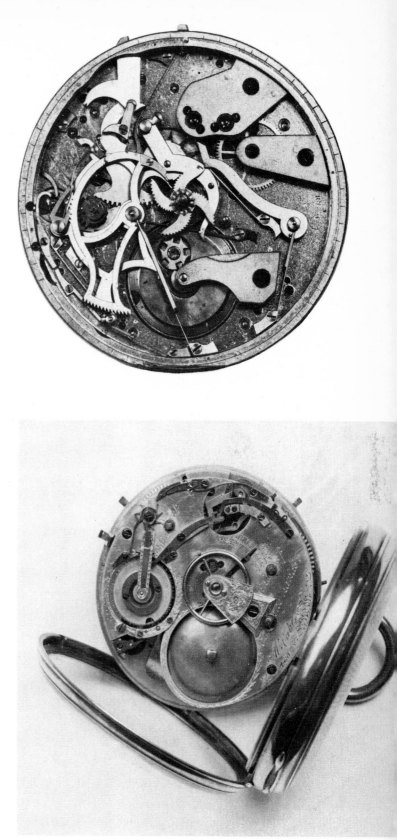

Carillons of bells operating upon this system have been associated with quite early church clocks, as well as with rather smaller creations. There is in the British Museum, for instance, a carillon clock by Nicholas Vallin dated 1598, which, with an overall height of only 23 inches, cannot have been intended for public use. This clock, the earliest known clock with a carillon to be made in England, albeit by a Flemish craftsman, plays a tune on thirteen bells just before each hour, a short phrase at the quarters and a slightly longer fragment at the half-hour. As for carillons in larger clocks, it is known that the original Strasbourg cathedral clock, built in the fourteenth century, incorporated such a mechanism. The oldest surviving one, however, is probably the clock said to date from 1542, which was taken from the church of St Jacob, in The Hague, and which is now preserved in the Clock Museum in Utrecht.

Musical watches were being made in London by a certain John Archambo early in the eighteenth century, the tunes being played upon sets of hemispherical bells set upon a common stem and concealed in the back of the watch case. Inevitably, however, such watches were large, and musical watches did not really enjoy much of a vogue until the early nineteenth century, when the tuned comb was adapted from the musical box. Two types of musical watch, both made principally in Switzerland, are known from this period. In the first, the action exactly replicates that of a musical box, with a small pin-barrel revolving against tuned steel teeth set parallel to one another. The other version, which is the more common, as well as enabling the watch to be made thinner, utilises instead of a pin-barrel a revolving disc, in which pins are inserted upon both sides. The separate teeth of the comb have their feet planted around the outer circumference of the movement, where they are out of the way of the mechanism proper; the effect, however, is to form a wedge of steel rods pointed at the disc, which would be quite incapable of operation were it not for the fact that alternate ones pass above and below it.

This musical watch by James McCabe which dates from about 1800, is a throw back to an earlier era when makers such as John Archambo, in the first half of the eighteenth century, were making large watches which played tunes on bells. This very much smaller watch nevertheless employs five hammers striking on four bells. Museum of the Worshipful, Company of Clockmakers, Guildhall, London.

The earliest surving domestic carillon clock is almost
certainly this one by Nicholas Vallin which is dated 1598.
The carillon consists of thirteen bells. British Museum,
London.

This view shows more clearly the operation of the carillon with its vertically mounted pin-barrel. Visible in the centre foreground is the striking count wheel. British Museum, London.

The church of St Jacob in The Hague originally possessed a clock with what is believed to be the earliest surviving carillon mechanism, which is attributed to the year 1542. The pinned drum which operated the carillon is visible towards the end of the mechanism. It is five feet in diameter and fifteen inches wide.

Other musical forms incorporated into clocks and watches at various times have included organs, singing birds and even a barking dog, if that can be classified under this heading! Almost any combination of complications is possible – and has probably been made, at some time or another –

so that it is understandable that terms like 'triple-complicated watch', which means a watch incorporating chronograph mechanism, repeatingwork and a calendar, should come into use, ugly though it may sound. There must be some slight sense of loss, however, that such objects are unobtainable new and, as antiques, are prohibitively expensive. They added some quality, springing from pure craftsmanship and the pride taken in its practice, to daily life which nowadays is totally absent, and which is certainly missed by discriminating people.

Great Clocks of the 'Iron' Age

As has been mentioned before, the precise – or even the approximate – moment of breakthrough which gave birth to the mechanical clock has so far escaped the historians of science. There are a few established milestones which it will be helpful to review, even though any final conclusion is likely to be elusive.

The single feature of a mechanical clock which must identify it beyond any shadow of doubt is the escapement. When, in the previous chapter, allusion was made briefly to a hydro-mechanical timekeeper of exceptionally early provenance, the clock in question was Su Sung's great astronomical clock of about 1090, although it is apparent that there were other mammoth Chinese clocks in existence and such technology clearly preceded anything that had, up to that time, come into use in either the Arab or European world.

The evidence upon which our knowledge of Su Sung's clock is based is contained in an early Chinese book, of about the date above-mentioned, the significance of which was first discovered by Drs Joseph Needham, Derek Price and Wang Ling in the 1950s. They published their evidence in 1960 (see the Further Reading list on page 254).

Su Sung constructed his clock in the Palace at Kaifeng; it is certain that it was actually built, and that it operated satisfactorily for a number of years. In essentials it was a great astronomical clock-tower, over thirty feet high and surmounted by a bronze power-driven armillary sphere which would have been used for astronomical observation. Below this was a rotating celestial globe – also powered to work automatically – with which comparison could be made from the observations carried out above it. Beneath this again was a five-storeyed pagoda-like structure, each stage of this carrying a procession of automata, ringing bells and gongs and otherwise indicating the hours and special times of the day and night.

Needless to say, all this action required a not inconsiderable power source to drive it. Therefore, also contained within the tower was a great water-wheel, the vanes incorporating scoops to contain the liquid, and this was sufficient to drive all the shafts actuating the various devices. However, from the horological viewpoint, the significant component was the checking mechanism which prevented a scoop descending under the weight of the water it contained until it was full. This device utilised a kind of weighbridge, together with a trip-lever and parallel linkage system, the first to ensure uniformity in filling the scoops, the remainder to stop the wheel at another point so as to bring the next scoop into position on the weighbridge.

This procedure, cumbersome and noisy though it probably was, took place each quarter of an hour; and, although the clock was driven hydraulically, it nevertheless provided for the release and locking of a wheel for the eventual purpose of nudging forward the time-indicating contrivances, step by step, in precisely the manner of any other mechanical escapement. It is a quite remarkable piece of advanced technology, considering its early date; but whether there is any tangible link between it and the clocks of conventional wholly mechanical construction with which we are all familiar, or whether it is a single isolated and individual example of that great genius which typified the Chinese culture at that period, remains to be seen.

Turning now to other considerations regarding the advent of the mechanical clock, it has often been held that, because the first mechanical clocks of which we have any real knowledge are associated with religious institutions, it is reasonable to suppose that it was in such cloistered surroundings, where the tender bloom of philosophical invention might be best expected to flourish, that one should look for the particular spark of

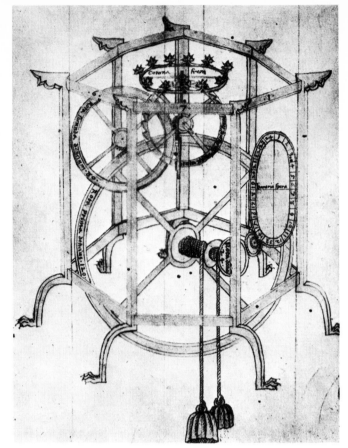

This modern reconstruction of da Dondi's clock, which followed his manuscript in the minutest detail, was carried out under the supervision of the great English horologist, the late H. Alan Lloyd, and was made by Thwaites & Reed of London. The clock itself is now in the Smithsonian Institution, Washington, D.C.

above right
This schematic representation of da Dondi's clock is the earliest known illustration of a weight-driven clock.

creative brilliance that added an escapement to the sum total of mechanical knowledge as it then existed. There are, indeed, in monastic records from very early times innumerable references to 'clocks' described by various linguistic derivatives of the Latin word *horologium*, but what sort of clocks these were is but rarely made clear from the context. Where it is made clear, the reference is invariably to a sundial, a clepsydra or some other kind of non-mechanical timekeeper.

Another school of thought inclines to the belief that clocks somehow arrived in Europe from closer Oriental cultures. The Arabs in the Near East, who were doubtless descended from the Biblical astronomers of Babylon and Chaldea, themselves studied and mapped the heavens and were certainly supreme in designing and manufacturing such essential scientific time-calculating instruments as astrolabes and nocturnals. But so far evidence is lacking as to their mechanical prowess.

What other evidence, of any substance, is left to be considered? There is some documentary evidence that the mechanical escapement had not been discovered by 1277, in which year a remarkable work entitled *Libros del Saber de Astronomia* appeared under the patronage of Alfonso the Wise, King of Castile. Essentially a set of astronomical tables, this work also included an account of past and present inventions for time-measurement, and it is very unlikely that the mechanical clock would have been omitted, had it then been in existence. Yet by 1350 the documentary evidence is of such familiarity with mechanical clocks as to suggest that they had been in common use for some time. It is quite possible that very early clock mechanisms have gone unrecognised since they would have had no dial: indeed only the telltale escapement would reveal to the knowledgeable that they were dealing with a clock.

As to early records, there is a tradition that a clock was erected at Westminster as early as 1288 while in 1286 a record exists of the payment of beer and bread to the 'Orologius' of St Paul's cathedral. There is also a record that a big clock was set up in Canterbury cathedral in 1292. Until comparatively recently it was believed that this series of records, deriving from the twenty years between 1280 and 1300 – in all of which the term for timekeeper remains *horologium* – must have been referring to clepsydrae rather than any mechanical device; but there has recently been a complete reappraisal by experts in this field, as a result of which it is now thought more likely that the mechanical clock first appeared in Europe some time between 1277 and 1300, and that many of these records refer to it. Furthermore, it has long been thought most likely that the clock made its first appearance in Italy or elsewhere in Central Europe. This opinion is also now being revised, since it seems on sound evidence that England may well have been in the van of this technological advance, and that she was certainly no less well informed than other countries at the relevant time. Even so, the first clockmakers were probably so thin on the ground as to make it necessary for them to travel widely in order to pursue their craft, and it is a clear possibility that those working in Britain may have come there from elsewhere in Europe.

The first clocks, therefore, seem certainly to have been used in religious institutions; they may only have been forms of alarm, perhaps with no dial as such, but just a simple means of ringing a bell after a certain period had elapsed; they warned the sacristan of his duties, and they were probably on the ground, rather than hoisted in a tower, as we nowadays expect to find church clocks.

It was not long, however, before true public clocks started to make their appearance in Italy, France and Germany, even though these took the form of belltowers under the control of a bellringer, whose actions in turn were controlled by the sort of mechanical alarm that was used in the monas-

This reconstruction of Su Sung's astronomical clock tower of AD 1090 shows the large water wheel used to drive the various motions including a rotating armillary sphere on the top level and a celestial globe immediately below.

left
In order to test the feasibility of the hydromechanical escapement of Su Sung's clock, this scale model was made in 1962 by Mr J. H. Combridge, an engineer. It proved conclusively that the escapement not only worked, but worked very efficiently. Science Museum, London.

The famous clock at Wells cathedral originally had no dials but now possesses one outside the church and one inside. This is the outside one.

above right
The twenty-four hour astronomical dial – graduated in two periods of twelve hours – at Wells cathedral, is one of the finest medieval dials of its kind in the world. Added to the clock about a century after this was built in 1392, it shows hours, days, dates and moon phases. It also incorporates automata, having four jousting knights above it as well as the oldest *jaquemart* known as Jack Blandifer.

teries. He was required to ring the curfew each night, as well as such other warnings as might become necessary from time to time.

Soon after this, it became possible to substitute a machine for the man ringing the bell – perhaps one of the first instances of automation – and by making it and the bell on a big enough scale and hoisting them up in the air, to provide a time service for the surrounding countryside.

At some quite early moment in the history of mechanical clocks, the mainstream of development split into three separate, even though related, directions. We have so far been following the simplest line – the primitive monastic alarm leading to the eventually somewhat more sophisticated turret clock, which, it might be argued, reached its peak of perfection during the nineteenth century in such masterpieces as the great clock at Westminster. During the period covered by the present chapter, however, such mechanisms were produced in wrought iron by techniques substantially based upon the blacksmith's craft in which hot metal was roughly shaped with the hammer, and files were used for finishing and rounding up. These clocks would have had two trains of gears – at first, perhaps, going and alarm, but soon changing to going and striking – and these were placed end to end; not until several centuries had passed and pendulum control had been introduced were they to be planted side by side. The earliest extant examples of these relatively simple mechanisms include a so-called 'belfry alarm' – of the type, that is, used to alert a bellringer – which is in the Mainfränkisches Museum in Würzburg and is said to date from about 1380; and the original clock of Salisbury cathedral, which can be reliably dated at 1386. This clock, which was most carefully restored in 1954, and then installed on the floor of the cathedral where it can be inspected by visitors, strikes the hours yet has no dial. It is controlled by a large foliot, with a period of oscillation of about four seconds.

In order to follow another subdivision of the mainstream, that of the monumental medieval astronomical clocks, of which, happily, a number of examples still exist albeit in varying states of their original condition, we must revert to the years between 1348 and 1362. During this time a quite remarkable clock was designed and made; and the inventor's description, which has come

The astronomical clock of 1389 at Rouen possesses the earliest surviving quarter-striking work. It is also very much larger than the clocks of either Salisbury or Wells. Considered to have been built originally by Jehan de Felains, the clock was modified at some unrecorded time, being converted to a verge with pendulum as well as being given some new wheelwork.

The quarter striking train of the Rouen clock of 1389.

65

opposite page
At Holy Trinity church, in the Suffolk village of Blythborough, stands this bearded warrior in mid sixteenth-century armour, nowadays disconnected from the clock so that he strikes the bell only when a cord is pulled. Jaquemarts of this kind were once commonplace.

left
Salisbury cathedral possesses one of the two earliest extant church clocks in England, dating from 1386 (see page 65).

below
The other famous early church clock in England at Wells cathedral dates from 1392. Unlike Salisbury, it possesses a quarter striking train which is thought to be contemporary (see page 67). Science Museum, London (on loan from the Dean and Chapter of Wells cathedral).

down to us intact, enters into such fine detail that it has proved possible within recent years to construct a facsimile of the clock with complete confidence that it is indeed a faithful replica. This work was carried out in 1960 under the direction of Mr H. Alan Lloyd, by the specialist firm of Thwaites & Reed of London; the clock itself is now in the Smithsonian Institution in the U.S.A.

The inventor of this clock was Giovanni da Dondi, who was born in 1318. The son of a doctor, he became a doctor himself, being appointed personal physician to Emperor Charles IV in 1349. He lectured in astronomy at Padua university, and in medicine at Florence; and he died at Genoa in 1389. In what was clearly a very full life, he yet found time to design and record in detail a clock the complexity of which was such as had never been seen before his time and which, indeed, was not to be attempted again for two centuries.

Two aspects of this clock are of importance in considering the historical development of clockwork. First, the complexity: the movements of the heavenly bodies, and especially the astrological and religious significance of such motions, were matters of enormous interest to God-fearing peoples – and it is arguable whether astrology necessarily deserves the reputation for absolute charlatanism that it enjoys today. Secondly, the technology employed: it will be remembered that iron was the customary material used for clocks at this early period – yet da Dondi's clock was made from brass, with some parts cast in bronze, and at no point in the manuscript is there any mention whatever of ferrous metal being used.

In the century from 1350 to 1450, very many big clocks were built in the cities of western Europe; there is some record, even if only documentary, of at least sixty. Many of these were simply time-keeping and time-sounding. Clocks striking the hours were more or less commonplace, and of the two English clocks included on the above-mentioned list from this period, both that at Salisbury – which has already been described – and the other, at Wells cathedral and dating from 1392, possessed this facility. The latter, in addition, has a quarter-striking train which is thought to be contemporary; and this extra facility compares, chronologically, with a similar feature in the clock at Rouen, which predates Wells by a handful of years, there being clear evidence that it was already completed and working by 1389. So, by the turn of the fourteenth century, public clocks already possessed the basic attributes which we expect of them today.

In addition, however, the clocks at both Wells and Rouen were fitted with astronomical dials, the former being one of the finest medieval dials in the world. Above this dial which was probably fitted a century or so after the clock was first built, since Wells – like Salisbury – originally had no dial,

there is a scene with automata, of four knights mounted on horseback who, at each hour, indulge in a joust during which one knight gets knocked off his steed. Other examples of very early clocks with astronomical dials in Britain include those at Exeter cathedral, Ottery St Mary, and Wimbourne Minster. Some of these fine machines, too, have automata figures, often called 'Jacks' (*jaquemarts*), which strike the hours and quarters, the one at Wells being known as 'Jack Blandifer'.

Perhaps the best-known large astronomical clock in the world is the one in Strasbourg cathedral; perhaps not so well known is that it is the third of its kind. The series started with a clock made about 1350, of which virtually nothing is known

This massive church clock from Cassiobury Park was almost certainly made in the fourteenth century and possibly for the abbey of St Albans; and there is even a possibility that it once belonged to Richard of Wallingford (see page 75). British Museum, London.

save that it was enormous – at least thirty-eight feet high, with a width at the base of about thirteen and a half feet. The only feature of this clock that is still extant is the great cock which crowned it and which, every day at midday, opened its beak, put out its tongue and crowed, simultaneously flapping its wings. One of the engineering miracles of this bird, which, together with the train and bellows operating it, is in Strasbourg Museum, is that each separate one of the primary feathers splayed out when its mechanism was working.

When the first clock was replaced after more than two centuries, the cock was found to be in such excellent condition that it was incorporated into the new design, as were also three pinned drums used to operate the carillon, although the tunes were changed. This second clock was built by Isaac Habrecht (1544–1620), a fine maker of complicated clocks, who took three years to construct it, finishing in 1574. He worked to the technical designs of the then Professor of Mathematics at Strasbourg university, one Conrad Hasenfratz,

sometimes called by the latinised version 'Dasypodius' – his name literally means 'Hare's Foot'. Habrecht, who came from a great clockmaking family – there are said to have been twelve such exponents of the craft within the compass of three generations – may well have been helped by his younger brother Josias and he subsequently made two smaller versions of the Strasbourg clock, both of them still surviving. One of these is in the British Museum and the other in Rosenborg Castle, Copenhagen, while all that remains of his cathedral clock is in Strasbourg museum.

Eventually, the second Strasbourg clock fell into disrepair in its turn – and it seems extraordinary to learn that, two hundred years after it was built, it proved impossible to find anybody to repair it, but that is said to have been the case. It remained out of action for many years, until J. B.-S. Schwilgué, sometime Professor of Mathematics at the College of Silestat as well as in business with a partner making portable scales, balances and turret clocks, was invited by the Mayor of Strasbourg to submit proposals to rectify the situation. He prepared three alternative solutions, starting with an estimate for repairing the old clock, which would, however, never be other than inaccurate and unreliable. Secondly, he proposed the replacement of certain parts of the old clock with new and more functional components; and finally, he offered to build a new clock. Eventually, his third proposition was accepted, then shelved because of the cost; but at long last, in 1832, it was revived although the contract was not finally signed until 1838. Schwilgué started work on 24th June in that year. He was compelled to fit his clock into the old clock case, already *in situ*, which did not please him as it left him no latitude to display his new machinery. His clock was set going for the first time on 2nd October 1842, simultaneously with the opening of the tenth Scientific Congress in France.

Before leaving early turret clocks, either on churches or on other public buildings, mention might be made of one other feature that is often a source of fascination to laymen. This is the very long pendulum. There are a number of churches in Britain where the pendulum can be seen swinging below the ceiling under the tower. Nearly always these will be found to have been a late eighteenth-century modification, except for the pendulum beating 1¼ seconds and corresponding to a length of five feet, which was first tried in longcase clocks at the end of the seventeenth century. The longest pendulum at present working in a turret clock in Britain is probably the one with a period of oscillation of 4 seconds, corresponding to a length of nearly 65 feet. This is installed in a clock dating from 1912, in St Stephen's church, Stockbridge, Edinburgh.

Finally, there is a third subdivision of the mainstream, the first appearance of the domestic clock.

As we have seen, the earliest public clocks were made of iron, and the first domestic clocks were, in essentials, small-scale versions of these, housed in rectangular frames that were reminiscent of those of their bigger brethren. These clocks are called 'Gothic' clocks or 'chamber' clocks, or just iron clocks, and they are usually associated with southern Germany, Switzerland, France and Italy. Technically, it became necessary to extend the gear train, in order to reduce the distance that the weight had to drop in order to drive the clock for a reasonable duration; the alternative would have required that it be hung so high up as to be not clearly visible to those wishing to read the time. These fine iron clocks were controlled by a foliot or a wheel-balance, and they were made over a considerable period, really only dying out after the pendulum had risen to prominence in clockwork.

The longest pendulum on a church clock in Britain measures 65ft and forms part of the clock built in 1912 at St Stephen's church, Stockbridge, Edinburgh. It has a period of 4 seconds.

They continued to be made of iron long after the introduction of brass as a common material in clockmaking; and it is generally believed that they were made by smiths who were accustomed to working on smaller scale objects – probably locksmiths and gunsmiths – than the blacksmiths who made the turret clocks. Gothic clocks generally have an iron dial, with a painted hour circle – more usually called a 'chapter ring', after the chapters or offices to which the monks were summoned by the very first clocks in monasteries – and springing from the tops of the four-posted frame a skeletonised superstructure containing one or more bells, surmounted, often enough, by a spire. Time is shown by a single hand, which may rotate in the normal manner, or remain stationary against a moving dial; the bells are used to strike the hour and sometimes to provide an alarm.

Weight-driven clocks were restricted anyway in their portability, and were quite unsuitable for use on the person, so that the obvious prerequisite for further development was a substitute power source

This small domestic clock of the late Middle Ages is simply an alarm clock. Weight-driven, it probably required winding every twelve hours, and the dial revolved against a fixed hand. The alarm is set by putting a peg in the appropriate hole in the dial which, in the course of its revolution, eventually lifts the arm which releases the alarm mechanism. British Museum, London.

opposite
Of much the same period as the previous example, this domestic iron clock is remarkable for its castellated superstructure and for its painted dial incorporating, at the bottom, a bird on a leafy branch. Attribution of this clock is difficult, although it is almost certainly northern European. British Museum, London.

below

The construction of this late fifteenth-century clock clearly follows that of larger public clocks of the time, with its posted frame and curved corner posts carrying rosettes. The primitive dial is a pierced iron plate with painted hour figures. The whole is surmounted by quite an elaborate canopy supporting a bell. Museum of the Worshipful Company of Clockmakers, Guildhall, London.

right

Of similar attribution to the previous illustration and of similar construction, this clock is nevertheless somewhat simpler. It incorporates a dial wheel with twenty-four holes and a pointer, and an alarm could probably be set off by inserting a pin in the appropriate hole. Museum of the Worshipful Company of Clockmakers, Guildhall, London.

of greater convenience. This was the mainspring, probably developed somewhat earlier, but first applied only during the last half of the fifteenth century. It is possible that the earliest springs may have been beaten out of brass, although steel was always the preferred material; but a major difficulty must have been to make it. Iron has to be made to absorb extra carbon to become steel, and this is done essentially by hammering and reheating. Then there was the associated problem of beating out a ribbon of steel that remained constant in width and thickness throughout its length. Inevitably the reject rate must have been inordinately high.

From evidence in contemporary paintings, the earliest spring clocks may well have looked like their forerunners, the Gothic wall clocks. However, they were soon to diverge into a variety of clearly recognisable types, from one of which it seems likely that the watch was evolved.

Although it has proved impossible up to the present time to pinpoint the invention of the

Unusually in clocks of this type, this example is signed
'Ulrich Andreas Liechty, Winterthur' and dated 1599. It
provides striking and alarm facilities, as well as phases of the
moon. British Museum, London.

mechanical clock with great accuracy, some clues can be gained from consideration of the times and conditions of the society in which it appeared. As Professor Cippola remarks in his book *Clocks and Culture 1300–1700*: 'It was not entirely by chance that the mechanical clock and the cannon appeared at approximately the same time. Both were the product of a remarkable growth in the number and quality of metalworkers and . . . many of the early clockmakers were also gunfounders'. In those times there was neither sufficient demand for clocks nor sufficient craftsmen skilled in their making to allow for the formation of guilds of specialists in this field. Furthermore, there can be no doubt that making any kind of clock was a very expensive operation, so that only rich individuals or corporations could afford it; and, in countries where metalworkers with mechanical knowledge were rare, it quite often happened that foreigners with the necessary expertise were imported to undertake the work. Thus it seems quite likely that both the Salisbury and Wells cathedral clocks were made by craftsmen brought to England specifically for the purpose by Bishop

Ralph Erghum, who himself came from Bruges, but who was Bishop of Salisbury from 1375 to 1388, in which year he was translated to Wells. At that particular point in time, large clocks were certainly more common on the continent of Europe than in Britain.

Before that time, though, there had been without doubt mechanical expertise of a high order in England, mainly among the monks. A certain Friar Richard of Wallingford is said to have constructed a complicated astronomical clock about 1320 which, when viewed by an experienced traveller two hundred years later, was not only still going, but was still remarkable enough to draw forth the comment that its like was not to be seen anywhere in Europe. Probably the observer who made this remark had not seen da Dondi's clock, but there can be no doubt that Wallingford's was earlier in the field. So Britain can no longer be lightly dismissed from consideration as a pioneer among European countries in experiments with clocks.

Iron chamber clock with right-handed train and large
balance. Possibly Flemish, about 1570. British Museum,
London.

right
Apart from his *magnum opus* in Strasbourg cathedral, Isaac
Habrecht is particularly known for two smaller astronomical
clocks. This one is in the British Museum, London (see also
page 54).

The Age of Brass and the Birth of the Watch

Fig. 10.

A detail from this plate, which appears in the celebrated eighteenth-century work *La Grande Encyclopédie* of Diderot and D'Alembert, shows one of the first stages in early springmaking with the metal being hammered out by hand.

The appearance upon the horological scene of the spring as a principal power source is of prime importance; but it will be realised by now that, when reviewing the early history of horology, one takes it almost for granted that, whatever else may have survived, inventors' names have not been passed down to us. Thus, most of what we know about the early history of the mainspring is based upon two paintings, both of which unmistakably show spring-driven clocks among the furnishings. The first, depicting a gentleman of the Burgundian Court, is to be found in the Museum of Fine Arts in Antwerp. The portrait dates from 1440 or thereabouts, and there is a spring-driven clock in the background. Another portrait, this time of Louis XI of France and dating from about 1475, includes among the detail a small hexagonal spring-driven table clock.

The first spring-driven clocks seem to have continued the fashion of previous styles, being designed to hang on the wall like weight-driven chamber clocks. It was not long, however, before they gave rise to a change of fashion since they were inherently so much more adaptable than those with weights. The styles that eventually developed, however, were recognisably national, so that designs can be fairly readily identified as originating from particular clockmaking 'schools'.

The two pre-eminent centres of early clock- and watchmaking in Europe were the south German towns of Augsburg and Nuremberg. England, prior to about 1600, had virtually no native industry, relying entirely upon foreign imports or foreign workmen brought into the country to pursue their craft. Thus, its domestic clocks at this period were generally imported iron chamber clocks, copied occasionally by English craftsmen in the smithing tradition, who sometimes also added a sheet metal casing to exclude dust. Apart from Germany, however, there was also, at this

77

time, a substantial interest in spring-clocks among French and Flemish craftsmen, and in Italy; each developed individual styles.

Although apparently first applied many decades before, the mainspring does not appear in quantity production, so far as can be judged, much before 1500. At quite an early date – perhaps somewhere in the second quarter of the sixteenth century – the watch 'stream' must have split away from that devoted to clocks; but this was anyway a period during which enormous creative effort was being applied to the design of timekeepers in general. It is likely that the new latitude provided by the compact spring drive gave impetus to this effort.

Of the two principal German centres of the craft, Augsburg enjoyed an unrivalled reputation for the enormous variety and superb craftsmanship of its spring-driven clocks, while Nuremberg concentrated mainly upon watches. The Augsburg makers had an insatiable appetite – and presumably also a bottomless market – for clocks incorporating automata which they produced in seemingly endless variety and with the greatest imaginable ingenuity. The fabulous *nef* described in chapter 2 and made by Hans Schlottheim for Emperor Rudolf II – or so it is intelligently surmised, since this magnificent object bears no signature of any kind – is, of course, an outstanding yet not a unique example; there is, for instance, an almost identical *nef*, only perhaps a little later in date because its mechanism is slightly more sophisticated, in the Conservatoire des Arts et Métiers, in Paris. Excluding such extreme examples of the craft, even the average specimen of the output of the Augsburg 'school' was more likely to involve some fabulous

above left
The weight-driven wall clock (this example was made in Germany about 1550) demonstrates the next stage in posted frame design incorporating top and bottom plates. This clock has clear similarities with the English so-called lantern clock, even to the pivoted sides, although this example is very much smaller. British Museum, London.

above
A late sixteenth-century chamber clock, almost certainly of German origin, this example, while preserving the posted frame construction that was normal at the time, has sheet steel sides with the front containing an engraved hour circle and central wavy-rayed sun. The steel arrow hand tells the hours, while the plain hand operates an alarm. The pierced steel balustrade is an interesting feature. The original verge and balance escapement has been replaced by a pendulum. Museum of the Worshipful Company of Clockmakers, Guildhall, London.

above right
The construction of this clock is interesting in that the movement and dial slot into the case. The latter, of gilt metal, is engraved with arabesques, in the manner of Hans Holbein the Younger, and surmounting the whole are 'Jacks' which strike the bell at the hour. The clock was made either in Germany or possibly in England about 1540. British Museum, London.

right
Early Italian clocks are by no means common, and this sixteenth-century example is steel throughout apart from the brass dial; it is controlled by a foliot. British Museum, London.

or actual beast which performed one or more functions automatically; or perhaps a little scene involving several people, such as the milkmaid milking the cow under the friendly eye of the farmer – the diversity of these clocks is endless. They also used religious motifs, such as the well-known types called crucifix, monstrance and tabernacle clocks; clocks of the two last-named types are often multi-dialled and extra complicated, with astrolabes and similar accessories incorporated.

Mention of Hans Schlottheim and his connection with the *nefs* – which, incidentally is based upon written evidence that he did supply such an object to the Emperor in 1581, while three years later he was certainly in Prague and actually working for him – brings to mind another celebrated clock with which he was associated. This is usually described as the Tower of Babel clock; it was and presumably still is in the Grünes Gewölbe in Dresden. This clock must have represented one of the earliest attempts to use a rolling ball as a time standard, a principle which was to be further exploited in succeeding centuries. In Schlottheim's arrangement, the mechanism was contained within an octagonal tower some four feet high. Above a base which contained the dial and main part of the machinery were two galleries surmounted by a lantern. The galleries were connected by a track spiralling through sixteen complete turns between one level and the other, and each minute a crystal ball rolled the whole length of this track, taking a minute to do so. On reaching the bottom the ball was raised by the clock mechanism once again to the upper level; but in the meantime another ball had started its down-

The preference of French makers for the two-tier table clock movement has already been demonstrated, but at least two London makers shared their views. This square table clock signed by Bartholomew Newsam was made about 1580–90. The dial-plate is a modern replacement. British Museum, London.

above right
A complicated version of another early clock style, this drum clock is attributed to Paulus Grimm of Nuremberg and is dated 1576. The dial is made up of eight concentric bands giving a variety of astronomical information. British Museum, London.

left
This elaboration of the cylindrical or drum-shape style of clock, which was made by Hans Gutbub of Strasbourg about 1590, incorporates an automaton figure on top of the bell which moves its arm at the hour. The case is decorated with hunting scenes in relief. British Museum, London.

ward journey. As if this were not enough of a novelty in itself – and the continual rolling of balls must have made a noise reminiscent of the early tramways, making it easy to see how the clock acquired its popular name – there were automaton figures of musicians simulating the sounds of an organ which was incorporated into the mechanism, and other figures were also deployed elsewhere upon the structure. Schlottheim started this clock in Dresden in 1592, and it is said to have taken ten years in the building; and unlike the *nefs*, where the actual clock forms but a tiny part of the whole and incorporates no new principles of design or craftsmanship, the Dresden clock is a milestone in horological terms.

Schlottheim was not the only clockmaker towards the end of the sixteenth century to appreciate the possibilities in a rolling ball, which was anyway based upon a fundamental concept of Galileo. Another maker interested in this device was a Viennese, Christof Margraf, who went so far as to take out a patent in 1595. Then, a few years later, Christolph Rohr of Leipzig made a most elaborate rolling ball clock, now in the Herzog Anton Ulrich Museum in Brunswick. Dated 1601, there is a variation of the original principle in this

clock, in that there is only one ball, its periodicity being taken to include not only the length of time it takes to roll down the inclined track – not a spiral this time, but running around the four sides of a flat-topped pyramid – but also the time taken to restore the same ball to its starting point again by lifting it in a cup on an endless chain. Once again, this total period is one minute. As an added attraction, the platform surmounting the runway contains, under a cupola, a carrousel of figures which is set in motion every three hours. Incidentally, the rolling ball as a time standard is not to be confused with the rolling ball as a power source, to which reference will be made in another chapter.

No survey of the great clocks of the sixteenth century, however brief, would be complete without some reference to the work of two other makers. Schlottheim and his contemporaries, by building so much novelty into their masterpieces, may be said to some extent to have equated time-measurement with entertainment, for this is what the adoption of automata on the grand scale must signify. Two centuries earlier – even though a considerable advance on its time – there had been one monumental scientific clock, made for the most serious of purposes between 1348 and 1362, the

left
The designs engraved on this hexagonal copper gilt French table clock are scrupulously copied from those made in the year 1528 by an engraver who signs himself 'I.B.' The clock, therefore, probably dates from 1530–40 and bears the signature on its base 'LOIS F'. This maker has not been identified. British Museum, London.

above
A very much more elaborate hexagonal table clock, this French product is dated 1545. Aside from the sculptured quality of the case with its figures in the roundels on the upper level, the clock has three dials, one below the hour dial showing the day of the week, and a third dial, shown in the photograph, for setting the alarm. There was originally a fourth dial, above the bell, which recorded certain astronomical data, but this is now missing. British Museum, London.

work of Giovanni da Dondi. Was there no comparable equivalent, even by this later period?

The answer to this is to be found in the work of Eberhart Baldewin, who was court clockmaker to Landgraf William IV of Hesse about the middle of the sixteenth century. He made two large astronomical clocks, the first between 1559 and 1561, and the second somewhat later, as well as, in 1575 or thereabouts, a mechanically operating celestial globe. His earlier astronomical clock as well as the globe are now in the Hessisches Landesmuseum in Kassel, while his second clock, which Landgraf William IV subsequently presented to the King of Saxony, is now in the Staatliche Physicalisches und Mathematisches Salon in Dresden. The background to his astronomical masterpieces is to be found in a work entitled *Astronomicum Caesarium*, published in 1540 by Petrus Apianus in Ingolstadt, which incorporated devices called volvelles. These are neither more nor less than rotatable paper discs, from which the position of the planets at any time can be simulated. Landgraf William not only conceived the idea of a clock which should provide this same information mechanically – the project with which

Baldewin was entrusted – but, together with his chief astronomer Andreas Schoener, he himself made fresh calculations of the positions of the chief stars. The decorative work on Baldewin's clock – that is to say, the case and all the associated engraving – was executed by Hermann Diepel of Giessen.

The second important sixteenth-century clockmaker of whom mention must be made is Jobst Burgi (1552–1632). Although born in Switzerland – in Lichtensteig, which is in Toggenburgh – he also entered the service of Landgraf William IV of Hesse, in 1578. There he remained until the Landgraf's death in 1592; and in 1604 he was appointed Imperial Clockmaker to Emperor Rudolf II in Prague.

Burgi's reputation as an outstanding craftsman in the making of globes has been recognised for generations; rather more recently he has come to the fore as a master clockmaker, and this only as a result of research by Professor Dr Hans von Bertele of Vienna. Again Landgraf William IV seems to have been the motivator; his dedication to astronomy necessitated ever more accurate timekeepers, which it was Jobst Burgi's pleasure to

strive to provide for him.

Professor von Bertele discovered three clocks – two in Kassel and one in Dresden – which, although unsigned, are on a number of technical grounds the forerunners of a fourth clock, which is signed. The numerous innovations directed to improved timekeeping performance to be found in this series of clocks include not only long duration – one clock goes for three months at each winding – but also the use of a form of remontoire. This is a device, of which any number of designs have been postulated over the centuries, which is directed towards ironing out idiosyncracies and inconsistencies in the power drive to a clock by converting it into a constant force, usually by using it to rewind a small ancillary spring, which then acts as the direct power source to the clock. This small spring, being frequently returned to maximum tension, exerts a well-nigh constant pull upon the mechanism.

Burgi's principal claim to horological fame, however, rests upon his remarkable development of what is now called the cross-beat escapement. In the third quarter of the seventeenth century the famous astronomer Hevelius mentions an escape-

opposite page, left
One of the more elaborate constructions to emanate from Augsburg, this hexagonal astronomical clock has a case made from gilt metal and silver. It is doubtful if the relatively simple clock mechanism, unfortunately missing, could possibly have lived up to the ambitions exhibited in the profusion of dials. British Museum, London.

opposite page, right
Eberhart Baldewin, clockmaker to the Landgraf William IV of Hesse, made this remarkable astronomical clock, completing it in 1651. The clock has three trains and a thirty-hour movement with quarter striking; it has dials on all four sides.

above left
The other side of Baldewin's clock.

above
Like Baldewin, Jobst Burgi also worked for Landgraf William IV of Hesse. A celebrated craftsman in the making of globes, he also made some outstanding clocks. This one is known as his experimental clock no. 1 and dates from about 1595.

left
This style of clock is generally described as a tabernacle clock, and it was probably made about 1600, in Germany, by makers who signed themselves 'SA.HA'. British Museum, London.

above
Burgi's second experimental clock predates 1600. His outstanding horological invention was the cross-beat escapement.

above right
Burgi's third experimental clock was made about 1605. For more details on this series of clocks see page 89 *et seq*.

ment for which he claims the greatest accuracy then attainable, referring to it as '*libramentum duplice*'. The ordinary escapement of that time – which can only have been the verge – is described simply as '*libramentum*'. Until Professor von Bertele's discoveries, nobody had unravelled this mystery, but it is now quite clear that it is to the Burgi cross-beat escapement that Hevelius was referring. The term '*duplice*' encompasses the two independently pivoted arms, geared together and each having one pallet, which take into an escape wheel having a large number of finely cut teeth. The arrangement permits of much closer adjustment of the escapement than in the case of the simple verge, which thus operates with increased efficiency.

Apart from the appearance of the mainspring, there were two other technical developments around this time of which it is necessary to take account. The first was the gradual assimilation of brass into the craft, as a suitable material for certain components in clock- and watchmaking. Brass is an alloy of copper and zinc, and it seems first to have been used for clocks on the continent of Europe about the middle of the sixteenth century;

Spherical and tambour-cased watches seem to have
originated at about the same time and are the earliest forms
of watch known. This German clock-watch, about 1550, has
the striking and going trains one above the other, and the
movement is fitted with a stackfreed. Ashmolean Museum,
Oxford.

left
Dating from about 1600, this exquisite silver gilt enamelled
table clock stands only 3¼ in high: a rare and fine example of
court craftsmanship, it probably emanated from Augsburg.
It incorporates both striking and alarm facilities. British
Museum, London.

opposite page
The diminutive clock built by Schlottheim into this elaborate
dinner table entertainment piece or *nef* is represented by the
small silver and enamelled dial which can be seen at the foot
of the mainmast (see page 41). British Museum, London.

but it did not spread to England for some little while thereafter, probably because there was no native brass industry and, even with government aid, it took many years to establish one. Thus it is not usually found in English practice until the beginning of the seventeenth century.

As clock materials go, brass is softer than iron or steel and worked differently. It cannot be hardened, like steel, by heating and then quenching, but only by hammering, or, where appropriate, drawing it into wire or rolling it. The early clockmaker probably cast his own brass; and, although it was at first used mainly for cases and dials, while the movements remained principally of steel, it was not long before brass became accepted as the material of choice first for the framework of the mechanism and subsequently for the wheels. Eventually, brass was adopted as standard for wheels, while steel remained the material for the pinions with which they are meshed. This usage is based upon the proven concept that two surfaces in contact suffer less friction from rubbing against one another if they are made from different metals than if they are the same. The pinions have to withstand more potential wear than the wheels, hence they are made from the harder substance; but the danger is always that dirt, and especially particles of metallic grit, can embed themselves in the softer substance that comprises, *inter alia*, the teeth of the wheels. This can then act as a cutting medium upon the steel pinion leaves, which start to show wear even though the teeth that are doing the damage appear completely unaffected.

The second technical development which should be noted was the appearance of what is generally called the 'plated' movement. The earliest clocks – and the design persisted for several centuries – were of that type which is commonly described as 'posted' or 'framed'; that is to say, the movements were deployed between metal strips containing the pivot holes for the arbors, and themselves supported within frames of, usually, rectangular open construction top and bottom, separated by four vertical posts, one at each corner. This arrangement had the advantage of great simplicity, both of original construction and when put into operation; the whole movement was so accessible that every part could be observed and adjustments were easy. Furthermore, when cleaning and overhaul were necessary, the main frame could generally be left intact; it served no purpose other than to hold the mechanism together and, as such, needed no maintenance.

In an illuminated manuscript of Flemish or Burgundian origin, of about 1470, there appears for the first time an illustration of a small clock without its outer casing, so that there can be no doubt about the unorthodox manner of its construction. In this new style, the mechanism is contained between two solid metal plates, which are maintained at the correct distance from one another by four pillars. The plates, however, are fundamental to the mechanism because the arbors carrying the wheels and pinions pivot in them – except for the balance wheel, that is. It follows, of course, that when this type of clock requires cleaning, the plates themselves, with their integral pivot holes, have also to be cleaned. The great importance of the movement contained between plates is that, once they were made sufficiently small, they became to all intents and purposes watches and could be carried conveniently on the person.

Every century, certainly up to the end of the nineteenth, has seen great strides in the development of mechanical horology, and the sixteenth was no exception. Reference has already been made, when dealing with the rudiments of clockwork, to two inventions – one only short-lived, but the other both theoretically and practically perfect and surviving for centuries – designed to correct the uneven pull exerted by a mainspring. The stackfreed probably only remained in use for fifty years or so, and was employed almost solely by south German makers. The origin of the word itself is unknown; but it is said to have come into use, being probably a corruption of Low German or Dutch, only in the mid eighteenth century, some two hundred years after the device itself had been abandoned.

The antecedents of the fusee, however, are somewhat better established, as befits the invention that provided both the first and best solution to the problem. The term itself is said to derive from the Latin *fusus*, a spindle, a definition that is not wholly irrelevant in its horological application. It was believed for many years that the first indication of the existence of this device was contained in certain drawings of Leonardo da Vinci that can be dated to about 1485–90. However, this date has been superseded as a result of the discovery of an illuminated manuscript in the Bibliothèque Royale in Brussels which can be dated, on various other grounds, around 1450–60, and which includes, among several clocks, sundials and other associated items, a table clock which unquestionably incorporates a fusee; thoughtfully, its outer case has been removed by the artist, so that the movement can be inspected in some detail. No example survives, of course, that approaches within even reasonable reach of that date. Until comparatively recently it was held that the earliest surviving spring clock with fusee was by Jacob the Zech (the last word means 'miner') of Prague, which is dated 1525, and is owned by the Society of Antiquaries in London; until three decades or so ago, this same craftsman was even credited with its invention, an interesting indication of how horological research has progressed of late. Now, however, pride of place goes to the fragmentary remains of a clock in the Bavarian National Museum in Munich, of which little more than the plates, spring barrel and fusee remain. This clock is signed with four initials and the date '1509'. Apart from this, there is a drum-shaped clock in the Musée des Arts Décoratifs in Paris which purports to date from 1504; but the third digit of this

This delightful drum-shaped clock in its rock crystal case is probably French and of late sixteenth-century provenance. It has an attachable alarm, which is positioned above the dial when in use and incorporates a lever projecting downwards in such a manner that it will be tripped by the hour hand when the latter reaches the appropriate time. British Museum, London.

opposite page, left
Burgi's greatest masterpiece is known as the Vienna Crystal Clock and was made about 1615.

opposite page, right
This view of a Burgi cross-beat escapement is taken from his second experimental clock illustrated on page 87.

In the Bavarian National Museum in Munich, these fragmentary remains of a clock dated 1509 represent probably the earliest surviving example of the fusee.

left
The rolling ball as a time standard has been used at various times in horological history. This elaborate example by Christolph Rohr of Leipzig is dated 1601. Only one ball is used, and the time it takes to descend the long track and reach the top again is one minute. Herzog Anton Ulrich-Museum, Brunswick.

opposite page, left
It is possible that portable watches were developed from small clocks in circular canister cases, such as this one of German origin, dating from the second quarter of the sixteenth century. Each of the hours on the dial is fitted with a touch-pin so that the time can be told at night. Museum of the Worshipful Company of Clockmakers, Guildhall, London.

opposite page, right
The movement of the canister clock previously illustrated is mainly of steel, and the only two brass wheels are almost certainly replacements. Museum of the Worshipful Company of Clockmakers, Guildhall, London.

date is suspect, and it would not be safe to rely upon it. The Jacob the Zech clock remains the earliest surviving complete example. The early form of fusee tends to be much too sharply tapered, as presumably the theory had not then been completely worked out; and not until the seventeenth century, when the scientific aspects of horology became more predominant, did the outer curve of the grooved cone become shallower and more flattened out.

The question of regulation – making the clock run faster or slower – was not dealt with at length as part of the rudiments of clockwork, since, in its simplest form, the method must be self-evident. It is necessary only to vary the force of the driving power, for example by increasing or reducing the weight, to obtain what is certainly fairly coarse, rough and ready, regulation of a simple clock; and this is indeed what was done in the earliest times. In addition, of course, the arms of the foliot were supplied with small movable weights, which could be brought nearer to, or removed further from, the centre of oscillation, providing a somewhat finer degree of control. Another method is known as hog's-bristle regulation, of which a clock of about 1500 in the Germanisches Museum in Nuremberg has the earliest surviving example. The method, subsequently applied to early watches as well as to clocks, caused the extent of the swing in either direction – or the amplitude, as it is usually called – of the balance to be limited by interposing in its path two bristles, to catch in turn either side of the balance arm or crossbar. The hog's-bristle was often used in conjunction with that type of balance in which a flat rim had been added to the simple crossbar, to make it a sort of flywheel; this type, and the true foliot, with or without adjusting weights (in the latter case the arms are terminated by rounded bobs which have led to its sometimes being called a 'dumb-bell' balance), seem to have

been used indiscriminately from earliest times, and there is no evidence to show that one superseded the other. It can be appreciated that the bristles possessed their own in-built resilience, so that when limiting the amplitude of the balance, they exerted quite a gentle restraint, much to be preferred to any system which brought the balance to a sudden jarring stop when it had swung as far as it was deemed necessary that it should do. Furthermore, there had of necessity to be provision for the bristles to be adjustable in their proximity to the balance bar at the limits of its swing, otherwise there would be no latitude for regulation. There is, incidentally, another interesting feature in the Nuremberg clock referred to above, and that is the use of screws and nuts, a very early example of this facility being used in horology, and only postdating by about fifteen years Leonardo da Vinci's sketches of a tap and die for making metallic screws.

Over the years, there has been much speculation about the origins of the watch. Two technical requirements were necessary before it could become a practical proposition – the development of a successful spring-drive to power it, and some better arrangement for framing the movement than the open-work, posted method used in the earliest static forms of timekeeper. Both these developments eventually came to pass, and, amongst the plethora of clock-types and shapes that must have poured out of centres like Augsburg, there gradually evolved two basic designs. One of these provided for a movement that was essentially deployed in a vertical plane with a dial likewise, and the other, which is often called the drum or canister type, has the dial and movement arranged horizontally. It is further held that the next stages in clock design sprang from the first, vertical system, while the drum clocks – many of which, from the middle of the sixteenth century

A good example of the second form of tambour case, in which the outer surfaces are curved. The protective cover over the dial is pierced to allow the time to be read, a fashion which preceded that of fitting a glass cover. Museum of the Worshipful Company of Clockmakers, Guildhall, London.

above right and opposite page
This spherical French clock-watch is by Jacques de la Garde, and, like the rather smaller German clock-watch shown on page 89, dates from about 1550. Unlike the German example, this incorporates a fusee. National Maritime Museum, Greenwich.

right
The stackfreed, as a means of evening out the pull of the mainspring, was an interesting, albeit ineffective, device used almost exclusively on watches and on a few horizontal table clocks, all of German provenance. It is almost unknown in small vertical clocks such as this one, which is dated 1612 although thought to be actually somewhat earlier.

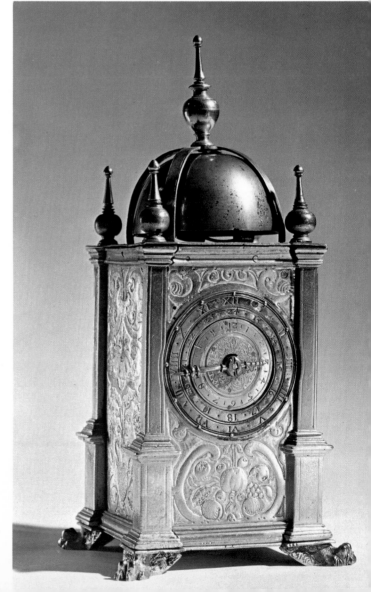

The earliest type of tambour watch-case had a flat top and bottom and a flat band, a fashion which continued till about the end of the third quarter of the sixteenth century. This German clock-watch, an example of this earlier style, also incorporates an alarm. Ashmolean Museum, Oxford.

if not earlier, were already being made quite small enough to be carried on the person – were the progenitors of the watch.

However this may be, the earliest watches seem to fall into two groups. One was indeed a modified form of the drum clock described above: it was flatter in contour, often a little larger in diameter, with hinged covers to either side which were engraved and pierced, as was the band of the case, to allow the sound of the hours being struck to issue forth. Nearly all such watches had an added attachment, usually either alarm or hour-striking – the latter, in other words, were clock-watches. The band of the case – that is, the part separating the back and front covers – might be flat or curved in profile, and the covers flat and overlapping the band or domed and butting with it. Cases with flat bands and overlapping flat lids are usually called tambour cases, preceding the other variety which did not appear until the last quarter of the sixteenth century.

The second style of early watch is spherical. It is extremely rare – probably no more than half a dozen examples survive in the world – but it is clear even from these few specimens that this type of watch was made both in Germany and France. The earliest of all dates from the second quarter of the sixteenth century, while the earliest French model is dated 1551. The latter is by Jacques de la Garde, and is in the Louvre in Paris. A similar, but larger, version by this same maker, dated the following year, is to be found in the National Maritime Museum at Greenwich.

Once upon a time it was unanimously held that the spherical watch was the prototype although recent research tends to suggest that both early types of watch arrived more or less simultaneously. The basis of the earlier belief derives from one Peter Henlein of Nuremberg, a locksmith who was clearly rather more of an artist than his trade description might imply. He first figures in a published reference dated 1511; he is later credited with making 'the small watch works which he was one of the first to make in the form of muskballs . . .' Since he must have been one of the first genuine watchmakers, later historians, even in this present century, also credited him with inventing the mainspring, although we now know this to have been a complete fabrication.

It is a curious thing that all surviving sixteenth-century watches are cased in gilt bronze. There are contemporary inventory references that show that gold and silver were used for this purpose as well, but none have come down to us. It may be that there were restrictions placed upon the use of precious metals for such purposes by the guilds concerned – this happened at a later date, certainly – which made such objects rare even in their own time.

By far the greatest number of extant watches

The stackfreed of the clock shown on page 94. The cam is original, but the curved spring and roller are replacements.

Back view of the movement of the watch on the opposite page shows a stackfreed and a foliot with a bristle regulator. Ashmolean Museum, Oxford.

from this period are German, as has been mentioned – and Nuremberg was unquestionably preeminent in this respect from quite early in the sixteenth century. However, research among archives in Italy shows that small clocks – and almost certainly watches too – were being made in that country before 1490, while there was a watchmaking tradition in France from 1525 or a little before. The styles of German and French watches, so far as it is possible to judge – since no French watch survives from before the mid century – were substantially different. There are no French watches in the tambour type of cases; of the mere half dozen or so that predate 1590, nearly all are spherical or oval. Piercing of the case, required to allow the sound of the bell to be heard, is confined to the band and the covers remain solid. The heavy chiselled decoration of German watches is replaced, in the French usage, by fine engraving. Towards the end of the sixteenth century, both France and Germany inclined towards octagonal cases, some of the rather more elegant elongated variety, while from 1590 France produced some of the first watches in oval cases with slightly domed

covers back and front. Although watches were certainly known in other European countries – England, Holland, and Switzerland, in particular – before 1600, the native craft in such countries had barely appeared, so that, in many cases, watches must have been imported into them from one or other of the major producers.

One remaining feature of many – perhaps most – sixteenth-century clocks and watches was the employment of touch-pins. These were placed around the dial, one at each hour, so that after dark, when the generating of any kind of light would have been tiresome and time-consuming, the position of the single hand could be related to its nearest touch-pin; this in turn had to be referred back to the twelve o'clock touch-pin, which was more prominent than the others and clearly distinguishable from them on that account. The same system has prevailed ever since, in watches designed for the benefit of the blind. *Montres à tact*, as the French call them, are but another example of an invention in horology that goes back to the beginnings of the craft, yet has never been bettered.

The Seventeenth Century – The Golden Age of Clocks and Watches

The title of this chapter has no connection with some particular horological application of a precious metal; the phrase is used metaphorically, yet any student in this field will recognise its validity. The hundred-year period between 1600 and 1700 has come to be known as the 'golden age' not only because it offers a far wider spectrum of decorative techniques and materials, and an infinitely higher standard of overall craftsmanship – especially towards the end of the period – than ever before, but also because it saw the birth and ascent to the peak of their prowess of some of the greatest names in the history of the craft. The real uniqueness of this century lies in its production of clocks and watches that were both functional and inherently beautiful, the perfect combination of art and craft. Later periods were to see timepieces become ever more accurate as such, while the quality of their decorative appeal all too noticeably degenerated. Finally, of course, the seventeenth century saw the introduction of possibly the two most significant horological developments of all – the pendulum and the balance spring.

As the century started, the commonest domestic clock was still the iron posted-frame 'Gothic' clock, weight-driven and relatively uncomplicated. Certainly the output of Augsburg, with its preference for spring-driven timepieces, cannot be discounted: too many superb examples remain to please us. But for the average European household – those that could afford it, that is – the iron clock, probably imported from south Germany although perhaps copied locally, gave a better showing than some of the more elaborate timepieces that were available. However, soon after 1600, the English established their own native craft which quickly rose to such prominence as to require proper organisation. One outcome of this was the granting of a Royal Charter in 1631, giving formal approval to the founding of the Worshipful Com-

pany of Clockmakers of the City of London. This was rapid progress for its time – it is difficult indeed to discover native English horologists before the start of the century, the only two names that readily spring to mind being those of Bartholomew Newsam and Randolph Bull, who both made clocks for Queen Elizabeth I and enjoyed the appointment of Royal Clockmaker; yet within thirty years the craft was clamouring for recognition.

The first outcome of this upsurge of activity was the emergence of a purely British style of domestic clock, the lantern clock. Nobody seems to know quite how it got that name – it may well have customarily been hung from a beam in much the way that lanterns were, and it is said that some ships' lanterns were of similar appearance – but it has been conjectured that the word is a corruption of 'latten', or 'laiton', the French word for brass. These clocks are also called 'Cromwellian' clocks, despite the fact that they were in use long before the Protector came to power. The first such clocks were somewhat shorter than the Gothic clocks from which they derived, and there was a large proportion of brass used in their manufacture. The movement continued to be of 'four-poster' construction, with the going train in front and the striking train behind, surmounted by a bell hung from a canopy. The great change was the addition of sheet brass sides, usually easily removable but nevertheless very efficacious in excluding dust.

The lantern clock was made throughout the seventeenth century and into the eighteenth, lasting even longer in provincial usage; and it occurs in the form of 'period reproductions', now either spring-driven or with electric movements, right down to the present day. As seventeenth-century technology progressed, so too did the mechanical design of the lantern clock. Originally these were made with wheel balances and, seemingly, never with a foliot; but soon after the introduction of the pendulum, not only was the wheel balance superseded, but earlier models that incorporated it were converted to the newer form of controller. Early lantern clocks with their original wheel balances are consequently very rarely encountered.

Stylistically, early lantern clocks had a narrow chapter ring, which was confined within the width of the clock frame. As the century progressed, however, the chapter ring became wider, projecting beyond the frame; such clocks are customarily called 'sheep's-head' clocks. Yet another variant, a short-lived fashion lasting about twenty years in the latter half of the seventeenth century, was the 'winged' lantern clock. The pendulum of such clocks was constructed in the shape of an anchor, the flukes acting as the pendulum bob. Extensions – 'wings' – were added to the sides of the case, and sometimes even surmounted with decorative cresting. As the pendulum swung, the flukes appeared momentarily in alternate 'wings', at least demonstrating that the clock was going!

Clockmaking in France, admirable though it was at certain times, enjoyed a rather chequered existence. French craft guilds tended to be organised by localities, and proliferated in numbers between the sixteenth and eighteenth centuries. The first guild of clockmakers was formed in Paris in 1544, but in Blois not until 1597; other centres blossomed at Lyon, Rouen, Dijon and elsewhere. Apart from the mere three royal clockmakers who were allowed in office at any one time – and who were considered outside guild rules and regulations – there were innumerable associated crafts with fringe interests in clockmaking, such as cabinetmakers, gilders, casters, chasers, bellfounders and so forth, all of whose special interests had to be protected. Despite this, and contrary to the practice in other countries, the French clockmakers were able to obtain permission to work in precious metals; this is without doubt the reason why so very few French Renaissance clocks have survived. Once they went out of fashion, they were melted down for the value of their cases, whereas the gilt bronze ones, favoured in Germany and elsewhere, survived in tolerable quantities. Such French examples in base-metal cases as do survive from time to time are mainly of the upright hex-

above
Although unsigned, this octagonal crystal-cased watch is probably French and dates from the first decade of the seventeenth century. Museum of the Worshipful Company of Clockmakers, Guildhall, London.

right
Transitional stages between the Gothic and lantern forms of domestic clock are rare, and this example dates from the first quarter of the seventeenth century. The posted frame of forged steel still incorporates Gothic detail. British Museum, London.

the seventeenth century? One explanation that has been advanced, particularly in regard to French clocks, is that carrying a watch for display – and this must have been the principal intention since while they were beautifully made, using the richest materials, they were still appalling timekeepers – became so compulsive among gentlemen of fashion that table clocks, at any rate, became superfluous. There were also extraneous influences. The German industry, for instance, suffered so grievously during the Thirty Years War (1618–48) that it took two hundred years to recover.

There is another 'grey area' in our knowledge of this period, and that concerns exactly how watches were worn. Renaissance watches seem to have been carried on a cord about the neck or, more rarely, at the waist. In England, at any rate, pockets, introduced fifty years earlier, were confined to the breeches until 1675, and watches carried therein would have been subjected to such jarring as to render their already temperamental motions well-nigh inoperative. Yet it is rare indeed to find a watch being visibly worn in a seventeenth-century portrait.

In England, whatever may have been going on elsewhere, the making of clocks – principally lantern clocks – thrived, and alongside it, during the first twenty-five years of the seventeenth century, the making of watches became sufficiently established to see the gradual emergence of a national style which was to last for several decades, as well as to lay the foundations for the supremacy in this field which English watches were to enjoy somewhat later on. At first, they appear to have been based upon French designs – elongated hexagons and ovals of highly engraved gilt brass or silver, sometimes with an added band of contrasting metal. Mechanically very little was to change for seventy-five years, and the surest way of placing a watch from this time in its right category is by its decoration – yet the English national style, for at least three decades from about 1620, was to be devoid of such artifice, at least externally. The 'Puritan' watch, as the style has come to be known, represents a total rejection of everything that had gone before. In round or oval form, and in gilt brass but perhaps more generally in silver, the watch case – and its second, outer case where such is provided – is completely plain, while the dial consists of a simple chapter ring engraved upon an otherwise featureless flat metal surface. The single hand is of steel, with a 'tail' extending back from the centre and balancing the pointer, the whole carrying the barest minimum of turned and chiselled ornament.

The only decoration that was applied to such watches was upon the movement, which largely resembled what had gone before. The balance cocks of such watches were oval, with no sign of a rim to the irregular edge, and they were attached

agonal type, of exquisite quality and comparable with anything produced elsewhere. The only traces of their more intrinsically valuable counterparts are the mouth-watering descriptions of them which abound in contemporary documents. Towards the end of the sixteenth century, the French clockmakers tried out various new shapes – at first upright cylinders and squares, and, as always in French artefacts, possessing obvious architectural overtones. However, by the beginning of the seventeenth century the accent was turning squarely towards the production of watches with a consequent decline in the output of clocks, which, to all intents and purposes, died as a French craft industry until after the mid century.

Elsewhere in Europe at this time, too, clockmaking flagged as a craft. The Italian practice tended to be intermittent and fragmented, while Holland was yet to achieve fame and individuality with the rise to prominence of its great physicist, astronomer and mathematician Christiaan Huygens, but again only after mid century.

Why should clockmaking, a relatively new technology, have stumbled so badly at the beginning of

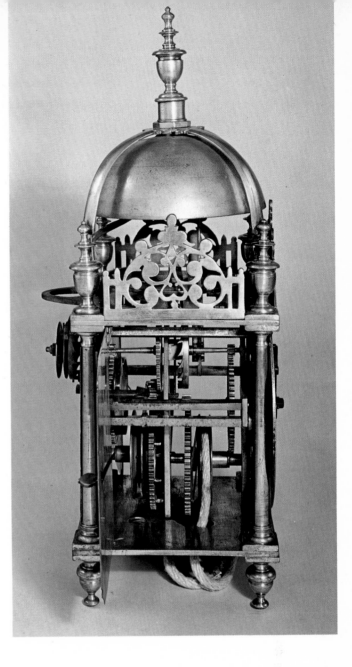

opposite page
This lantern clock, which is unsigned, has wings on either side (sometimes they have cresting on top, as here), in which the anchor-like flukes constituting the pendulum bob appear. This style was short-lived, lasting only about twenty years towards the end of the seventeenth century.

above
This clock, which dates from about 1640, exhibits the narrow chapter ring which is typical of early lantern clocks. It was made by William Bowyer. British Museum, London.

above right
This lateral view of the previous clock, with sides removed to show the movement, reveals the typical fourposter frame, the trains placed one behind the other and alarm mechanism at the rear. The pillars are now brass instead of steel as are the finials and frets. British Museum, London.

to the back plate of the movement by means of a block or tenon, fixed to the plate, which fits into a squared hole cut into the neck of the cock. The tenon and the neck of the cock have been drilled to take a pin which, when in position, makes an adequately firm fixing. Such cocks were decorated with pierced scrollwork and foliage. The mainspring set-up, also located upon the back plate of the watch, was made the site for decorative steelwork, both when this function was performed by the ratchet wheel and click and later, from about 1635, when it was superseded by the worm and wheel arrangement.

The 'Puritan' watch probably reflected the feelings of the times, and it can also be argued that it foreshadowed the English trend towards unadulterated functionalism that was to predominate as the scientific approach to time-measurement took hold. Nevertheless, elsewhere among those nations, mainly European, who were building up a horological heritage, the period from 1625 to 1675 is renowned for producing some of the most fabul-

101

opposite page, above
Signed 'Edm. Bull In Fleetstreet Fecit', this oval watch is engraved in the centre of the dial with Venus and Cupid. It dates from the first quarter of the seventeenth century. Victoria and Albert Museum, London.

opposite page, below
David Ramsay, who was born about 1590 and died about 1654, was the first Master of the Clockmakers' Company in 1632. He was an outstanding watchmaker, and this star watch is one of his finest creations; it was made about 1625. Museum of the Worshipful Company of Clockmakers, Guildhall, London.

left
Another of David Ramsay's watches. The outside of the case is engraved with religious scenes, and the movement is signed 'David Ramsay me fecit'. Victoria and Albert Museum, London.

below
This watch made by Ramsay about 1630 reveals his Scottish background, being signed 'David Ramsay Scotus me fecit'. The octagonal case is in rock crystal mounted in gold. Museum of the Worshipful Company of Clockmakers, Guildhall, London.

ous watches ever seen. It was the supreme era of the decorative watch, and it may be useful here to review some of the many techniques and materials that were used while this fashion was at its height, although we must not lose sight of the fact that, throughout the whole period, the timekeeping properties of the objects upon which so much expensive craftsmanship was being lavished were, to say the least, minimal. They were, in other words, essentially items of personal jewellery.

There were a number of techniques available for working upon raw metal. One that became popular towards the end of the seventeenth century and throughout much of the eighteenth was repoussé work, in which a design is hammered out from the back, using a variety of different punches. In extreme cases, the relief obtainable can be really three-dimensional. Similar techniques but used upon the front of the metal are known as chasing. Sometimes these two techniques will be found to have been combined on the same watch case, generally upon early rather than later specimens. Classical and allegorical scenes were particularly favoured for depicting by these methods; and where a repoussé watch case is of the very highest quality, it is not unusual to find an additional outer case, consisting simply of two bezels, or rims, hinged together, one of them fitted with a convex glass. In position, the repoussé back of the watch case was covered by the glazed bezel through which it could be examined, yet it was fully protected from accidental damage or from rubbing or scratches in the pocket. Decoration similar to repoussé work can, of course, be cast, although it is difficult to obtain the high quality thereby.

Other methods of decorating metal include piercing, chiselling and engraving. Early German watches combined the first two of these, the depth of the chiselling being sometimes quite unusual; but, except in relatively low relief, chiselling gradually died out, to be superseded by engraving. Cast metal decoration has often to be tidied up by manual means, frequently chiselling, in order to improve the definition of the subject matter.

Enamelling upon metal is a means of decoration of considerable antiquity. In its simplest form, enamel is a special type of colourless glass, known as 'flux', to which colour can be imparted by the addition of metallic oxides. The melting temperature can be varied according to the amounts of the ingredients used, to produce so-called 'hard' or 'soft' enamels possessing different properties, mainly relating to brittleness of surface and retention of colour. Two of the most usual methods of decoration by enamelling are known as cloisonné and champlevé. In the first of these, thin strips or fillets of metal – usually gold – are formed to the outline shape of each colour of the design and fixed in position, often simply being set into a thin layer of enamel covering the whole surface of the article concerned. The compartments thus formed, which will together make up the finished design, are each filled with powdered enamel mixed to give their relevant colours, and the whole object is then fired in a furnace. In champlevé enamelling, the other and commoner form, the compartments are formed by scooping out metal from the object itself, rather than by adding fillets of metal to it; otherwise the process is similar.

A third variant, known as enamel painting, started around 1630. Here there was no attempt to form compartments or cells; a smooth enamel surface was laid down, suitably painted and fired. Because of the expansion of the metal carcase and its possible effect upon the decorated surface, gold was most frequently used; but notwithstanding this, it was usually found desirable to enamel the whole watch case, inside and out, rather than risk cracking. Where this has been done, the reverse protective enamelled surface is called 'contre-émail'. The earliest 'school' of enamel painting was at Blois, closely followed by that at Geneva from about 1650. The most famous watch case

103

painters in this genre, the Huaud family, originated in the latter city; their watch cases are always signed and have great individuality, although experts consider their work inferior to the very best turned out at Blois.

There were several other processes involving enamelling in use at various times – for example, the painting in enamel pioneered at Limoges, as opposed, that is, to the painting on enamel outlined in the preceding paragraph. Then there were combination procedures like basse-taille. This involves enamelling over an incised pattern, often engine-turned or, as the French expressed it, *guilloché* with geometrical figures; this became very popular in watch cases towards the end of the eighteenth century. Another method used on watch cases is niello, which is effectively a method of filling up the compartments in a champlevé surface, usually of silver or steel, with a black molten filling of various metallic sulphides. The contrast can be very effective.

So far, the carcases of all the watch cases described have been metal, but other materials were used from time to time. One of the richest was

Edward East, remarkable for the general elegance of his work, did not neglect to make his own signature outstanding, as this example from another of his watches demonstrates.

The most commonly encountered oval form of Puritan watch is seen in this example by Edward East which dates from about 1630. Museum of the Worshipful Company of Clockmakers, Guildhall, London.

rock crystal, fashioned in a considerable variety of forms, the material itself being generally the clear variety although, occasionally, the rarer smoky type is found. Apart from 'form' watches, to be described in the next paragraph, crystal-cased watches are usually octagonal or round, the two halves of the case set in gilt metal bezels hinged together. Very much more rarely, the bezels are omitted, and the two crystal segments are connected directly by a hinge on one end and a catch on the opposite one. Curiously, crystal is almost never used plain. Round cases are divided into lobes, hexagonal cases are cut with large facets, and so on.

'Form' watches is the term used to describe the multitude of seventeenth-century watches specially cased up to represent something quite different: cross watches, tulip watches, skull watches, book watches and many more. Cases were cast and chiselled in the form of pomegranates, cockleshells, Tudor roses, doves and, in some cases, incorporated rock crystal in combination with silver or gilt metal. Many of these cases were not of the highest quality; but those that were are superb.

Watches like the foregoing were obviously among the most expensive obtainable, but with so much attention being paid to the exotic it would be strange if some change did not rub off on the more everyday product. The English 'Puritan' timepiece remained fairly static until mid century although, with such craftsmen as Edward East putting their names to them, they were as good of their plain and unadulterated kind as it was possible to find. They did aspire to an outer protective case – in order, presumably, to exclude dust since there was nothing decorative to take care of – as did also many of those watches that could be described as works of art. Sometimes, this case was just to deposit them in when not in use – like a jewelbox – but after about 1650, outer cases were made to be worn with the watch, and watches so equipped came to be known as pair-cased watches. These outer cases, in their turn, came to be made in both plain and decorative versions, the latter often employing attractive materials like horn, tortoiseshell and leather moulded to a base-metal carcase, and further decorated with underpainting or inlaying with gold or silver in the fashion known as piqué.

Other details of the watch changed greatly during the seventeenth century. At the beginning, the metal dial plate had a simple hour ring engraved upon it, or the engraving was done on a separate metal ring which was then attached to the plate; occasionally a disc was used in preference to an applied ring. Such rings were narrow, occupying little enough room on the dial plate and the rest of the area was covered in close engraving. Later on, the hour ring became wider, leaving much less room for decoration. Plain white enamel dials started to appear about 1675, but they are nowhere common before 1700 and, in England, not until 1725. Hands are generally of steel and well made, and glasses over the dial came into use at some time during the century, replacing the earlier pierced covers; but since it must always be open to question whether a particular watch glass is original, it is difficult to say when this happened. The recognisably round watch, as opposed to the other shapes that had gone before, became the norm from about mid century.

Up to the middle of the seventeenth century, then, watches according to the English usage were, as a rule, outstanding for their lack of decoration,

This watch in the shape of a cross, from the second quarter of the seventeenth century, is by Didier Lalemand of Paris and is a typical example of a form watch. British Museum, London.

while the complete reverse applied to those from other manufacturing centres. Clocks came in three principal styles – the lantern clock fitted with its wheel balance, the travelling or coach clock, which was simply a greatly oversize watch, and the table clock with its horizontal dial, largely unchanged from its inception. All such clocks were, of course, survivals from the past, as indeed were the tabernacle clocks with their vertical dials and their three or more trains driving added complications, which were still being made by the Germans and Italians in the style of a century earlier. It was as if the industry was awaiting a sudden flash of inspiration, an invention of genius which would bring the making of clocks and watches to life again after seemingly stultifying for so many decades.

The invention, which was the application of the pendulum to clocks, when at last it came, was in fact the result of applied logic coupled to exceptional scientific acumen, rather than some entirely new concept launched upon an unsuspecting world as a result of an explosion of brilliance never to be repeated. Such inventions are often the best kind. It had been appreciated for a century and more that a pendulum had a capability for keeping time which was much better than any foliot or wheel balance. Galileo, as a young man in 1581, had timed the swinging of a lamp in Pisa cathedral and noted that its period of oscillation – the time it took to complete each swing – was dependent solely on its length and not at all upon whether it was swinging in large or small arcs. This led to the measurement of short periods of time, in such

This mid seventeenth-century watch case combines the techniques of chiselling and engraving upon a carcase that was originally cast. British Museum, London.

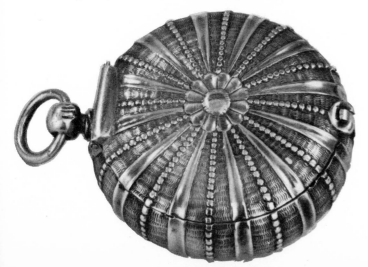

This clock-watch with alarm, a style which East made in various sizes up to and including coach watch, is in a beautifully decorated silver case and an outer case of wood covered with painted leather. Victoria and Albert Museum, London.

As befitted any maker with the Royal Appointment, East made some outstanding watches of which this pear-shaped crystal-cased example is typical. Victoria and Albert Museum, London.

fields as astronomy, being made by counting the number of oscillations of a weight on the end of a cord. Even before this time, the ubiquitous Leonardo da Vinci had sketched pendulums in connection with pumping machinery, while Galileo's son as well as, independently, several experimenters in Italy and Poland were working along the same lines. Finally, the obstacles to harnessing a pendulum to clockwork were overcome, and the problem to all intents and purposes was solved, by Christiaan Huygens, a Dutch physicist.

It is a remarkable quirk of fate that two such brilliant and versatile men as Huygens in Holland and Robert Hooke in England should have shared the same century, let alone almost the same period of it for their life spans. Christiaan Huygens was born at The Hague on 14th April 1629, the son of a poet and statesman of considerable stature. At first he studied law, but then he devoted himself to mathematics and astronomy and quickly built a high reputation. His improvements in telescope lenses led to important gains in observational astronomy, while at the same time he was experimenting to perfect the control mechanism of clocks. He visited England in 1660 and 1663, in the latter year being elected a Fellow of the Royal Society. Subsequently for nearly twenty years he lived under the patronage of Louis XIV of France, and in 1673 published his celebrated work *Horologium Oscillatorium*. In effect, this was the first attempt to apply dynamics to bodies of finite size; later, it was to be of great value to Newton. Other matters to which Huygens applied himself included the wave theory of light – by which he explained reflection and refraction – and polarisation of light, a phenomenon which, despite its discovery by him, he was unable to explain. Huygens died at The Hague, to which he eventually returned, on 8th June 1695, leaving behind him a corpus of work which, when published, occupied twenty-two weighty volumes.

Huygens' great contribution to horology was his investigation of the theory of pendulums – both the ordinary vertical type and the conical, which has a circular instead of a lateral motion – as a result of which he was able to revise Galileo's previous postulation that the only determinant for a pendulum to 'beat' equal periods of time was its length, the size of the arc being of no consequence. This quality, usually called isochronism, is also dependent, so Huygens proved, on the arc described by the pendulum bob being that of a cycloid rather than a pure circle. A cycloid is the curve traced by a point on the circumference of a circle as it rolls along a straight line; in practical terms, a curve of this kind is rather more U-shaped than the curve of a circle.

Huygens translated his ideas into reality by means of pendulum clocks made by a well-known clockmaker at The Hague called Salomon Coster.

The case of this remarkable enamelled watch by East is unusually shallow for the period. With a light blue ground enamelled on gold, the edges of the case are decorated with small flowers in relief, while the interior pictures are landscapes with ruined buildings and figures again on a blue ground. Victoria and Albert Museum, London.

The cycloidal curve of the swinging pendulum bob was achieved by suspending the pendulum on a silk thread hanging between curved 'cheeks' which, in theory, were to cause the arc described by the bob to steepen at each end of its swing. In fact, it was soon discovered that, though theoretically correct, the cycloidal curve caused more problems than it was supposed to solve, and for all normal purposes its effects could be ignored. Finally, Huygens assigned to Coster the right to make pendulum clocks for twenty-one years.

The application of the pendulum of necessity brought about a quite fundamental change in the clock designs obtaining at that time. A vertical pendulum presupposes a movement laid out in a vertical plane, with a vertical dial, as opposed to the horizontal table clocks that had hitherto been so popular. The plates between which the movements of clocks like this were confined would therefore be best described as 'front' and 'back' in place of 'top' and 'bottom'. A whole new generation of clocks was poised upon these mechanical improvements.

More or less coincidentally, John Fromanteel, a member of a famous Dutch clockmaking family based in London, happened to be working for Coster only a matter of days after the Huygens pendulum clock was patented and lost no time in absorbing the requisite technology. Extraordinarily quickly his family in London, headed by Ahasuerus Fromanteel, started advertising the

below left
This form watch by Richard Masterson dates from about 1630, and the silver case is cast in the form of a cockle shell. Museum of the Worshipful Company of Clockmakers, Guildhall, London.

below
The form watch resembling a tulip is found in various sizes, this being quite a small one made by F. Sermand who is probably the same as the maker of the watch on page 110. Its silver case has three crystal windows, and the watch dates from about 1640. Museum of the Worshipful Company of Clockmakers, Guildhall, London.

right
The silver case of this watch by Benjamin Hill is cast in the form of a pomegranate. It dates from the mid seventeenth century. Museum of the Worshipful Company of Clockmakers, Guildhall, London.

far right
Disguised in the form of a dove, the watch is only revealed when the lower part of the body of the bird hinges outwards. Made about 1685, this watch is probably Swiss and is signed 'Soret et Jay'. Museum of the Worshipful Company of Clockmakers, Guildhall, London.

availability of this new kind of timekeeper – this was in October and November 1658 – and from that point on the new development gathered momentum. In the process, it gave England such an enormous technical advantage as to ensure its supremacy in the field for generations ahead.

In the form in which, at this early stage in its history, it was commonly adopted by Fromanteel and many another London clockmaker, the pendulum rod was ten inches long and terminated in a pear-shaped brass bob, which could be screwed up or down the rod to effect regulation. Such pendulums had a period of oscillation of about half a second, and they were applied to two basic types of clocks, one spring-driven and the other powered by weights.

Salomon Coster's first clocks with pendulums were spring-driven, in ebonised black wooden cases with pediment tops, and with two trains placed side by side, for going and striking, both powered by going barrels and both winding through the dial. In England, spring clocks – or bracket clocks as they have come to be known, although many of them never sat on a bracket but on a table or sideboard – and weight-driven hooded wall clocks, both with a strong architectural influence discernible in their design, were the first results of the adoption of the pendulum; they remained in fashion for about fifteen years from 1660 to 1675. The hooded wall clock, by the way, might be described as looking like the top of a grandfather clock, fixed on the wall and with the weights hanging down underneath. These types of clocks did not copy their Dutch progenitors in decorative detail: English clocks never boast velvet-covered dials with applied metal name plaques and chapter rings, but favour gilt metal dial plates, their centres matted or sometimes engraved with the then fashionable tulip type of ornamentation, that flower being adopted instead to reflect the increasing Dutch influence in design. English spring clocks, incidentally, favoured the fusee from the beginning – probably another example of the national emphasis placed upon accurate performance.

Very shortly after these initial styles, the English cherub spandrel appeared to fill the four corners of the dial, outside the chapter ring. In its earliest examples, and especially in those very rare ones where the spandrels have been cast in silver, it is an object of great beauty in its own right. But, like most popular ornamentation, constant copying and insufficient hand-finishing cause deterioration of the effect; this is detectable in English clocks even before the end of the seventeenth century. The other dial feature on English clocks at this time is the maker's signature. Until about 1675 this appears across the bottom of the dial plate, below the chapter ring, and it is frequently in a Latinised form. It might also appear on the otherwise perfectly plain back plate of the movement. Later the name is found in a plaque inside the chapter ring, or on the chapter ring itself – this was eventually the most favoured site for this feature – and after about 1675 back plates became the focus of overall engraved decoration, mainly various arabesque forms and sometimes incorporating a cartouche containing the maker's signature.

Once the architectural styles of clock cases, with their pediment tops and side columns in classic

arrangement, and often with gilt metal capitals and bases, the whole upon a suitable plinth, had been superseded – and this was a relatively short-lived style – a more notably English style came into use. It has been said that the period up to about 1680 was the period of experimentation, while makers were struggling to perfect the styling that was appropriate to the new technology; the use of the pendulum clearly bespoke spatial requirements which needed to be reflected in the case design, and it was natural, at first, to seek solutions deriving from a discipline that is wholly concerned with the best use of space, i.e. architecture. However, this was the short answer; the longer one must inevitably have been to discover a recognisable English style, more especially because of the supremacy already gained in the field, which

This watch combines two decorative materials – crystal and enamelling – to great effect. It dates from about 1660 and is by Sermand of Geneva. British Museum, London.

above right
This watch has a square silver-studded leather case and is by Francis Rainsford. Dating from about 1700, it shows the continuing fashion for novelty of shape. Museum of the Worshipful Company of Clockmakers, Guildhall, London.

right
This engraved silver skull contains a watch signed 'Moysant Blois' and has its original shaped protective leather case. Tradition says the watch belonged to Mary Queen of Scots, but the existing mechanism postdates her execution by at least fifteen years. Museum of the Worshipful Company of Clockmakers, Guildhall, London.

110

needed to be consolidated. So architectural cases were not made much after 1675, apart from the occasional use of barley-twist pillars and the stepped panel top during the following few years. Instead an essentially upright rectangular case became the norm, with glazed doors front and back, mounted upon a shallow moulded plinth with four simple feet, and surmounted by either a bell or basket top. A handle on the top enabled the clock to be carried most easily from room to room, and especially upstairs to bed at night; for a clock was an expensive item so that only the very rich household would contain more than one. Ebony is by far the commonest wood used for bracket clock cases at this period; of the others occasionally found, walnut is the rarest, while, very infrequently indeed, cases were made entirely of metal, usually gilt.

Case decorations include the fret above the door – to allow the sound of the bell to emerge – which, after about 1685, was made of metal rather than wood, as were also those inserted at the top of the side panels of the case, and sometimes also replaced the glazed rectangles in those panels which had been the original style. Similarly, metal frets with the wood cut away behind them were applied to the front and sides of the shallow domed structure placed lengthwise across the top of the case – the bell top, as it is usually called – which

left

The silver gilt case of this watch by William Clay has been cast in the pattern of a Tudor rose which is carried round on to the bezel. The watch dates from about 1640. Museum of the Worshipful Company of Clockmakers, Guildhall, London.

above

Another flower-shaped form watch. The cast silver case shaped like a bud has three outer petals, one of which forms the cover over the dial. The watch itself is by Henry Grendon and dates from the second quarter of the seventeenth century. Victoria and Albert Museum, London.

superseded the architectural top after about 1675; and when occasionally this entire top structure is covered with pierced metal embellishment, it is called a basket top. By the end of the century there were other minor alternatives to this superstructure – a variant of the bell top, known as the inverted bell top, simply added another moulded level to the original, in exactly the same way as did the so-called double basket top – although the great makers, such as Tompion, never allowed ostentation to be confused with elegance. His cases have a restraint which conveys great individuality by comparison with many others of that period, although the foregoing describes in brief the outward appearance of the conventional English bracket clock as it was to remain for a long time to come, albeit with some development of fine detail.

One specialised form of spring clock which has appeared spasmodically from the period under review almost into modern times is the 'night clock'. Most variants of this type substitute a revolving dial with cut-out hour numerals for the conventional hands indicating the time upon a chapter ring. A lamp placed behind the dial at the point where the correct time will always be registered permits of this being read off in the dark, obviating any need to kindle a light. Some of these clocks had a silent escapement, one of the acting surfaces being made of gut. Such clocks, before 1700, are extremely rare.

So much for the English prototype spring clocks. The longcase clock – which is often called in England a grandfather clock, and in America a tall clock – seems to have been a wholly English inspiration, for the earliest known clocks of this kind are all English, and the fashion never seems to have become popular elsewhere, save for its adoption by the Dutch. There are no longcase clocks before 1659, and for the ensuing twelve years or so such clocks all had the short half-seconds pendulum and verge escapement of the bracket clock.

above
The overall enamelling of this watch case is notable for its restraint, the pattern of white flowers and foliage in relief with black markings contrasting with the white enamel dial, the centre of which is decorated similarly to the case. Signed 'Goullons A Paris', the watch dates from the middle of the seventeenth century. Museum of the Worshipful Company of Clockmakers, Guildhall, London.

right
Another watch combining rock crystal with enamelling, this dates from about 1625 and is signed 'John Ramsey fecit'. There is no evidence that this maker was related to the famous David Ramsay, and indeed nothing is known about him except that perhaps he may have worked in Dundee. Museum of the Worshipful Company of Clockmakers, Guildhall, London.

The immediate ancestor of the longcase clock was, of course, the hanging hooded wall clock. Many of these were simple thirty-hour duration mechanisms of the lantern clock type; but once the pendulum had been introduced, eight-day duration became the standard. This required much heavier driving weights than its predecessor, so that the overall mass of the clock may have been too great to suspend from a wall bracket with safety. Certainly hanging clocks of the earlier kind but running eight days continued to be made in the period 1660–75, and all with the then current architectural type of case. At the same time, however, it is likely that a free-standing clock case, which would not only enclose weights, pendulum and mechanism and protect them from dust and interference, but relieve the strain on not always very robust walls, must have been considered highly desirable. Some such considerations are likely to have given rise to the longcase clock.

Until 1675, many of the factors relating to bracket clocks apply also to longcases. Architectural styles prevailed, probably for the reasons of experimentation already postulated. A longcase has three main sections – the plinth, the trunk and the hood – and, in the earliest specimens, it is general to find that the plinth is a plain box-like structure, while the trunk is panelled. At the top of the trunk and around its three exposed sides is a convex moulding, upon which the hood rests – this is an important feature in assigning a period to a clock, for after 1700 these mouldings are almost

invariably concave. The back of the trunk is continued upwards almost to the clock's full height, its outside edges running in grooves in the hood, which has to be slid upwards to obtain access to the mechanism. This was necessary because, at this early period, hoods had no forward-opening door although, subsequently, many were converted, the door becoming usual after about 1700. The lift-up hood was generally lockable by a special device which cannot be released until the trunk door is opened, giving useful additional security.

These early longcase clocks were usually about six feet high, with dials eight to eight and a half inches square. Dial arrangements followed closely those already described for bracket clocks. The half-seconds pendulum almost never occurs with a subsidiary seconds dial; bolt-and-shutter maintaining power is commoner on longcase than on bracket clocks.

Cases in general follow the spring clock fashion in being made of dark wood, usually ebony, more rarely laburnum or lignum vitae. The pure architectural style of the hood, with its triangular portico top and discreet gilt metal embellishment in the tympanum and in the framing of the dial, sometimes extends also to pillars and bases.

There is one other type of longcase clock which deserves brief mention, if only because it may constitute another connecting link with what had gone before. Very much more primitive than those described hitherto, it consists of little more than a posted movement of the lantern clock type, with a duration of thirty hours, which is wound by pulling down a chain or rope inside its longcase. Such clocks were made provincially whenever the long-case was in fashion, and generally with the longer pendulum; but occasionally a famous early maker indulged in such modest work, and there is an example by Thomas Tompion in the collection of the Worshipful Company of Clockmakers in London which is dated at about 1672. It has the short bob pendulum of the time and is housed in a plain black ebonised case of which the hood is topped by uncommon cresting. It also had an alarm train, now missing.

Huygens' application of the pendulum to clock-work was inhibited by the deficiencies of the escapement – the verge – to which it was allied. Thus, however he might strive, by the use of such devices as cycloidal cheeks, to bring it to perfec-tion, the verge escapement itself has inherent mechanical shortcomings the nature of which eluded him; however, it did not elude the English craftsmen who were so assiduously developing his invention. Their contribution was the application of a new clock escapement, to which could be allied the thirty-nine-inch seconds-beating pendulum.

There are two contenders for the claim actually to have invented the anchor escapement, and argument has continued over the years between their respective supporters. The first is a respected craftsman clockmaker, William Clement, who – if indeed he did nothing more – made a clock with this escapement for King's College, Cambridge, which is the oldest specimen of its kind to survive. The clock is signed and dated 1671, and was trans-ferred to the Science Museum in London, where it is shown working, only in the present decade. Clement's claim is substantiated by John Smith, one of the earliest writers in English on horology, who states in his *Horological Disquisitions* of 1694 that Clement was 'the real contriver of the curious kind of long pendulum which is at this day so universally in use among us'. As against this, pro-tagonists of the second claimant point out that Clement never showed any other special merit as an inventor, whereas the anchor escapement was an entirely new and novel departure from what had gone before and thus an invention in every possible sense; and furthermore they draw atten-tion to the fact that Clement seems to have made no attempt to claim the invention as his own dur-ing his lifetime, which any craftsman with pride in his work surely would have done.

The second contender for whom credit is claimed in this connection is Robert Hooke. He was mentioned previously as having shared roughly the life-span of Huygens; and in an age in which brilliance almost seems commonplace, he was one of the giant intelligences. Living from 1635 to 1703, he ranged his mind over science and mathematics as those disciplines then existed,

The white enamel chapter ring of this watch surrounds a central enamel portrait said to be that of the Duchesse de Montpensier who was born in 1627. The watch is signed 'Jean Hubert A Rouen' and dates from about 1650. Museum of the Worshipful Company of Clockmakers, Guildhall, London.

opposite page, left
This beautiful small clock dating from the end of the first quarter of the seventeenth century is the work of Henry Archer who was one of the first Wardens of the Clockmakers' Company. The case of the clock was possibly imported from France. Museum of the Worshipful Company of Clockmakers, Guildhall, London.

opposite page, right
The movement of Archer's clock showing the extensive decoration with which it is embellished. Museum of the Worshipful Company of Clockmakers, Guildhall, London.

115

making numerous contributions in a variety of fields, including several in horology. However, he was said to have been a secretive man, of a morose and melancholy nature, sleeping little, while being insatiably active and restless. He seemingly had a habit of throwing off ideas of great inventiveness in which he immediately lost interest; but only let someone else develop them into worthwhile realities, and he was the first to claim credit for the entire creation from start to finish.

Hooke was Curator of Experiments to the Royal Society and sometime Secretary to that august body. He was experimenting with long pendulums as early as 1664, and in 1669 had progressed to one some thirteen feet long and beating once in two seconds, but the escapement was certainly not an anchor. His own diaries do not start before 1672, nor is there mention of the escapement, as such, in any of the Royal Society's Proceedings. Yet it is inconceivable that Hooke played no part whatever in such an important advance in a field in which he was substantially involved. At the present time it might seem most likely that the idea of an anchor escapement started with him and finished, in its fully functional state, with Clement. This is the only theory that meets all the facts as at present understood, but it is to be hoped that more information will eventually come to light on the subject.

Before leaving Robert Hooke, it might be illuminating to review his other contributions to horology. In the field of pendulums, he was the first to postulate the flat steel spring suspension to replace Huygens' silk thread, and he successfully demonstrated this to the Royal Society in 1666. Some years later, in 1672, he produced his wheel-cutting engine, successfully mechanising a procedure which had been hitherto partly manual and consequently liable to some inaccuracy. Finally, he seems to have been the first to suggest using the different coefficients of expansion of brass and steel as the basis for compensating against temperature changes in horological mechanisms, although it was to be another half century before this device underwent further development.

The incorporation of the one-second pendulum and anchor escapement in longcase clocks caused their dimensions to increase in almost all directions. Thus after 1675 the eight-inch square dial grew to ten inches, where it remained for almost the remainder of the century, although before 1700 eleven- and even twelve-inch dials began to appear. Heights of cases grew to seven feet, aided by the fashion for higher ceilings; this extra height in the clock case was achieved by adding to it a shallow domed top equivalent to the bell top of a bracket clock. This feature, accompanied often by finials at the two forward corners and with sometimes a third on top, is nevertheless not as pleasing as the flat top, embellished on occasion with cresting, the latter being just an alternative method of accomplishing the same objective.

Details of the hood and dial settled down by 1690. The use of columns at either side of the dial followed the same progress as in the bracket clock, alighting eventually upon the slim round column that was to last throughout the ensuing century.

above
This table clock with its fine architectural case, was made by Samuel Knibb; the narrow chapter ring, all-over engraved dial and fine simple hands suggest the period round 1665. Museum of the Worshipful Company of Clockmakers, Guildhall, London.

right
The back plate of the movement of Knibb's clock bears no decoration but the maker's signature in a beautiful flowing style, together with some engraving on the count wheel. Museum of the Worshipful Company of Clockmakers, Guildhall, London.

far left
This clock signed 'Pieter Visbach Fecit Hagae met priuilege' gives a good impression of the first clocks made for Huygens – to whom the 'privilege' refers – by Salomon Coster. The silk suspension to the pendulum and the cycloidal cheeks are typical of such early Dutch pendulum movements. Museum of the Worshipful Company of Clockmakers, Guildhall, London.

left
Even relatively little-known makers turned out fine clocks in the last quarter of the seventeenth century, as this specimen by Edward Bird shows.

From about the same date, too, the maker's signature appeared upon the chapter ring rather than upon the dial plate. The lift-up hood lasted until about 1700, even with the taller generation of clocks. Seconds dials became customary, of course, almost as soon as the seconds pendulum was introduced. The larger dials required a rather bulkier corner ornament than the hitherto ubiquitous cherub spandrel, so that designs embracing two cherubs supporting a crown, or sometimes a woman's head within an arabesque arrangement, are commonly encountered.

Unlike the bracket clock, ebony and ebonised finishes for the longcase clock faded out of popularity in the final quarter of the seventeenth century. Olivewood and walnut succeeded them, together with special effects like the 'oyster' pattern, which is veneer cut across the grain of the wood, in this case often laburnum. Panels of inlaid decoration and, after 1690, all-over inlay were much favoured. The earliest variety of this kind of decoration, known as parquetry, is very rare in clocks; it involves building up patterns with straight edges – such as diamonds, squares and similar shapes – and arranging them as a design. It was followed by marquetry, the usual type of such embellishment on clock cases, in which complicated designs of birds, flowers and other motifs were built up from veneers of different coloured woods, the colours often being obtained by staining, and sometimes with the additional use of ivory and bone.

The trunk of the longcase was of necessity closely related to the pendulum, its proportions

This magnificent basket-top spring clock possesses a strangely asymmetrical dial, with the apertures for the winding squares apparently displaced to the left. There is also a substantial engraved band above the dial which might seem to serve no obvious purpose. However, there exists a second clock by the same maker, John Clowes of London, which is virtually identical to this one, and which has these same curious features. The overall displacement seems to have resulted from certain unusual mechanical elements in the movement, and this was probably not appreciated at the design stage.

right
The architectural design of this hooded wall clock, with its pointed pediment, specially turned columns and rising hood, is typical of the period about 1680. Made by William Clement, it has a striking movement that runs for eight days. British Museum, London.

reflecting the length and arc of swing. Square-topped trunk doors further extended the lines of the square dials – for the arch had not yet invaded the clockcase – and, as if to encourage inspection, it is common to find a bull's-eye glass, called a len-ticle, set into the trunk door at the level of the pendulum bob, and through which it can be seen

swinging.

Rare among clocks in this final quarter of the seventeenth century were some interesting experimental examples by William Clement and several other makers, still striving to improve the performance of the pendulum. In these, a pen-dulum having a length of sixty-one inches and beating 1¼ seconds was employed. Inevitably, the pendulum bob of such clocks was swinging within the plinth; some such clocks, therefore, have another door at that level, to give access to the bob for adjustment and regulation, done by raising or lowering it on the rod by means of a rating nut. At the very least a lenticle is set into the plinth, for purposes of observation. An obvious feature of such clocks, too, is the seconds dial, divided into forty-eight instead of sixty. No further clocks of this type were made after about 1700.

The seventeenth century saw the first appearance in England of the kind of superb native craftsmanship that was needed to breathe life into the inventions of contemporary scientists such as Huygens and Hooke. Strangely, most of the great workmen from this period spanned the end of the century, many only reaching the peak of their attainment in the succeeding one. One, however, lived out his life wholly within these five score years. He was Edward East.

East was born in 1602 and lived to the ripe old age of ninety-five. He came originally from Southill in Bedfordshire which, by a curious coincidence, is only a few miles from Northill, birthplace of Thomas Tompion. He was apprenticed to a goldsmith, being admitted to the Freedom in 1627; but switched shortly after, to become the junior member of the first Court of Assistants of the Clockmakers' Company, newly formed in 1631. He was Master of the Company in 1645 and 1652. His work is characterised by its extreme elegance and simplicity, enhanced by his ability to work in precious metals gained from his training as a goldsmith. He became Royal Clockmaker, first to Charles I and later to Charles II. The latter regularly presented watches by East as prizes for tennis played in the Mall, London. East seems to have spent the last few years of his life at Hampton in Middlesex.

By contrast, a second Royal Clockmaker of the Caroline era remains something of a mystery.

Robert Seignior was born in 1645, the son of a tailor. Entering into an apprenticeship in 1660, under John Nicasius – a well-known craftsman of the day – he was duly admitted to the Freedom in 1667. He never subsequently served any office in the Company, and his output must have been minimal; a bare handful of clocks and watches bearing his signature seem to have survived. Yet all are of the highest quality. Furthermore, he was a friend of Hooke and Tompion, figuring in the diary of the former. In 1674 he was granted a Royal Warrant 'without ffee, until the Death, Surrender or other Determinacion of Edward East. And then to enjoy the same place with ffee . . .' However, he never did enjoy the 'profitts, allowances and priviledges thereto belonginge', for he died in 1686, and East survived him by more than a decade.

One of the unusual features of clockmaking in the seventeenth century was the way the craft seemed to attract whole families to its practice. The Fromanteels were one example. Edward East lived so long that for years it was believed that there must be at least two of him. But perhaps the best-known craft family of that period were the Knibbs. Samuel Knibb, born in 1626, started as a clockmaker at Newport Pagnell, becoming accredited to the Clockmakers' Company in 1663, soon

Standing 6ft 10in high, the longcase of this clock by Thomas Tompion, which dates from about 1680, is a superb example of the use of olivewood inlaid with star medallions in ebony and satinwood. The movement is of one month duration. British Museum, London.

after he moved to London. The very few clocks identified as made by him are of the finest quality. His cousin Joseph (1640–1711), having been apprenticed to him from 1655 to 1662, set up in business at Oxford, where his first clocks reflected the influence of Fromanteel's work which he had certainly acquired from his time with Samuel. However, he soon revealed evidence of his own original thought. Meantime, in 1664, he took as apprentice his own younger brother John (1650–1722), and in 1668 another cousin Peter. The work of Joseph Knibb remains outstanding, even among the general excellence of the work of the other members of his family; he seems to have prospered certainly up to 1697, when he retired to Hanslop, continuing to make a few clocks until he died in 1711.

The greatest craftsman of his day – indeed, his admirers would say, the greatest of all time – was Thomas Tompion, who has often been called the 'father of English clockmaking'. As has been said already, he was born at Northill in Bedfordshire close to Edward East's birthplace, although not until 1639. Little is known about his activities until his admission in 1671 to the Clockmakers' Company, of which he became Master in 1703. Tompion's reputation rests entirely upon his supreme abilities as a craftsman and designer of complex clocks; his standards were emulated by many another fine London maker, albeit not always with complete success, but there is no doubt that the supremacy enjoyed by English horologists of his time owes more to his example than to anyone else's. By contrast, his name is not connected with any specific invention directed to improving timekeeping, and in this regard his friend and partner George Graham exerted a more lasting influence. Tompion became known to Robert Hooke soon after arriving in London and was subsequently commissioned to make clocks and watches of special design for him. Curiously, he never seems to have enjoyed the Royal Warrant although, for example, he made a fine equation clock for William III. Tompion worked with two partners during the latter years of his life. Edward Banger, a relative by marriage, joined him in 1701, the partnership lasting about seven years; a number of works bear their joint signatures. George Graham, another relative by marriage, had worked for Tompion since 1696 and was subsequently taken into partnership. They too maintained all the standards in their work which Tompion had initiated. Finally, Tompion died in 1713, being buried in Westminster abbey and, nearly forty years later, his grave was reopened to receive the body of his last partner, George Graham.

In fact, Graham survived until 1751, thus playing a large part in maintaining the craft practices and standards pioneered by East and Tompion. Many other fine seventeenth-century makers lived

The ebonised pinewood longcase surmounted by cresting encloses a posted movement signed 'Tho. Tompion, Londini fecit'. It is an early example of this master craftsman's work which appears to date from about 1672. Museum of the Worshipful Company of Clockmakers, Guildhall, London.

Made about 1695 for William III, this year clock by Thomas Tompion incorporates the first examples both of equation work and of a break-arch dial. Royal Collection.

on well into the eighteenth century – Daniel Quare until 1724, Joseph Williamson until 1725, the Windmills family even longer – and it may be more convenient to consider these in the succeeding chapter. They provided a continuity within the craft at a time when nothing could have been more important.

Although it will be dealt with more fully in a later chapter, an important milestone in the history of chronometry took place during the last quarter of the seventeenth century and will be mentioned now in order to preserve events in their correct sequence. In 1675, in order to initiate studies in astronomy directed to aiding navigation, Charles II established an observatory in Greenwich Park, installing as his first Astronomer Royal – a title which prevails to the present time – a certain John Flamsteed. An outstanding feature of this new observatory was the pair of year-duration weight-driven clocks commissioned from Tompion. The need for accurate timekeeping in observatory circumstances such as these being so great, the famous craftsman went to enormous lengths, within the limitations of horological knowledge then current, to achieve precision. Thus their long duration was intended to avoid errors due to frequent winding, while their fourteen-foot pendulums, beating two seconds, reduced considerably the small cumulative error deriving from pendulums with a shorter period. These two clocks

must certainly be numbered among the world's great timekeepers since, as scientific instruments, they played their part in advancing human knowledge in the fields of astronomy and navigation.

The application of the pendulum to clocks was exactly matched, in the latter half of the seventeenth century, by the invention and application of the balance spring to watches. In their different ways both offered the same facility, a means of regulating the timekeeping without altering the main driving force of the timepiece. This latter method, at the best of times, can provide only a coarse adjustment.

There is no doubt that the perceived advantages of the one improvement led directly to the other, and indeed, the dramatis personae are the same. Huygens published, in 1675, his claim to the invention of the balance spring, only to be met with a counter-claim from Hooke, stating that he had originated the same device in 1658. The craftsmen of the day sat on the sidelines watching the course of events, except for Tompion, personally involved by Hooke, who claimed he had commissioned him to make a watch with such a spring. The two designs, even so, were not identical. Huygens' spring had a pinion built in to enable the balance to make much larger vibrations – an arrangement which is usually called a 'pirouette' – whereas Hooke's much simpler arrangement is virtually the same as the one in use to this day. The dispute

far left
The night clock is a comparatively rare form, and this one by Joseph Knibb of about 1670 is a particularly fine example. British Museum, London.

left
Remarkably few clocks and watches by Robert Seignior are recorded despite the fact that he held the Royal Warrant 'without ffee'. This striking and repeating spring clock was, from internal evidence, completed in 1688, although Seignior himself died two years before.

The celebrated 'Mulberry Tompion' longcase clock, of about 1700, stands 8ft 2in high with an 11in square dial. The case is of oak finely veneered with mulberry and inlaid with ebonised stringing. British Museum, London.

has never been finally settled; but whereas Hooke's design was implemented at once, Huygens' device is very rarely encountered and not in examples made directly under his aegis. It is a fact that Tompion was making watches with balance springs soon after 1675, and that George Graham subsequently quoted Tompion as authority for crediting the invention to Hooke.

In the next fifteen years a number of events had their effect upon watchmaking. The waistcoat came into fashion, so that watches ceased to be hung round the neck or from the waist and were stowed comfortably away, where they would be likely to come to far less harm in wear than formerly. This was a happy conjunction of events because, while previously the timekeeping was haphazard and size was of no importance, so that many watches were quite small, the new balance spring watches tended at first to be uniformly large and would have been a nuisance if permitted to swing loose.

Another significant event had political and religious origins. Watchmaking in continental Europe had had spasmodic beginnings – in France, and in Germany until her problems with the Thirty Years War, in Switzerland after 1550 or thereabouts, and in Britain rather later. The two latter centres at least offered a haven to Protestants as well as a prosperous market for fine timepieces, and had already benefited from the great craft skills of the Huguenots, who, in their efforts to escape persecution, had settled in both countries and were peacefully plying their trades. This movement was suddenly given unexpected and enormous impetus by the revocation in 1685 of the Edict of Nantes by Louis XIV of France, which had protected Protestants there. As a result, Huguenots already settled in England and Switzerland were augmented by the sudden arrival as refugees of thousands of their French contemporaries.

With a balance spring of only two turns and a cock with irregularly shaped foot, this watch movement of Edward East's was made about 1680 and reflects the earliest stage in the application of the balance spring. Museum of the Worshipful Company of Clockmakers, Guildhall, London.

Both pendulum and balance spring do much more for their respective timekeepers than simply supply, as mentioned earlier, a convenient vehicle for effective regulation to obtain accurate performance. The pendulum is continually moving from one extreme to another – from the outermost points of its swing, whence it has been impelled by the escapement, to its zero vertical position, under the influence of gravity – and this overall action is a rhythmic one. Similarly, the effect upon a watch escapement of incorporating a balance spring is to make the action rhythmic and consistent: just like a pendulum under the influence of gravity, the balance spring is continually trying to return the balance wheel to zero – in this case, its natural position of rest. Previously, the action, already

inherently erratic, could be violently affected by sudden movement or positional changes. Henceforth the watch could be made to perform rhythmically – and accurately – when positioned in any plane, and whether static or mobile.

As the benefits of the balance spring became obvious, very many earlier watches were 'converted', a procedure which the modern purist collector often deplores, but which must have made an enormous difference to watch-users at that time. But the increased accuracy obtainable now made it worthwhile to indicate minutes as well as hours, and this of itself occasioned some most interesting developments.

The employment of two hands on a watch dial to tell us the time is such a familiar arrangement, which it is entirely second nature for us to read,

Daniel Quare made a few magnificent year equation clocks similar to this example in a walnut case standing 9ft 10in high, which is reputed to have been made for Hampton Court Palace about 1695. British Museum, London.

that it is difficult to appreciate the extent of the problem for people who had never been brought up to enjoy this amenity. Children learn to tell the time with both hours and minutes, as part of a normal upbringing, but the need to educate whole nations in such a technique must have been comparable to the recent British experience of adopting decimal coinage and 'going metric'. The conventional system of concentric hour and minute hands soon caught on – even though the mechanical arrangements under the dial to accommodate them are sufficiently ingenious as to suggest that they cannot have been invented overnight – but this was seen by watchmakers at the time as merely one of a number of dial arrangements with which they were experimenting to find the most practical, convenient and easily assimilable. Of the others, some are very rare, while one system at least is fairly common and might therefore be considered the 'runner up' to the two-handed method.

This is the variation known as the 'sun and moon' dial. The upper half of the dial contains a semicircular aperture, around the curved edge of which are engraved the hours starting from VI at one side, arriving at XII – in the place where it would be on a conventional dial – and extending on to VI again at the far side. Behind this aperture is a revolving disc, upon which, diametrically opposite each other, are engraved representations of the sun and the moon, and this disc revolves once in twenty-four hours. Thus, at sunrise – say at six a.m. – the sun appears at the extreme left-hand edge of the aperture, indicating the hours through the day to six p.m. As it disappears from view on the far side, the moon rises at the VI on the near side, performing the same function through the night hours until the whole procedure starts again at six a.m. the following morning. The minutes are indicated separately upon a minute band running around the extreme outer edge of the dial, upon which the five-minute figures are usually engraved upon polished plaques, the long minute hand revolving from the centre in the normal way. This kind of watch may be said to be unusual in showing day and night hours separately, even if such information is self-evident.

Another type of dial utilising a cut-out aperture is called the 'wandering hour' watch. This time, around the edge of the semicircular opening are shown the minutes from 0 to 60, the five-minute divisions again being shown on polished plaques. Revolving behind this aperture is once again a disc, with two circular 'windows' cut into it directly opposite one another. Behind this disc and pivoted to it are two small discs, one engraved with the even hours, the other with the odd, in such a way that as the parent disc rotates, whichever window happens to be in view upon the dial shows the correct hour against the minute band. Supposing this to be an 'odd' hour, the next – even – hour

A dial divided into six hours instead of twelve provided much more space for the accurate reading of an outer ring calibrated in minutes, all with the use of a single hand. This example from about 1680 is signed 'Will Bertram London'. Museum of the Worshipful Company of Clockmakers, Guildhall, London.

opposite page, above
The commonest of the experimental dials associated with early efforts to indicate minutes, this sun and moon dial watch is by Joseph Windmills and was made about 1700.

opposite page, below
Another experimental dial from the same period was the 'wandering hour', and this specimen signed 'Sinclare Dublin 146' dates from about 1690. Museum of the Worshipful Company of Clockmakers, Guildhall, London.

will have been set up meantime beneath the opposite circular window but, of course, will remain out of view until the current hour has passed the '60' mark on the minute band. This type of watch was probably inspired by the night clock of this period.

A third variation used experimentally to show minutes had the main dial divided into only six hours instead of the conventional twelve. Therefore, on the 'six-hour dial' watch, the single hand revolved twice in each twelve-hour period; but, since each hour division was necessarily twice as large as on the normal dial, it was correspondingly much easier to divide them to show minutes, calibrated in twenty minute divisions upon a polished outer band. In order to cope with the hours 7–12 on watches of this kind, it is usual for 1–6 to be shown in large Roman numerals, with 7–12 in smaller Arabic numerals superimposed upon them.

These and other similarly eccentric forms of dial devoted solely to ascertaining the best way to indicate minutes are found not only upon English watches but also upon watches from other parts of Europe. Most may be dated between 1680 and 1700, although outside Britain some of the versions died a long death. It is not unknown, for instance,

A large and beautifully made watch by Benjamin Bell of London. Its outstanding feature is the outsize subsidiary seconds dial and steel tulip hands. Its date is about 1690. Museum of the Worshipful Company of Clockmakers, Guildhall, London.

to find a six-hour dial watch with an enamel, as opposed to an all-metal, dial. Like many another manifestation in horology, too, it is probably true to say that the 'novelty' watch, as a concept, was newfangled several centuries back, and that nothing wholly new or original has been seen since.

Before leaving watches with such strange dials as some of these, brief mention must be made of the 'pendulum watch' – almost a contradiction in terms – which occurred for a short time around 1700. This variety of watch is always supposed to have been inspired by the universal belief among non-scientific people in the quasi-magical properties of the pendulum. The movement of such

watches was so arranged as to reveal the balance vibrating, either through an aperture cut into the balance cock or, a much to be deplored practice, by moving the escapement to just beneath the dial, through which an opening was cut to reveal the balance wheel. In both cases a spurious 'bob' was added to one arm of the balance wheel, and this, seen swinging backwards and forwards through the opening, whether in front of or behind the movement, was intended to give the impression that a pendulum was at work. Nowadays such an example of misplaced ingenuity would simply be dismissed as a gimmick, and probably it was originally intended mainly to boost sales. Even so, Dutch makers as well as some French ones exten-

This fine spring clock was made by Thomas Tompion about 1700. The subsidiary dials in the upper corners are for regulation and strike/silent. Museum of the Worshipful Company of Clockmakers, Guildhall, London.

sively adopted the practice of the cut-out balance cock to show a 'bob' swinging on the back of the watch movement during the eighteenth century.

As the title of this third chapter indicates, the most decorative watches predate 1700. The last quarter of the century saw the beginnings of the popularity of repoussé work for outer cases, at this early stage often no more than flutes radiating from a central boss. Tortoiseshell was another favoured material, being decorated with silver or gold piqué work. Silver and gold filigree is also known but very rare. Stone or crystal is only found – and then exceptionally rarely – framed in otherwise gold cases; cornelians particularly were employed in this style.

So far as other European styles were concerned – and the foregoing has tended to concentrate upon English styles in view of their importance in the history of the craft at this time – certain features are prominent and should be noted. Dutch watches came to favour the so-called 'arcaded' minute band – that is to say, instead of being a complete circle it was broken by twelve equally spaced arches. This feature is even reflected in watches made by English makers for export to that country and is immediately detectable. French dials were quite different from usage elsewhere in that the hour numerals were displayed upon separate enamel plaques, which were in turn mounted upon a decorated metal dial plate. This rather heavy arrangement nevertheless suited the style of French watch known as the 'oignon', a near spherical single-cased watch with overall engraving, generally made in gilt metal, which can suffer badly from wear. Enamel cases are now rare except in France and Switzerland.

The movements of English, French and Dutch watches cannot be easily confused once their styles have been noted. French watches for a long time before and after 1700 employed a winding system actuated by a square projecting through the dial centre. The balance wheel is protected not by a cock, but by a balance bridge, the latter being fixed to the back plate of the movement by two screws, one each side, rather than the single fixing through the cock foot favoured in England. This bridge is generally very large and is the focus for all the decoration applied to the back of the movement; the only other feature visible on such movements is the small regulation dial, simply retained in position by a small bar or arm rather than forming part of a slide plate. On Dutch watches either a cock or a bridge may be found, but, in the latter case, the design is quite different from that of the French. The Dutch bridge will often have two projecting arms through which it is screwed down into position; it is much smaller in size than the French, and the dial for regulating more prominent, eventually being incorporated into a slide plate in the English style.

About 1700 a short-lived fashion arose presumably directed at the more gullible and purporting to show watches controlled by a pendulum. This was nothing more than a metal disc fixed to the crossbar of the balance which, as in this case, was sometimes sited to show through an aperture cut in the dial. This watch was made by David Lesturgeon of London. British Museum, London.

The other version of the pendulum watch involved cutting an aperture in the cock table to allow the disc on the crossbar of the balance to show through. This version is by Richard Howe, Dorchester, who died in 1713.

Another aspect of clock- and watchmaking to which little attention is paid, but which is of signal importance in any general study, is methods of production. Thomas Tompion, most of whose working life was spent in the seventeenth century, is credited with producing altogether around six thousand watches and six hundred clocks – at least, this is the number that may be supposed to have borne his signature, even if they have not all survived. A presentday craftsman, handmaking a single watch – even with all the benefits of modern machine tools and precision equipment – takes upwards of two thousand hours upon the task.

Therefore clearly Tompion employed a workshop of skilled men who must have specialised in their tasks. In other words, even by the later seventeenth century, there must have been considerable division of labour. Furthermore, from long before this time there are clear indications that certain parts of watches, especially dials, were imported from one country to another – it is not uncommon to find an English and a French watch from the earlier part of the seventeenth century with dials as identical as hand-produced parts can ever be; clearly they came from the same workshop. Research has not, as yet, thrown much light upon exactly when a single craftsman ceased to make every part of the watch or clock carrying his name, but in the event it may well turn out to be very much earlier than most students would consider likely.

Progress Towards Precision
-The Eighteenth Century

By the year 1700, most of the fundamental inventions necessary to the construction of a timekeeper with modest pretensions to accuracy had been perfected. The pendulum had been applied to clocks for sufficiently long a period as to have run itself in; the corresponding device for watches, the balance spring, although of more recent origin, was also now in general use everywhere. For clocks, the anchor escapement had revolutionised timekeeping, and a static clock with a pendulum beating seconds coupled to this escapement was, of its kind, every bit as good a timekeeper as would normally be required for ordinary household purposes at the present day, three hundred years later. Many period clocks with this mechanism are still cherished domestic possessions, performing both a decorative and a functional role effectively, and their owners would certainly not swap them for something more up to date.

The only substantial gap in the technology was a better escapement for watches. The verge escapement, the earliest known for both clocks and watches, had been superseded in the former; but there was still no alternative for use in the latter. The verge is in many ways an admirable escapement – and, even at the present time and despite enormous research, much misunderstood by a lot of antiquarians. It is robust and relatively fault-free, going for long periods without maintenance or any kind of attention. It is constrained simply by its design – during its cycle of operation, it is not at any point wholly detached from its balance mechanism, so that the latter is never able to swing free of its influence. In theory, the more 'detached' from contact with the escapement, apart from the moment of impulse, that a balance – or, for that matter, a pendulum – is, the better the timekeeping. So it is not surprising that the eighteenth century should turn out to be the century of escapements, among much else – for the changing life of the ordinary individual, as well as the demands of certain branches of science, was going to require rather more precise time-measurement than had been necessary before.

The second half of the seventeenth century had given England a technological lead that was to last substantially throughout the eighteenth century as well. As has been indicated, other European countries had had their problems. What was the situation in the principal centres of clock- and watch-making outside Britain?

In France, from the beginning, a clock was always seen to be – and deliberately designed as – part of the furniture first, and as a timekeeper only second. French clockmaking underwent a traumatic decline in the middle of the seventeenth century, and when it as dramatically revived following the successful introduction of the pendulum, the first native style to appear was the 'pendule religieuse'. This style was at first clearly modelled upon Salomon Coster's first clocks, and mirrors the strongly architectural approach, although it was not long before they achieved an individuality as well as a splendour which is all their own. Made either to stand on feet or to hang on the wall, these clocks became the standard domestic French design until well into the eighteenth century, although some canister clocks were still being made almost until 1700. These clocks were the forerunners of the famous round French clock movements that became increasingly popular in the eighteenth century, and which achieved virtually a monopoly of production in the nineteenth. The French equivalents of the finest English practitioners, all of them working in Paris, were the families of Thuret and Martinot, Louis Baronneau, Nicolas Gribelin and Pierre Gaudron. Of the cabinetmakers of the day – who were much involved in the casing-up of clocks – mention must be made of André Charles Boulle, famous for the

inlay of brass and tortoiseshell named after him.

The 'religieuse' – supposed, incidentally, to have been so named because in shape it resembled a French nun in her habit – underwent substantial development in the latter part of the seventeenth century, the architectural style gradually disappearing in favour of more free-ranging decoration, which included basket and inverted bell tops, with highly embellished side columns, the whole often surmounted by a gilt figure as opposed to the earlier vases or finials. Such clocks gradually merged into what has come to be known as the 'Grand Style', in which the rectangular basic shape has given way entirely to an arched form; and this quite rapid evolution laid the foundation for the galaxy of styles, exuberant often, yet always elegant according to the French taste, which was to burst upon the world in the eighteenth century. Invariably, however, the French clock was first a piece of furniture. Thus, the French equivalent of a longcase clock required that it should look like a mantel clock standing upon a pedestal – which, of course, was actually the lower part of the case and housed the pendulum. Even when, later on, long-

case clocks were made in one piece, they looked nothing like those to be found in England. Straight lines disappeared finally in the Régence period (1715–23) to be replaced by curves, which gradually developed into the true Rococo style of Louis XV. The mantel clock and such hitherto unknown types as the 'cartel' clock, a wall clock in a frame of highly gilt carved wood or cast bronze, kept pace with the ever increasing tendency to elaborate decoration, utilising groups of figures and animals – Philippe Caffieri is a particularly celebrated artist in this regard – allied to a wide range of decorative techniques. Boulle has already been

mentioned, and this form of marquetry of tortoiseshell and brass enjoyed huge popularity. Gilding was contrasted with bronze in the castings for
cases, which come in infinite variety. Another form
of decoration to become very popular towards the
middle of the century was 'Vernis Martin', a form
of lacquerwork which added the ingredients of
colour range, hitherto lacking, to the armoury of
the Rococo designers.

Eventually, however, the passion for Rococo
passed, and the second half of the eighteenth century saw a return to symmetry and the straight

The earliest type of Dutch pendulum clock, a Haagse klokje,
made by Salomon Coster in 1657 to Huygens' direction. The
chapter ring and cartouche containing the name are set upon
a ground of blue velvet. Every minute is numbered.
Netherlands Clock Museum, Utrecht.

right
The cartel clock epitomises the exuberance of French
clockmaking in the mid eighteenth century. This example
has a case made by C. Cressent and a movement inscribed
'Guiot, Paris'. Wallace Collection, London.

A pendule religieuse by the famous Paris maker Isaac Thuret, about 1675. Science Museum, London.

line, fine workmanship and a great reduction in elaborate decoration. Bracket clocks were largely superseded by mantel clocks, and white marble, with gilt bronze applied decoration, became fashionable. Dials generally were made smaller and of one-piece white enamel, instead of the style previously favoured, in which the hour and five-minute numerals appear as raised enamel plaques on a gilt metal plate, the centre also being of enamel. Several new types of clock appeared – for example, the 'column' clock, in which the central element, the clock itself, is slung beneath a portico top supported upon side columns. Another particularly graceful version is usually called the 'lyre' clock.

Contrary to popular belief, Switzerland has always concentrated upon watches rather than clocks, but even though she was making these in Geneva as early as the sixteenth century, her influence has always been indirect, and she was very late in formulating anything that could be described as a national style. In the earlier periods she is best known for the work of her émigré craftsmen, like the Vulliamys and Emery, who went to England, and Lepine, Berthoud and Breguet, who worked in France. Throughout the eighteenth century most of her production was for export, and was not of the highest quality.

Holland failed to take advantage of the tremendous potential lead given to them by Huygens' genius. However, there must have been much cross-fertilisation of ideas between the Dutch and the English; for example, the longcase clock, generally thought to have originated in London, was very quickly copied and adapted for use in Holland. Seventeenth-century Dutch longcase clocks are much like their English equivalents, except that they follow Coster's style in cladding the dial in velvet; but by the eighteenth century they have veered away, great emphasis being placed upon complications of every kind, with music, phases of the moon and tidal dials becoming quite commonplace and often allied to simple automata which either moved continuously in phase with the escapement or only when the music or striking trains were in action. Typical of such visual additions to the clock's normal function was the ship rocking on the waves, the windmill with rotating sails and the fisherman catching a fish. At the same time, Dutch longcases became much more elaborate – and, many people would say, much less elegant – than their English counterparts. The bases became bulbous, with elaborate paw feet and hoods surmounted by all kinds of exotic figures: Atlas holding the world, with trumpeting angels on either flank, is a typical example.

Perhaps more essentially Dutch than the longcase clock could ever be are a range of hanging weight-driven wall clocks whose detailed design as well as outward appearance differ according to the localities from which they originate and the periods when they were made. First and nowadays most prized is the Zaandam clock, from the industrialised district of Zaan, north of Amsterdam. Zaandam clocks are noted for their highly finished wooden cases with glazed sides, dials backed with velvet showing off with distinction the silver chapter rings, and hollow wall cases which accommodate the pendulum. This type of clock was made from about 1670 until the middle of the following century.

A simpler version of the Zaandam clock originating from Friesland is known as the 'stoelklok'. Appearing first about 1700, it is supported upon a wall bracket with a roof above to exclude dust; sometimes a linen runner is added to this latter feature, hanging down on either side. Both dial and bracket of such clocks would be brightly

This clock is known as the Avignon clock because that city presented it to the Marquis de Rochechouart in 1771. Here the clock is enveloped in statuary rather than separated from it. Wallace Collection, London.

139

painted, and the movement was fundamentally similar to that of a Zaandam clock except for fine detail, like the use of chain rather than rope to suspend the weights. Most were fitted with alarm trains, as well as striking at hour and half-hour.

Finally, about the middle of the eighteenth century, there appeared the 'staartklok'. The movement is contained in a hood like a longcase clock, and has an anchor escapement with pendulum, the latter contained in a flat case splayed out at the bottom to accommodate the pendulum bob, the whole lying flat against the wall. The weights hang on chains in front of this case. Clocks of this kind often have automata, as well as calendar- and lunarwork.

In Austria, the main historical centres of clock-making were located at Vienna, Prague and Innsbruck. Originally following the southern European taste, Austria quickly recouped herself after the Thirty Years War; and from 1680

This style of clock represents a complete break with the Dutch tradition which influenced the pendule religieuse; it was made by Jacques Thuret who worked from 1694 to 1712. Wallace Collection, London.

below
French clocks frequently incorporate statuary in their composition, and this mantel clock by Jean André Lepaute employs reclining figures, after Michelangelo, representing Night and Morning. Wallace Collection, London.

onwards, for at least a century, the English influence is clearly marked. Starting with posted movements, sometimes allied to complicated astronomical trains as well as conventional time-measuring machinery, the Austrian spring clock, by the early part of the eighteenth century, followed English patterns but coupled them with Austrian Baroque ornamentation. The Austrian longcase clock, however, favoured the bulbous style of French provincial work. It was not until about 1780 that a truly native style emerged. This was the 'Stutzuhr', and consisted essentially of a substantial base from which sprang the clock upon a slender support, with flanking ormolu ornamentation and often surmounted by a gilt figure, or sometimes an imperial eagle. Beneath the clock, in the space above the plinth, swings the pendulum bob, and behind it is generally a mirror. The effect can be most attractive.

Finally, mention must be made of clockmaking in the Black Forest. The great feature of clocks from this area is the use of wood for every part of the mechanism, except in those rare places where it simply cannot be made to work. The reason was economic – the peasants in that locality, taking to clockmaking in the middle of the seventeenth century, had of necessity to use readily available local materials, among which brass and steel did not figure. Their first clocks, then, had a foliot balance and a single hand; and, apart from the verge itself, the escape wheel teeth – which were simply metal pegs – and the pins forming the leaves of the lantern pinions, everything was wooden. Power was provided by a stone driving weight. These clocks had painted wooden dials, and only later were their movements boxed in. Striking mechanism was not added until about 1730, nor was the pendulum substituted for the primitive foliot until roughly the same period. Indeed, specimens still incorporating the latter form of controller are found as late as 1760. The popular feature peculiar to Black Forest clocks is the cuckoo bird call to sound the hours, which, contrary to popular belief, is not of Swiss origin. Although cuckoo clocks were undoubtedly made in the eighteenth century, few have survived that can be dated prior to about 1840, and they more properly belong, therefore, in a later chapter.

So inevitably it is necessary to return to England to find the mechanical ingenuity that was so necessary to propel horology in the direction in which developments in other branches of science and technology were to demand that it should go. For, while the French experimented with extremes of decoration on clocks and furniture alike, the Dutch regionalised their styles and the Austrians adapted other national styles to their own usage, it was the English who continued to experiment with mechanical improvements to make time-measurement ever more accurate and reliable, as

Another French clock style, the pedestal clock, is shown in this example by Vidal à Paris about 1750. Wallace Collection, London.

141

well as to retain throughout the eighteenth century the supremacy which their skills had earned them in the previous one.

An instance of this is the provision of special mechanism to indicate the equation of time. This, it will be remembered, is the name given to the difference – which varies from day to day – between solar time, as read from a sundial, and mean time; and the facility depends upon a specially designed cam, called the 'kidney piece' because of its shape, connected to the main mechanism.

The first equation clocks all bear famous English craftsmen's names – Tompion, Quare and Williamson – and the last-named claimed to have invented the principle involved. Tompion, however, can claim to have been first in the field with a clock for William III made about 1695; and the likelihood is that both he and Williamson, who claimed also to have made such clocks for Quare, obtained the idea of the kidney piece from Huygens. The great Dutch physicist wrote a letter to his brother Constantan, then working for William III, in which he explained the principle he had evolved, and it is conceivable that this was the starting point for both Tompion and Williamson.

Astronomy was catching the popular fancy then much as it does today; but it was also serving a much more serious purpose. The equation clock was an example of the scientific solution to a commonly encountered problem, for people had noticed, since the advent of the anchor escapement and the much more accurate performance of their clocks stemming from it, what a substantial effect the equation represented: the sun could be as much as a quarter of an hour fast or slow, by comparison with their clocks. More serious purposes were served by astronomical clocks such as those built, forty years or so apart, by Samuel Watson and Henry Bridges.

Samuel Watson was Mathematician in Ordinary to Charles II. Relatively little is known about him, his claim to fame resting upon at least three astronomical spring clocks, all different in design, one of them made for the King, and one or both of the other two reputed to have belonged to Sir Isaac Newton. These were the first such clocks to have been made for a very long time; and apart from the creation of Richard of Wallingford, known to us only by literary reference. Watson's were the first such masterpieces by an English craftsman.

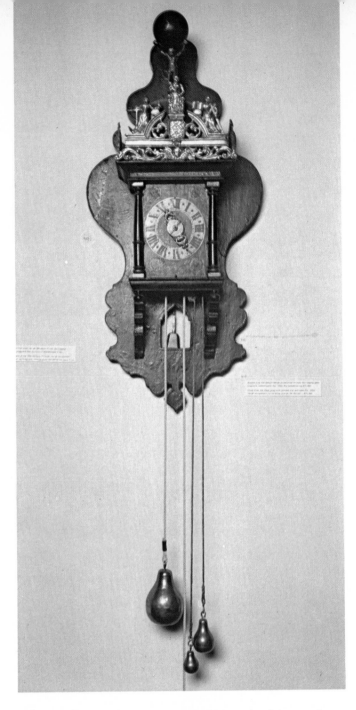

Zaanse clocks originated in a district north of Amsterdam, near the River Zaan, and were made for something over fifty years from about 1670. This example by Groot dates from the latter end of that period. Netherlands Clock Museum, Utrecht.

opposite page
The simplest European clocks – they were constructed almost wholly of wood – originated from the Black Forest and were virtually a cottage industry. This nineteenth-century 30-hour example has a shield dial.

right
This typical late seventeenth-century Dutch longcase clock, an eight-day example, incorporates Dutch striking and alarm and is signed 'Jac. Hasius, Amsterdam'. British Museum, London.

143

Watson's royal clock was ordered by Charles II
in 1683 and was probably completed about 1690.
However, his original client having died before
completion – and his successor abdicated – Watson was left with this highly complex machine on
his hands. He apparently even went so far as to
offer it as the first prize in a raffle, but seemingly
this never took place for it had passed into the
hands of the Queen by 1694. It is in the Library of
Windsor Castle.

The main dial of this clock is twenty inches
square, divided into four quarters, in each of which
is a sub-dial. Taking them in order, that at top left
is for the sun and planets revolving around the
central earth according to Ptolemaic theory. At top
right, the lunar dial has the earth at its centre, with
the moon so arranged that, in its motions, its white
side always faces the earth. The sun, revolving
around the earth, is represented now only by the
pin which used to carry its effigy. The left-hand
lower dial indicates the year of the solar cycle and
the Dominical Letter – by the shorter of the two
pointers – as well as the day of the month, and the
month of the year. On its right, the fourth sub-dial
shows the Metonic Cycle or Golden Number, as
well as the Epact. As for the time, that is shown
only to the nearest quarter-hour by the small central dial.

Watson's two other astronomical clocks appear
to date from the last ten years of the seventeenth
century, and their provenance has been dealt with
in detail by the late H. Alan Lloyd in an article
in the *Horological Journal* for December 1948,
pp. 750–59. It seems likely that both may have
belonged to Sir Isaac Newton although they cannot be identified with certainty from existing
inventories of his belongings. Even so, they establish without any doubt Watson's claim to have
been the first maker of complicated astronomical
clocks in England; previously, the limit in such
designs had been the provision of a lunar dial and
calendarwork.

The fashion that he started continued during the
eighteenth century with a group of clocks by different makers, which varied in their essential purpose
from the academically serious to the popularly
scientific. Some of them fall into the category

which we should nowadays describe as exhibition pieces, but their purpose went rather further than pure novelty. In England at this time, among educated and even less educated people, curiosity was at last being aroused concerning the world – and even the universe – around them. Natural philosophy, a broad term covering the sciences of natural phenomena, was becoming the focus of attention not only of the well-informed professional but also of the amateur and the dilettante. Many of those who fit into the latter two categories were nonetheless highly intelligent and enthusiastic students, and, certainly in horology and astronomy, there are plenty of examples of important contributions to knowledge and understanding being made by just such people.

Careful inspection of this second of Watson's complicated clocks will reveal differences from that previously illustrated. None of the three clocks is identical one with another. Science Museum, London.

Outstanding among the group of clocks just mentioned is one known as the 'Microcosm'. It was of monumental size – ten feet high and standing upon a base six feet wide – and it was made by Henry Bridges of Waltham Abbey about 1734. His tombstone gives his age at his death in 1754 as fifty-seven, and apparently he was an architect; thus he is a good example of the brilliant amateur contributing to the scientific stream. Otherwise virtually nothing has come to light about him. The clock itself could not have been attempted unless

French clock of about 1770 by Ferdinand Berthoud, veneered in oak and ebony with a wheel barometer beneath the dial. Wallace Collection, London.

the maker had become an exceptionally competent workman in horological and allied skills; and its purpose seems to have been mainly to provide a source of income, by its exhibition. Thus, it is known that it was on view at the Mitre, near Charing Cross in London, towards the end of 1741, while in 1756 it had been taken to colonial America, where it was seen in Philadelphia as well as in New York.

The astronomical 'heart' of the Bridges 'Microcosm' consists of the two large dials, set one above the other; the top dial is based on the Ptolemaic system of celestial motions, and the bottom one on the Copernican. This is believed to be the only clock to embrace both systems, and it is perhaps strange – although in keeping with the new-found popular approach to science of the time – that allied to such academic profundities were the most elaborate automata, the whole being accompanied by music from an organ that either performed automatically or could be played from a keyboard. It is said that the mechanism embodied some twelve hundred wheels and pinions.

When the clock was exhibited, a descriptive leaflet entitled *A succinct Description of that Elaborate Pile of Art, called the Microcosm* was offered for sale; this of itself seems to have run to at least seven editions. The cost of viewing the clock varied from location to location, sometimes being as low as sixpence, yet on occasion as high as four shillings and sixpence. Immediately after Bridges' death the clock seems to have passed into the possession of one Edward Davies, for whom at least one edition of the descriptive leaflet was published. After returning from America – its final appearance there seems to have been in Boston – it was shown at Chester and Glasgow, and then seems to have disappeared completely. Eventually the astronomical movement was found in Paris in 1938 by the late Courtenay Ilbert, covered with a tarpaulin on the landing of a staircase in a furniture warehouse, and brought back to London by him, where it can now be seen in the British Museum. No trace has ever been found of the elaborate case or the automata.

An example of the more wholly 'exhibition' type of clock was that made by Jacob Lovelace of Exeter. Said to have taken over thirty years to build – Lovelace's dates in the eighteenth century are uncertain, although it is known that he was sixty when he died – this also was a monumental clock, measuring ten feet by five feet and weighing half a ton. It embraced all sorts of automata, including a moving panorama, an organ, a bird organ – whatever that may have been – and a belfry with six ringers, 'who ring a merry peal ad libitum'. The more serious content of the clock included a 'Perpetual Almanack' which was said to need regulation only every 130 years, the equation of time, and a leap year index revolving once every four years.

above
This broadsheet was issued to advertise the 'Microcosm'. Even given artist's licence, there can be no doubt that originally this clock must have been most impressive. Museum of the Worshipful Company of Clockmakers, Guildhall, London.

above right
This is all that now remains of Henry Bridges' 'Microcosm' which was discovered by the late Courtenay Ilbert in Paris. British Museum, London.

Another rather ingenious indication is located within the main twenty-four-hour clock dial, and shows the sun 'seen in his course, with the time of rising and setting by an Horizon receding or advancing as the days lengthen or shorten'. Within the same area was also located the age and phases of the moon.

The Lovelace clock is said to have turned up in a garret some while after his death, and thence to have passed into the possession of various persons in Exeter and thereabouts. It was frequently exhibited in the nineteenth century, notably at the Great Exhibition of 1851, and in 1888 it was proposed to purchase it for the City of London, but this was not carried through. By the time of the Second World War, it had found its way to the William Brown Street Museum in Liverpool, where it was believed to have been totally destroyed by a bomb. However, of recent years, parts of it have come to light again, namely the complicated dial, some of the chiming train, and an odd ornament from the case. Curiously, it would seem that the clock was never officially photographed during its 'lifetime' as a complete entity, and the only representation of it that is left is the rare lithograph by Hackett which was published in 1833. It would seem, from comparison with those parts that have so far been recovered that this rendering must have been fairly accurate.

Another clock with pretensions to being a scientific instrument, albeit not in the astronomical sphere, is James Cox's 'perpetual motion' clock. Cox was an exceptionally able maker of compli-

The remaining Watson clock has a dial layout totally different from the other two and is dealt with on page 144. Royal Collection.

cated musical automata clocks, invariably housed in the most lavishly ornamented cases, and frequently destined for China, where such extravagances were much to the taste of the rulers of that country. Cox had his workshop for many years in Shoe Lane, in the City of London, and, among other enterprises, he pioneered the Spring Gardens Museum at Charing Cross, which closed after a life of some six years, towards the end of 1774. The objects on show in this museum were of his own creation, and at the end there were some fifty-six of them; the fee for viewing was half a guinea. Cox obtained a private Act of Parliament enabling him to dispose of his museum exhibits, after its closure, by public lottery, and much of the information about them derives from the catalogues published in this connection. Cox himself died in 1788.

His 'perpetual motion' clock, exhibit no. 47 according to one catalogue, sets out to solve the insoluble, at a time when the concept of perpetual motion had caught the public imagination, and when indeed other clockmakers had tried – on paper, at least – to provide their own answers to a problem that almost seems to have overtones of the alchemist about it. Most of the other solutions were deliberately fraudulent, such as the one which wound a clock by the action of opening and shutting a door. Cox seems to have been serious about his, certainly to the extent of producing a most interesting as well as workable piece of machinery, which illustrated a principle – the use of small changes in barometric pressure to wind a clock – not finally adopted, despite its obvious utility, until the advent of the 'Atmos' clock nearly two centuries later.

Artist's licence has clearly been used in this print of Richard Greene's Lichfield clock which appears to tower over its observers.

The mechanism of Greene's Lichfield clock has been slightly modified over the years, and it has been fitted with a pedestal and superstructure. Described in contemporary accounts as an altar clock, it carries no indication of who made it. Victoria Museum and Art Gallery, City of Bath.

The date of Cox's clock is about 1760. Without going into the greatest detail, the winding arrangement depends upon two huge reservoirs of mercury – the weight of the liquid metal involved is about 150lb, of which the cost at the present time would be prohibitive – and these are in a state of unstable equilibrium, a kind of 'see-saw' action being involved. Even a small change in barometric pressure upsets the balance, which is enlarged by a lever system as well as given a uni-directional momentum, and applied to raising the weight which actually drives the tiny clock mechanism. The latter is, in fact, of the scale and substance of a watch. It appears that the mechanism worked well, and that the driving weight was almost always fully wound. Whether or not James Cox really believed that he had found an answer to the quest for perpetual motion must remain in doubt; the charge of half a guinea to inspect his museum was designed to prevent 'undue masses of the curious' from causing damage by congestion, and, presumably, reduced numbers enabled him to control their proximity to the clock to a nicety. Furthermore, despite his protestations that everything was clearly visible and that there were no hidden mysteries, the particular device which converts the upward or downward movement of the lever sys-

tem into a one-directional winding facility had been very carefully boxed in and hidden away. This might have been to stop professional competitors from cashing in on his invention, of course; we shall never know for certain.

One more unusual English clock in this general category – although completely outclassed by those already described – does deserve brief mention. It is usually referred to as 'Greene's Lichfield clock', although Greene was not the maker but the owner.

Richard Greene (1716–1793) was trained as an apothecary and surgeon, but seems to have abandoned any professional ambitions in such directions quite early in life, to devote himself to the amassing of curiosities and objects of unusual interest in every conceivable sphere of human knowledge or activity. He spent his entire life in Lichfield, of which he became Sheriff in 1758 and eventually one of that city's Aldermen. He was the first to set up a printing press there, but his fame undoubtedly rests upon his museum, to which visitors came from far and wide; even the great Dr Johnson, accompanied as ever by the voluble Boswell, inspected it on at least two occasions.

Among the vast mass of miscellanea set out in cases, closets, hanging from ceilings and so forth,

was a timepiece described as a musical altar clock. There is no indication, either upon the clock itself or from documentary references, as to who made it, although additions and improvements both to the structure and to the musical mechanism have been recorded. The clock is first described in the *Universal Magazine* of 1748, and is of good provincial workmanship; but it lacks that extra finish which always denotes the London practice.

The altar clock itself is about four feet high; but in 1768 it was provided with a pedestal and an outer superstructure which, when both are in position, give a total height in excess of nine feet. The prevailing religious flavour of the work is reflected in the various tablets, mainly of silvered brass, upon which appear the Ten Commandments, the Lord's Prayer and the Creed; this is further supported by statues of St John the Evangelist and St Peter, placed in niches either side of the clock dial, and there are a number of other statues positioned elsewhere on the clock. Above this again, a pavilion adorned with angels and cherubim contains an effigy of Pontius Pilate washing his hands, and around him process continuously three figures representing Christ going to his Crucifixion, the Virgin Mary and Simon the Cyrenian bearing the Cross, the trio making one complete revolution each minute. The clock is spring-driven; it incor-

porates simple calendar- and lunarwork. Besides striking the hours on a large bell positioned at the back and just below the topmost figure on the pinnacle – which is said to represent 'Fame, with wings expanded, holding a sword in each hand' – the clock has a musical action playing every three hours or at will. It is interesting that the pin-barrel operating the musical action has been repricked, presumably as part of the 1768 refurbishing, so that, where there were once eight tunes, now there are only five. The history of the clock once Greene died and his museum was dispersed – much of it was sold off between 1799 and 1821 – is not well established; but eventually it was bequeathed to the Victoria Art Gallery, in Bath, when that was opened in 1900.

This astronomical organ clock is the only one of Henry Jenkins's monumental masterpieces at present known to exist (see page 154). While the curious observer sits at the hinged bureau flap thoughtfully provided to support his notebook, the organ beguiles him with a selection of twelve tunes – six on each of the two interchangeable pin-barrels. In the opening exposed by the flap can be seen the two weights driving the main going and striking trains of the clock, while behind and to their right is the massive weight that powers the organ action. The reserve pin-barrel is stored on a shelf at top left of the opening.

Such are a representative sample of the variety of interesting and important large clocks being made for public approbation in England during the eighteenth century – for the only one of those described which could reasonably fit into any ordinary household would have been James Cox's clock. There were other clocks of this kind which have either disappeared altogether or of which little is known. Christopher Pinchbeck (1670–1732) made astronomical and musical clocks, as well as inventing the zinc-copper alloy which was used as a cheap substitute for gold, and which is usually called 'pinchbeck'. In his advertising, in 1731, he refers to his shop 'at the Musical Clock in Fleet Street', and there is an illustration of a typically large ornate machine complete with automata on at least three levels, which, it is reasonable to suppose, was one of his own productions. It seems unlikely that this clock can still exist, despite the remarkable survival rate that such mechanisms seem to enjoy, even if they are, in some cases, only partial entities. Indeed his son, also Christopher, made a superb astronomical clock for George III about 1768 which is still in the royal collection.

Another mystery surrounds the work of Henry Jenkins, who is said by Britten, in the sixth edition of *Old Clocks and Watches and their Makers*, to have flourished from 1760 to 1780 in various locations in London. This same craftsman published a book in 1778, entitled *A Description of several Astronomical and Geographical Clocks with an account of their motions and uses*, from which it is clear that he had made several extra-complicated astronomical clocks, with musical and other parts incorporated, and was in all respects a considerable craftsman. Yet until quite recently, he was known for one or two domestic clocks with astronomical complications, and his monumental clocks were thought to have perished.

Now, however, one has been rediscovered and restored to much of its original splendour and performance (see illustrations on pages 151, 154).

There remain two makers whose work should be mentioned, on account of their ingenuity and fine craftsmanship; in each case representative specimens still exist by which they can be judged. Charles Clay died in 1740. The date of his birth, somewhere in the West Riding of Yorkshire – for the family turns up in the registers of several villages within a few miles of Huddersfield – remains unknown. His claim to fame rests upon the design and production of a small handful of musical – usually organ – clocks, of which the finest, described by its maker as 'The Temple of the Four Grand Monarchies of the World', remains to this day in the collection of the Queen, at Kensington Palace in London. It says much for Clay's importance in his own time that he was able to invite established artists of the calibre of Rysbrack and Roubiliac, leading Baroque sculptors in the England of that period, as well as musicians like

above left
James Cox's celebrated experimental clock, whether or not he really believed in perpetual motion, received much attention in his lifetime as witness this contemporary print.

above
James Cox's clock, to judge by contemporary illustrations of it, is one of the best preserved of all experimental English clocks surviving from this period. Victoria and Albert Museum, London.

opposite page
The musical movement of the Lovelace clock after restoration.

153

Handel and Geminiani, to help him with the appropriate elements of his clock. Equally sad is the fact that, though the outer structure exists intact, so that one can appreciate what it must once have been, it is only a shell, for the whole of the interior has been gutted – probably by the Victorian clockmaker Vulliamy, who made a habit of such things – and the pedestal which contained the musical action has been replaced by an open-work stand on legs, wholly out of keeping with the object it supports. Even the small integral clock has been replaced. Of his other work, there is a fine clock in the royal palace in Naples, which is reasonably well preserved – including its tiny pipe-organ – although not working. Historically, the Duke of Sussex, a great horolophile, who had many clocks among his possessions when these came to be auctioned by Christie's on 4th July 1843, had a Clay organ clock; and in the description accompanying this lot, no. 127, Clay is described as having lived 'in the latter part of the reign of George I and the beginning of the reign of George II, and was a very celebrated maker of machine-organs'. Perhaps the only entirely complete and working example of his work to be seen in recent times was sold by auction in London in 1972. This particular clock seems to have been taken, soon after it was finished, to Amsterdam, where it became part of a notable collection; after that, it went to Portugal where it has remained ever since. It was clear that this clock must also have been one of Clay's important productions, for both the musical and artistic elements show unmistakable signs of collaboration with at least some of the celebrities already mentioned.

The second maker of whom mention must be made is Alexander Cumming. Born in Edinburgh about 1732, he died in 1814. He was an uncle of John Grant who was one of his apprentices, and went on to become one of the great precision clock- and watchmakers of the time. Cumming made a number of fine clocks and watches during his lifetime, being elected a Fellow of the Royal Society, as well as publishing a treatise entitled *The Elements of Clock and Watch Work* in 1766. He is probably best known, however, for his interest in coupling the phenomenon of barometric pressure with clockwork – not, like James Cox, to produce perpetual motion, but for more academically scientific ends, to produce the first successful self-

Apart from the clocks and watches they made in partnership, Tompion and Graham occasionally set their names to something rather more unusual like this orrery which shows visually the motions of the earth and moon around the sun. Museum of the History of Science, Oxford.

The frontispiece from Henry Jenkins's book *A Description of several Astronomical and Geographical Clocks . . .*, as it appeared in the second edition of 1778, gives a clear indication of this maker's individual style. It bears marked similarities to the clock previously illustrated, although clearly it is not the same instrument.

The dial of Henry Jenkins's clock reveals this maker's modest signature – Henry Jenkins, Cheapside, London – which is just discernible at the bottom of the dial-plate, left and right of centre. The dial itself transmits a variety of information, from the age of the moon and high tide at a range of different coastal towns, to the varying lengths of day and night throughout the year. Jenkins published his own description of his highly complicated clocks in 1760, with a second edition in 1778.

recording barograph. In 1765 he sold his first model to George III – it remains in the royal collection to this day – for which he was paid no less than £1,178, as well as an annual retainer of £150 for maintaining it. The following year he made a second instrument for his own use. These clocks display many fine original features, including a gravity escapement of Cumming's own design, which is fully explained in his published treatise.

Such is a brief outline of the more extrovert manifestations of horological ingenuity and excellence that took place in Britain throughout the eighteenth century. While these may seem to have occurred in a veritable explosion – and, for a small country, they represent a vigorous activity on quite a grand scale – it would be wrong to imply that nothing corresponding to this output was going on elsewhere. Vienna, for instance, was the centre for a small coterie of craftsmen building superb complicated clocks with an individuality all of their own. In the Bavarian National Museum can be found perhaps the finest example of this school, a

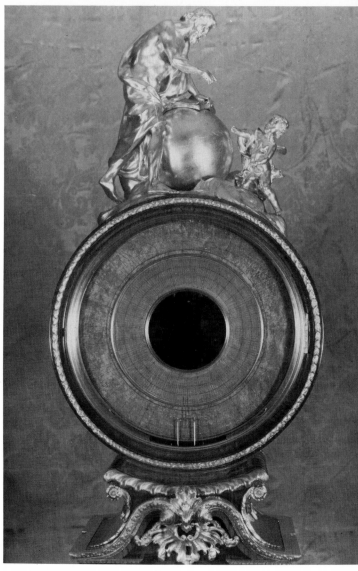

Alexander Cumming applied the idea of connecting clockwork and barometric pressure. This shows the dial of the self-recording barograph which he made for King George III in 1765. Royal Collection.

left
This year-duration clock was made by William Webster about 1720 and incorporates a slightly arched Vauxhall glass mirror into the trunk door. British Museum, London.

opposite page, top
The clock made by Aurelius in Vienna between 1760 and 1770 is depicted in this general view. Some authorities maintain that the clock case is the finest of its kind ever made. The clock is now in the Bavarian National Museum.

opposite page, below
The quality of the workmanship on the dial of the Aurelius clock is higher than even this photograph might indicate, while the complexity is self-evident.

monumental clock by an Augustinian friar, usually known as Aureliano, who taught mathematics and philosophy and, during the period 1760 to 1770, built this clock with his own hands. In essence it is an exceptionally complex astronomical clock, housed in a case, by an unknown maker, of a quality unequalled in any other known example.

Another Viennese clockmaker of eminence was David Caetano, a pupil of Aureliano, who built a month-duration astronomical clock of even greater complexity than that of his master. Completed in 1769, this clock is now in the Vienna Clock Museum. Work of the finest quality, though on a smaller scale than that of the two massive clocks just mentioned, was also coming from such other well-known makers operating in Vienna as Mathias Ratzenhofer, whose working life spanned the turn of the eighteenth and nineteenth centuries, followed early in the nineteenth by craftsmen of the merit of Brandl and Joseph Ettel.

Whatever else may be said, by way of wonder and amazement, about some of the clocks just touched upon, they contributed very little, in practical terms, to the timekeeping needs of the man in the street, being more often than not designed for some loftier scientific purpose which fell right outside his ken, or else simply as an exhibition novelty. Nevertheless, at a different level, a great deal was going on – mainly, but not wholly, in England – to refine the design and improve the performance of ordinary domestic timekeepers. This still resulted partly from the initiative of rich patrons – who had always hitherto been the springboard from which technological improvements had leapt upon the community, since a bottomless purse can be a great incentive to a comparatively impoverished craftsman – and partly from a gradually changing pattern of life, with the Industrial Revolution just around the corner. But the main impulse, as might be expected, was generated by scientific and humanitarian needs, such as that of accurate navigation, and the astronomical and horological implications associated therewith.

However, improvements occurred only at a very leisurely pace. In domestic clocks, for example, relatively little happened during the first twenty-five years of the eighteenth century. Longcase clocks gradually got larger – the six-foot case of the previous period grew to a norm of between seven and eight and a half feet, while dials expanded from ten inches square to eleven or twelve. Hoods were removed by being pulled forward on runners, and all had front-opening doors; the lift-up hood had disappeared altogether by 1700. On the top, flattened domes with three ball finials become usual and, where mouldings appear, these are now generally concave instead of convex. Marquetry inlay was popular, especially in the all-over seaweed pattern, but the finest clocks were mostly

housed in walnut. Lacquer is another finish in vogue at this time.

This period saw the rise to eminence of George Graham, who achieved a degree of elegance in his clocks that would be difficult to surpass. He also perfected the only mechanical innovation of note that occurred, the dead-beat escapement. Technical complexities apart, this escapement can always be distinguished from its near relation, the anchor escapement, by its lack of recoil in action. Observation of the seconds hand on any ordinary long-case clock reveals that, as it advances from division to division on the dial, each forward movement is immediately preceded by a momentary retreat, which is the recoil. With a dead-beat escapement, however, each forward motion of the hand is divided from the next following only by a pause: the hand is described as beating 'dead' seconds. Graham perfected his escapement in 1715, and his mercury pendulum in 1726: he utilised the consequential change in the volume of a body of mercury as a means of compensating for alterations to the length of a pendulum caused by changes in the ambient temperature, one of the principal causes

above
David Caetano was a pupil of Aurelius. He constructed a month weight-driven clock whose complexities needed dials at both front (left) and back (right). Clock Museum, Vienna.

left
Another innovation attributed to Ellicott about 1750 radically changed the appearance of the bracket clock by substituting a round dial for a rectangular one and by doing away with the necessity for spandrels. Museum of the Worshipful Company of Clockmakers, Guildhall, London.

right
Essentially of the period round 1790, this unusual painted satinwood eight-day longcase clock is by John Fordham of Braintree. During the nineteenth century the movement was modified by the addition of an eight-bell chime, necessitating a new dial centre and chapter ring.

This small bracket clock by George Graham was made some years after Tompion's death but still bears the unmistakeable hallmarks of the quality and individuality which they conferred upon their clocks. It stands only 13in high. British Museum, London.

Made about 1740 and standing 7ft 8in high, this fine mahogany longcase equation regulator clock by George Graham has his 'dead-beat' escapement and mercury compensated pendulum. It is of one month duration. See also page 31. British Museum, London.

of inaccurate timekeeping in ordinary clocks. These two innovations combined in the same clock formed the basis of the famous Graham 'regulator', which was in all essentials the finest clock of its type – that is, as an accurate timekeeper for observatory and other scientific purposes – until the last few years of the nineteenth century. Regulator clocks were simply timekeepers: any complication, even such as striking, which might possibly have upset the performance of the going train, was rigidly excluded. Despite these considerable advances, Graham made relatively few clocks and must have concentrated his attention mainly upon the roughly six thousand watches which carried his signature.

Spring clocks in England underwent relatively little change during the first half of the eighteenth century. Black was still the favourite colour for the wood of the case, which as a consequence was either ebony or ebonised pearwood, although for the more high-grade pieces walnut remained the

preference. Lacquer became increasingly popular, and dimensions overall started to increase. The most noticeable change in the style of bracket clocks throughout this time was the gradual appearance, starting about 1710, of the break-arch dial and case. This had been first introduced by Tompion fifteen years before in one special clock, his longcase year-duration clock with equation of time, made for William III; and when first introduced into bracket clocks, it was mainly employed to accommodate a strike-silent control or calendarwork. The other outward change of style that started during this time, but was not at all common before 1750, was the substitution of a round, instead of a square, window in the front door, which effectively eliminated spandrels and produced a somewhat severe effect. However, a new style had become highly desirable, the previous one having done duty with so little change for so long.

Longcase clocks, to judge from survivng examples, seem to have gone into a temporary decline in the two decades immediately prior to the mid century. The break-arch dial and hood, when seen in the longcase, predispose towards some change in the shape of the trunk door, the top of which was now generally arched, while the corners of the case are usually chamfered. Walnut, lacquer and japanning were customary for London clocks, while oak remained popular in the country; mahogany is almost unknown at this period. The top of the hood passed through a number of styles almost simultaneously; the break-arch top has been mentioned, but the inverted bell top was also fashionable, while country makers even tried to revert to an earlier fashion with an architectural flavour imparted by the broken pediment. This, however, gradually degenerated into a more Baroque form. Mechanically, mention has been made of Graham's important contributions to escapements and temperature compensation. Harrison, whose genius will be more fully described in the next chapter, made similarly substantial contributions in the same areas, his form of compensation being based upon the 'gridiron' concept. John Ellicott, not only a renowned clockmaker but also a Fellow of the Royal Society, devised yet another version of a compensated pendulum, using the same principle of the differential expansion of metals, although it seems to have found little favour with other makers.

The second half of the eighteenth century saw England's ascendancy in the specialised form of time-measurement known as chronometry, and much of the native talent of its best craftsmen was devoted to solving the complex problems associated with that discipline. Consequently, developments in the ordinary domestic clock were slow to occur and do not amount to substantial change until late in the century. While the popularity of the longcase declined in the south, it suddenly blossomed forth in the northern counties, from about 1760. Mahogany, a wood almost unknown in clock cases before that date, quickly gained popularity and monopolised the field. Virtually all other woods and finishes – except the countryman's oak for simple clocks – died out. Northern styles at first followed those last in vogue in London, and only later deviated into the broad proportions which have been generally considered a debased form, albeit sometimes very well constructed. Bracket clocks continued much in their previous form, and still with the verge escapement; the anchor, as modified for this type of clock, was not generally adopted until after 1800.

Growing alongside these traditional styles there gradually evolved a whole new series of shapes and sizes of clocks, a burgeoning comparable with what was happening in France; but these were only starting to take the fancy of the ordinary customer in the last two decades or so, and did not

This large travelling clock – its diameter is 3¾ in – was made by George Margetts about 1790. The three dials read hours, minutes and seconds respectively, the last two showing both mean and sidereal time. The polished wood protective outer box for this clock is a recent discovery. While possible not contemporary, it is unlikely to date from long after the beginning of the nineteenth century. Museum of the Worshipful Company of Clockmakers, Guildhall, London.

become really established until the following one. Thus, for longcases, a Chippendale design in which the clock itself sits atop a tapering case, something like an inverted obelisk, while exceedingly rare, is by no means unknown. This style is quite reminiscent of what was happening to such clocks in France. In more conventional styles, it was the dial that changed, either to a simple silvered and engraved plate, or to one painted white with numerals picked out in black. These fashions date from about 1775. Regulator clocks, in the style set by Graham, were not greatly different from other longcase clocks; but during the latter part of the eighteenth century these became much more severe and totally undecorated. Square silvered dial plates have the display of hours, minutes and seconds separated by splitting into sub-dials, and such an arrangement is usually called a regulator dial, even when it is used on a watch. The purpose is to avoid the additional friction resulting from having motionwork under the dial to support the usual arrangement of concentric hour and minute hands.

As for bracket clocks, we have already noted the style, pioneered by John Ellicott about 1750, in which the square front door has a round dial window and no spandrels. About 1770 the conventional bell top started to give way to a break-arch

163

top, a style which developed and extended well into the nineteenth century. Repeating facilities in bracket clocks had all but disappeared by 1750, but musical and organ clocks became popular. Such clocks can have as many as four trains, for going, striking, chiming and music. An entirely different form of clock – more, perhaps, for a mantel than a bracket – was the balloon clock. This first appeared as early as 1760 but took a long time to come into prominence; then it stayed in fashion until about 1810. These clocks are generally plain, with at most a panel of inlay below the dial and a pronounced waist.

Two other forms of clock remain to be mentioned. Coach clocks, the outsize watches made for the traveller to hang up *en route*, which were pioneered by such makers as Edward East in the

seventeenth century, continued to be made throughout the eighteenth. Almost invariably, they now have a pull-repeat facility.

The other type of clock is that popularly called the 'Act of Parliament' clock, after William Pitt's levy of 1797 on all clocks and watches. This so diminished the market for these commodities that innkeepers provided their customers with the right time, as an additional service, using a particular style of clock which, though quite attractive, could be cheaply made. A very large number of such clocks survive, and they can often be dated to several decades before the single year that Pitt's levy was enforced. Their popular name is clearly incorrect, therefore, and they were simply inn clocks of the second half of the eighteenth century. Mostly of mediocre quality, they include the occa-

164

far left
George Lindsay, who held the Royal Warrant from George III, was arguably the finest maker of musical clocks of his time. On pages 52 and 53 will be found an illustration of one of his organ clocks, spring-driven. This large weight-driven longcase clock has a third (musical) train which plays a selection of six tunes on twelve bells, but using thirteen hammers. The extra hammer permits a fast staccato effect on one of the bells.

left
Spring-driven regulator clocks are rare, and this one by John Grant, a famous London maker at the turn of the eighteenth and nineteenth centuries, is said to have been for his own use. It is of one month duration and has an unusual gravity escapement. Museum of the Worshipful Company of Clockmakers, Guildhall, London.

right
Grant chose to employ Ellicott's design of compensated pendulum for his regulator clock, and this close-up shows the pendulum bob which encloses the arrangement of a brass and iron component acting upon hinged levers. Museum of the Worshipful Company of Clockmakers, Guildhall, London.

sional specimen that is exceptionally fine, both in design and in execution.

When the progress of watchmaking in the eighteenth century is examined, it is clear that two attitudes of mind are at work. The English, preoccupied with precision timekeeping as part of their efforts in the field of chronometry, are poised to make many important mechanical discoveries applicable to watchwork. The French, on the other hand, are more concerned with the ultimate appearance of the watch and will direct their energies to improving this, so that eventually they can claim to have influenced its final metamorphosis into the modern watch.

Very little of any consequence happened, either mechanically or in any other respect, to the watch during the first half of the eighteenth century. The escapement, the heart of the 'movement', was probably still the verge although Graham had long since perfected his cylinder escapement, and used nothing else in his watches after 1727. Pair-cases, plain and unadulterated, with enamel or – now rather more infrequently – metal dials, were the norm. As the century progressed, watches became a little smaller and the dials lighter in concept, with minute figures gradually disappearing altogether. Seconds hands were often pivoted from the centre, which added sophistication to the appearance of the watch; but in no form were seconds hands yet common. Multiple dials were employed whenever complex astronomical, calendar or stopwatch information was to be displayed; in the last-named category, the stop action brought the entire watch to a halt, an arrangement which persisted throughout the whole century.

The thick pair-case watch was universally used in England certainly until 1775, and was still being made for another seventy-five years. Even when the best London practice was to dispense with it, the substitute did nothing to make the watch thinner; the first 'consular' cases were almost indistinguishable from pair-cases, and the movement was still hinged to swing out, but there was just one case instead of two. The French, however, moved rapidly towards the thinner watch in the last quarter of the century, and these were often wound through the dial to obviate the need of a double-backed case. Watch cases were now often completely plain, gold or silver, and such enamel work as is found has greatly degenerated from what had gone before. Similarly, repoussé decoration, at its best by mid century, persisted in increasingly debased forms until 1775. Guilloche, or engine-turning, started to come into its own from about 1770 and, in combination with over-enamelling, often edged with half pearls or paste, can produce a superb effect.

Mechanically, the second half of the eighteenth century saw the cylinder escapement further refined, in both England and France, by making part or the whole of the cylinder out of ruby. As made originally in steel, the cylinder is very susceptible to wear; with its bearing surfaces made of ruby in the English usage pioneered by Ellicott

At the end of the eighteenth century, a small handful of English and French watchmakers recommenced experiments with the lever escapement. Robert Robin working in Paris made a number of such watches about 1790.

and Arnold, or completely out of that same precious hardstone, as subsequently developed by Breguet, it seems almost impossible to wear the escapement out. However, the brittle nature of the stone makes accidental damage likely to have more serious consequences than with the earlier version.

Having some relationship to the cylinder escapement – they are all three so arranged that their escape wheels operate in a horizontal plane – are, first, the virgule and, secondly, the duplex. The virgule is only found in French watches and, as developed about 1780 by Jean Antoine Lepine, enjoyed a short vogue of only about twenty years. Today it is a collector's item indeed and only rarely encountered. Theoretical advantages of the virgule were largely offset by its inherent fragility, the difficulty of making it and its inability to hold oil. As a result, it wears quickly, so that its performance rapidly deteriorates. An even rarer version of the virgule known as the double virgule has survived in very few examples indeed, and these are almost exclusively in museums.

The third of the horizontally designed escapements is the duplex. To a greater or lesser degree it possessed all the faults inherent in the virgule: it too was fragile and difficult to make and to keep lubricated. But it was capable of providing great precision in performance, when built by the most skilled hands. Certain London makers specialised

in it almost to the exclusion of other escapements, most notably James McCabe, who was himself turning out fine examples towards the end of the eighteenth century while his successors continued the fashion even towards the middle of the nineteenth. The duplex seems to have acquired such a reputation during its heyday that it became the preferred escapement for the highest quality watches, despite the advent of the detent and the lever. And this reputation would not be contradicted by presentday experience, for there still remain plenty of fine watches with duplex escapements which, carefully maintained, give as good a performance now as when new, perhaps a century and a half ago.

The detent escapement was, of course, developed directly from the inventive 'stream' that was tackling the longitude problem and the navigational need for a high-performance timekeeper. While it can be perfectly well adapted to a pocket watch, the timing of its development was such that it could hardly have been available in any quantity for ordinary domestic use before 1800: all supplies were diverted to become deck watches for marine use.

The remaining escapement was the detached lever, invented during the eighteenth century and destined eventually to become the most important of them all, though unrecognised at its true value by its inventor and discarded. Thomas Mudge, a famous and inventive horologist with a particular interest in the field of chronometry, completed his prototype lever watch in 1759; George III, for whom it was made, gave it to Queen Charlotte, and it has remained in the royal collection to this day. It has often been called 'the most famous watch in the world'.

Mudge had the advantage of knowing about a prior invention, called the 'rack lever', which originated in France; and he must have recognised that the great disadvantage of the escapement in that form was the rack and pinion which continually connected the escapement to the train. It was his flash of inspiration to redesign that particular part of the mechanism, eliminating this feature altogether. He believed in his escapement to the extent of writing that in watches it could answer its purpose better than any other watch escapement then available. But he also conceded that it was very difficult to make, and few craftsmen would attempt it, let alone succeed.

This remarkable specimen can only be described as a skeleton clock, although it is quite unlike a normal one. Dated 1776, it is signed 'Jas. Merlin, Inventor' and therefore has associations with James Cox, for whom Merlin was principal mechanic. Unusual technical features of the clock include a dead-beat verge escapement with a crown wheel of sixty teeth, while the connection between the verge arbor and the centre wheel is by means of a worm pinion.

In fact, apart from Mudge's original watch, the lever escapement was the subject of further experiment in a very few watches made by a small handful of the best watchmakers towards the end of the century. Josiah Emery holds pride of place in this regard, although Leroux and Grant, as well as one or two others, produced their own versions of this mechanism, and similar experimentation was going on independently in France, by such makers as Robert Robin. It would be true to say, however, that the generality of watchmakers ignored the lever escapement until well into the nineteenth century, and the fully developed version, as handed down to our own times – which is known as the table-roller lever – did not become commonplace until at least 1830.

Technical features such as the balance spring were undergoing modification and improvement throughout this period, but they had at least been introduced. On the other hand, the other innovation of great importance in watchmaking was the equivalent to the temperature-compensated pendulum in clocks, the compensated balance. This refinement can hardly have been necessary until well into the nineteenth century for ordinary pocket watches which, in other respects, were not sufficiently accurate to justify such sophistication. But the chronometermakers did need it, and where they went the watchmakers were not slow to follow.

The first pocket watch with a lever escapement was made by Thomas Mudge for George III in 1759, but it was not for another sixty years or more that the escapement was to become commonplace. Royal Collection.

Marine Chronometry - 1675 to 1820

There is nothing mysterious about a chronometer: it is simply a special kind of timekeeper for use on board ship, where it is an important navigational aid.

In the usage of most English-speaking countries, the definition of a chronometer requires that it must have a particular type of detached escapement, which is known as the detent – or, sometimes, just as the chronometer – escapement. In Switzerland, however, a chronometer tends to be any timekeeper that has successfully passed stringent observatory tests. Marine chronometers are generally housed in brass drum-shaped cases, which in turn are slung in gimbals – so that, whatever the motion of the ship, the chronometer remains level – and these are fitted in a mahogany box with a glass-topped lid, as well as an outer solid lid. The time can be read, therefore, with the minimum of disturbance. The same specially accurate detent escapement was also fitted into watches, and in the early days these tended to be a little on the large side, when they were known as 'deck watches'; they too were often contained in specially fitted mahogany boxes with sliding lids, although not in gimbals. The original purpose of the deck watch was to enable the ship's 'box chronometer' – an alternative and self-explanatory term – to be set to time accurately, when the ship was in port, without having actually to move it from its normal position; the going of any timekeeper is affected to a greater or lesser degree by extraneous motion, and in the case of the ship's navigating timekeeper this was avoided at all costs. So the deck watch instead was taken to the nearest observatory where it was set to time by the regulator clock – which itself would be checked regularly by the observatory's transit instrument – and then brought back to the ship, where its time would be compared with the marine chronometer, and the latter adjusted as required.

But why was such an irksome procedure necessary? To appreciate this, it is important to understand one of the greatest hazards facing the mariners of those days, not a new hazard by any means but one that, in the more prosperous trading times of the seventeenth and eighteenth centuries was costing not only lives, then considered reasonably expendable, but also valuable cargoes, which were not. This hazard was simply the inability of a ship's captain, once out of sight of land, to be able to plot with any degree of certainty exactly where his ship was positioned. Some of the great voyages of discovery which took place before and during this time must, for their success, have depended upon a large slice of luck, however brilliant may have been the navigators conducting them. The alternatives to making a desired landfall were the likelihood of shipwreck or, perhaps even worse, slow death from diseases of dietary deficiency like scurvy.

Plotting a position at sea follows much the same pattern as on dry land; and anyone who has ever done any mapreading knows that, for the latter, one needs two coordinates. These are imaginary lines, one running north to south, the other east to west, and any position can be expressed in terms of the point at which two such lines cross. At sea, any navigator must know his latitude – that is, the distance north or south of that imaginary circle we call the Equator – as well as his longitude, which is his distance east or west of an imaginary meridian passing through the two Poles, before he can plot his position on a chart. Latitude is relatively easy to determine, by observation of the altitude above the horizon of certain of the heavenly bodies. Longitude is much more difficult, and any reliable calculation needs the services of an accurate timekeeper recording mean time on an internationally recognised meridian, such as Greenwich – which is Longitude 0° – for comparison with the

This high-performance longcase clock, signed by John Harrison's younger brother James and dated 1728, incorporates two of the innovations for which Harrison is celebrated – his grasshopper escapement and gridiron compensated pendulum. The movement is constructed almost wholly of wood. Museum of the Worshipful Company of Clockmakers, Guildhall, London.

local time of a ship, as again found by observation. When it was first decided to tackle this problem, neither the prime meridian nor an accurate marine timekeeper existed.

The first serious attempts to study and rectify this situation began in 1675, when Charles II established by Royal Warrant an observatory in his royal park at Greenwich, 'in order to the finding out of the longitude of places, and for perfecting navigation and astronomy'. Several first-class brains were involved in this matter from the start; the architect of the observatory was none other than Sir Christopher Wren, while the first 'observator' – forerunner of the office of Astronomer Royal – was a young man called John Flamsteed.

Flamsteed was a clergyman from Derbyshire; but he had already made quite a reputation for himself as an astronomer and mathematician before he started 'to measure distances in ye heavens' towards the end of 1676. The job cannot have been a sinecure for, although the Royal Warrant took care of Flamsteed's salary and even extended to that of an assistant, there was no provision whatever for purchasing equipment, so that, for the rest of his working life – and he died in 1719 – Flamsteed had to beg, borrow or buy out of his own pocket everything that he needed. At one time he was even taking in his students, giving them food, lodging and tuition, in order to make ends meet. Yet nothing deterred him. He seemed somehow to be able always to acquire what was necessary for his work, and over the years he amassed a formidable body of some 40,000 observations. These formed the basis of his star catalogue, a monumental work which was not published until after his death but which effectively established him as the founder of modern positional astronomy.

Notwithstanding all this activity – which was valuable in other directions – little was accomplished towards the principal objective of improving navigation. So in 1714 the Government offered a reward, by Act of Parliament, for 'such person or persons as shall discover the Longitude'. The prize was graduated according to the accuracy achieved, ranging from an upper limit of £20,000 if within half a degree, to £10,000 within a degree, upon a trial voyage from Britain to the West Indies. Translated into terms of precision timekeeping, a chronometer, to win the top prize on the six-week voyage involved, would need to keep time within three seconds a day; although this type of accuracy was within the capacity of the best static pendulum-controlled clocks at that time, such machines would have been quite useless at sea where the motion of the ship would have fundamentally disturbed their timekeeping. It required something special in the way of a timepiece to withstand such elemental forces and

Henry Sully, an Englishman who spent nearly all his working life in France and who died in 1728, designed this marine clock about 1724, and it was subsequently sent to George Graham for inspection. Museum of the Worshipful Company of Clockmakers, Guildhall, London.

This view of the movement of Sully's marine clock shows the big balance which in its oscillations acts upon a horizontal pendulum to which it is attached by a silk cord. Museum of the Worshipful Company of Clockmakers, Guildhall, London.

still keep good time; and such an instrument was not, in the event, to be proven in use for nearly half a century after the prize was first offered.

Despite what might now seem the obvious disadvantages of the pendulum in marine use, the earliest attempts to make a timekeeper for use at sea depended upon one, albeit specially designed. Huygens, already the pioneer of the pendulum and the balance spring, tried his hand at this as early as 1660, but the performance of his timekeeper was so erratic as to be worthless. Others, including Henry Sully, a very able innovator, worked along similar lines; but any attempt to associate any kind of pendulum with a ship was bound to fail, and the answer was eventually to be found in a balance controlled by a spring.

The great English pioneer – among a number of pioneers of stature, for England was to make an international reputation for herself in this field of 'the Longitude' – was John Harrison. Born into the trade of carpenter in the village of Barrow in Lincolnshire in 1693, Harrison and his younger brother James early in life started building simple clocks almost entirely out of wood. By 1726, what is more, they had constructed two regulator clocks of the most ingenious design, again employing wood as almost their sole raw material. Being carpenters, however, as well as inventors, they would

know how to make the most of the natural properties of their chosen medium; thus, for example, they used lignum vitae as an anti-friction agent, for this wood is considered self-lubricating. Their pendulums were of the temperature-compensating design usually described, on account of its appearance, as 'Harrison's gridiron'; the principle was so to arrange a grid of alternating rods of brass and steel that their changes in length with variations in temperature to all intents and purposes cancelled each other out, leaving the effective length of the pendulum unaltered. Their escapements, of the kind descriptively known as a 'grasshopper', were nearly silent in action and the most accurate – even though also the most complex and fragile – then available. These clocks – both of them still in existence, and still capable of giving an excellent account of themselves – had other highly sophisticated and quite new features that were also attributable entirely to the genius of the Harrisons, and without doubt, at the time, they must have been the most accurate clocks in the world. John Harrison himself noted that they kept time 'without the variation of more than a single second in a month'. What is more, in order to test the accuracy of their regulators, the Harrisons were not content with their own equation of time calculations – perhaps they distrusted the inherent accuracy of a

Harrison finally encapsulated his ideas on marine timekeeping within the two large watches known as H.4 and H.5, the first being completed in 1759 and the second in 1770. H.4 (left): National Maritime Museum, Greenwich. H.5 (right): Museum of the Worshipful Company of Clockmakers, Guildhall, London. H.5 was only completed when Harrison had reached the age of seventy-seven, and in appearance it is very severe by comparison with the decoration applied to H.4 (left, below).

sundial, with which such calculations had to be used – and instead made their own 'transit' observations of a suitable star.

Perhaps their experience with these two high-precision clocks led the Harrisons to decide to enter into the search for a longitude timekeeper. In any event, they early realised that they could no longer work in wood, and that they would need capital to underwrite the expensive purchases of brass and steel from which they would have to construct their machines. Luckily for them, the Board of Longitude – the body appointed to oversee the working of the Act of Parliament relating to the quest for the longitude, to make trials of timekeepers and to recommend the award of prizes – could advance money against the completion of designs thought to be particularly promising, in order thereby to alleviate just such circumstances as were facing the Harrisons.

Accordingly, John Harrison came to London for an interview with Dr Halley, who was not only Astronomer Royal – there is a well-known comet

named after him – but also a member of the Board of Longitude with particular responsibility for dealing with the inventors in the field. Halley sent Harrison on to see George Graham who, as both a Fellow of the Royal Society and a celebrated practising clockmaker, could give an expert opinion on the technical aspects of Harrison's work. Despite Harrison's thoroughly distrustful and truculent attitude of mind – like many another genius, he always thought others were trying to steal his plans – and even though he was always so inarticulate, to judge from surviving manuscripts, as to be quite unable to explain intelligibly to others what he was striving to accomplish, Graham was greatly impressed. It is said that they talked for ten hours non-stop, as a result of which Graham encouraged Harrison to build his marine timekeeper, to this end lending him money from his own pocket interest-free, and undertaking that, if the result turned out well, he and Dr Halley would support his approach to the Board of Longitude for development money to continue the good work.

Following Harrison's pioneering work, another innovator was Thomas Mudge who made three marine timekeepers of highly sophisticated design and obtained an award of £3,000 for his work. British Museum, London.

It took Harrison five years to build this first sea-going clock, and Graham's money was not of itself sufficient to finance the operation. However, other money seems to have been forthcoming, both from private individuals and from the East India Company, mindful, as always, of any way of reducing its losses at sea. Known as 'H.1', this first marine chronometer was a monumental machine by any standards, weighing about 72lb and occupying space equivalent to a cube of almost two feet.

H.1 had been completed probably about 1735, and was then tested on board a barge in local waters in order to fine-tune it. Accompanied by John Harrison, the great clock was next sent on a voyage from Portsmouth to Lisbon and back, in 1736, when the longitude calculated by reference to the timekeeper gave a position sixty miles nearer the correct one than the captain's own reckoning.

Despite its cumbersome bulk, H.1 set an entirely new standard in maritime time-measurement, and it has been calculated that, had the clock been assessed according to the standards which were eventually formulated as being the most accurate and informative concerning the performance of such a timepiece, it would at least have qualified for third prize from the Board of Longitude. Even so, that body was by no means unimpressed, and when Harrison asked for £500 as a grant-in-aid to build a second, improved timekeeper, the Board at once agreed. Being always canny about spending public money, however, it insisted that both H.1 and H.2, when completed, should be handed over to the nation.

Except for the escape wheel, all the wheels of H.1 were made of wood, and one of its exceptional characteristics is that it requires no lubrication whatsoever. H.2, which was essentially a refined version of H.1, was made with brass throughout but, in the event, was even more massive than H.1, weighing 103lb. Both brothers worked on H.2, which was finished in 1739, but it was never tried at sea since John Harrison seems to have determined to do even better before exposing his work to public scrutiny again.

At about this time too – and it may have had some bearing on John Harrison's attitude to the testing of H.2 – it seems that the brothers ceased their fruitful collaboration, and James Harrison gave up his interest in marine clocks altogether. John meantime had virtually abandoned H.2 and was already at work upon H.3; in 1741 he told the Board of Longitude that it would be ready for a trial voyage to the West Indies in two years and was given a further £500 on the strength of this assertion.

However, it actually took Harrison seventeen years to finish H.3, which was ready by 1757. Even then he was not satisfied, and asked that the trial be delayed while he finished yet a fourth – and

The chronometers Mudge made himself performed well although they were too complicated for large-scale production, and the copies commissioned by his son after Mudge's death did not stand comparison with the originals. This shows the back view of Mudge's marine timekeeper. British Museum, London.

left
Several representations of John Harrison exist including a cameo portrait by Tassie, and a mezzotint. This engraving from the *European Magazine* was published in 1788 and is perhaps less well known than some of the others.

far left
This first of Harrison's massive marine timekeepers was tested in 1736 on a voyage to Lisbon and was found to have an almost negligible error. National Maritime Museum, Greenwich.

much smaller – timekeeper. This was originally to have been an ancillary to the larger clock; but when it was completed, Harrison maintained that it would be a serviceable marine timepiece in its own right and that its performance was every bit as good as that of H.3.

H.4 was, in fact, much closer to the tradition of the travelling coach clock than anything Harrison had produced previously. It was, in effect, a large silver pair-cased watch, some 5·2 inches in over-all diameter, and it must have made a strange stable-mate for the three huge machines that had preceded it. Anyhow, when the time came to equip the trial ship, Harrison determined that H.4 should go on its own, and he himself, being then sixty-seven years old and perhaps no longer really fit for the privations of a long sea-voyage, stood down in favour of his son William.

This machine constituted Harrison's second design of marine timekeeper and was finished in 1739. National Maritime Museum, Greenwich.

So, on 18th November 1761, this most famous of Harrison's timekeepers was taken on board H.M.S. *Deptford*, which set sail from Portsmouth in bad weather, with the timekeeper resting on a cushion in the captain's cabin. Ten days out, amid conflicting opinions from the ship's navigator and other officers on board, William Harrison predicted the time at which they would sight a particular island in the area of Madeira. When this turned out to be correct, the ship's company were nothing if not impressed. Upon arrival in Jamaica it was found that the watch had performed well

within the most stringent limits required; and even when brought back again, in fearsome weather, to Britain, it still proved more accurate than anything else in the field.

However, the Board of Longitude, hitherto helpful and sympathetic to Harrison – he had had a number of small sums of money as grants from them to sustain his work – now seem to have turned against him. There followed years of wrangling and argument, much of it petty, with Harrison issuing pamphlets and getting up petitions in an effort to get himself a fair hearing, while the Board remained implacable in its antagonism to his demands. One of the chief protagonists was the Rev. Nevil Maskelyne, a member of the Board and eventually Astronomer Royal, who advocated an alternative method of finding the longitude based on lunar distances, and it was clear that for much of the time he carried the Board with him. It was not until 21st June 1773 that Parliament agreed to pay Harrison further money, bringing his total prize to £18,750; he had also had some £4,000 in grants over the years. He remained bitter and resentful to the end, which was not far away. He died at the age of eighty-three in 1776.

Looking back over the lifetime of this man, the major part of which he had willingly devoted to solving the longitude problem, one must marvel at his single-minded genius – especially in the light of his unpromising start in life – and clearly he must also have possessed the greatest determination, to enable him to carry on in the face of such adversity. Being deprived of the prize for so long meant that, for years, he was constantly short of money and living with his family in poverty since he could not work on his timekeepers as well as earn enough by some other means to support them. The demands made upon him by the Board of Longitude must strike anybody as going far beyond anything the Act required, let alone authorised them to do; they continuously demanded that Harrison hand over to them all his timekeepers, provide detailed drawings of them, make further copies to ensure they were capable of quantity production, and so on. Many of these demands came when Harrison was an old man – indeed, he made a fifth timekeeper, H.5, which he did not finish until he was seventy-nine – and even though he had the support of George III, who tested H.5 in his own private observatory in Richmond Park, it seemed he simply could not prevail. He may well have been a difficult and cantankerous man with whom to deal, but he deserved better treatment at the hands of his own country, whose reputation was to be enhanced by his inventions, than he ever received.

The single most powerful reason why his timekeepers were not fully appreciated in his own time – and this applies particularly to H.1, as its performance was appraised in 1736 – was the lack of understanding of corrections for rate. It was universally supposed at that time that a precision timekeeper must keep exact time day after day, whereas in practice, it is much better for a 'rate' to be laid down – that is to say, for it to be established with certainty that a timekeeper will gain or lose a certain number of seconds each day without fail – and for this correction to be applied consistently when making calculations from the timekeeper. If H.1 had been corrected by this means, its performance would have been seen to have been running within about three seconds a day, or within the lower limit for the prize money.

Harrison's five marine timekeepers were lost sight of for many years in the cellars of the Admiralty in London, but were rediscovered between the wars by Lt-Cdr R. T. Gould, who painstakingly

The third and last of Harrison's great machines won for him the Gold Medal of the Royal Society in 1749, but he was still not satisfied with its capabilities. National Maritime Museum, Greenwich.

restored them all to working order, an enterprise which occupied him for seventeen years. H.1, H.2, H.3 and H.4 are in the custody of the National Maritime Museum at Greenwich, where they can be seen working with all their original vigour. H.5 belongs to the Worshipful Company of Clockmakers and is on display with the rest of their collection at Guildhall, in the City of London.

While Harrison was undoubtedly the great inventive genius in the pioneering days of marine chronometry, he was surrounded – and was succeeded – by others of far more than average ability, both as designers and craftsmen. One of the more productive aspects of the Longitude Act, although it provoked a great deal of jealous animosity and petty bickering between all the leading makers of the time – for the prize was so big that few wanted to be left out of the running – was that it inspired such an atmosphere of competitiveness as to spark off every vestige of inventive ingenuity contained within the craft. The English, from very early times, were far more interested in accurate timekeeping than in any of the more flamboyant

Josiah Emery, an ex-patriate Swiss working in London, made four experimental chronometers, of which this is one, which he submitted for trial at Greenwich in 1792. Museum of the Worshipful Company of Clockmakers, Guildhall, London.

left
Emery's chronometer had a constant-force escapement and such advanced features as friction rollers for the balance arbor instead of the normal pivot holes. Museum of the Worshipful Company of Clockmakers, Guildhall, London.

opposite page, above
This fine deck watch by John Arnold dates from about 1776 and has his earliest form of detent escapement, the pivoted detent. Museum of the Worshipful Company of Clockmakers, Guildhall, London.

opposite page, below
This outstanding pocket chronometer by Larcum Kendall was made in 1786. It has a pivoted detent escapement, and noticeable on the back plate is the spiral bimetallic compensation curb. Museum of the Worshipful Company of Clockmakers, Guildhall, London.

approaches to horology – which, for instance, tended to put almost equal emphasis upon decoration – so that, in this sort of climate, they positively flourished.

One of these contemporaries was Thomas Mudge, whose major contribution to horology must be the original concept of the lever escapement, even though, as we have seen, he discounted its value. Born in 1715 he lived to a ripe old age, dying in 1794. He was a member of the technical committee which examined Harrison's timekeeper H.4 on behalf of the Board of Longitude. Harrison had had to dismantle his machine in front of the committee and explain the finer points of its working, so that they could determine its 'general utility', which probably meant how easy it would be to produce it in quantity. But Mudge had his own quite different ideas about the design of a marine timekeeper. He accordingly appears to have largely abandoned what must have been a most profitable business making high-grade clocks and watches, to concentrate upon his chronometers, of which he made only three. The first was completed in 1774. His chronometers were marvels of sophisticated mechanical complexity, which was one of their greatest drawbacks, since, while Mudge himself was a craftsman of supreme ability, head and shoulders above even the best of his contemporaries, any practical chronometer design had to be capable of replication by men of more modest talents. His three chronometers – two of them Mudge called 'Green' and 'Blue' after the colours of their cases – performed well while Mudge himself was available to supervise them, although even so they did not surpass Harrison's timekeeper. As Mudge himself became too old to continue the practical side of the work, his son organised a consortium of the best available craftsmen to copy his father's design of timekeeper, and between twenty and thirty of these marvellous machines seem to have been made. Mudge senior just lived long enough to see the first of them completed and running; his part in the project had been intended to be that of technical adviser, instructing the craftsmen involved on his own methods for making chronometers. As it was, none of the copies ever even approximated in performance to the originals, and the scheme eventually failed. The Mudges were not wholly ignored by an ungrateful nation for their contributions to finding the longitude: they received £2,500 from Parliament, although little enough encouragement from the Board of Longitude itself.

One other craftsman might be mentioned, from these same very formative years, if only to underline how great a fount of talent was available in England then. Larcum Kendall, another member of the technical committee that examined H.4, was subsequently paid £450 by the Board of Longitude to make a copy of it. The workmanship of this copy

was superior to that of the original – even Harrison, who did not customarily bestow compliments, acknowledged this – and the instrument performed superbly over a three-year voyage in the hands of Captain Cook.

Both Harrison and Mudge, in their different ways, had clearly demonstrated that the longitude problem was capable of solution, and the final conversion of their pioneering efforts into a form that was eminently practical, in that it could be produced in fair quantity and at a fair price, yet met all the technical requirements, was carried out at the inventive hands of two great English chronometermakers. Their work overlaps to some extent; and by this time a number of important and highly skilled makers in London were hard on their heels, so that, where they led, others were quick to follow.

John Arnold was born in 1736 and made his first chronometer in 1770. However, it was not until some years later that his experimentation enabled him to turn out a design for a chronometer that was wholly successful. His special contributions in this area include his design of spring detent escapement – that particular feature which, it will be remembered, distinguishes a chronometer from any other variety of timekeeper – as well as a succession of designs for bi-metallic compensated balances. He was also the first to fit his instruments with helical balance springs, which were often made of gold. His great inventiveness came to a head in the early 1780s with several important patents; and the quality of his work may be gauged by the performance of one of his pocket chronometers, worn over a period of thirteen months at around this time. Its total error was only 2 minutes 33 seconds, and its daily rate never varied more than 2 seconds.

Arnold died in 1799, but his work was ably carried on by his son John Roger Arnold. The Arnold chronometer factory at Chigwell, in Essex, turned out a steady stream of high quality timepieces. For ten years from 1830, Arnold junior had as his partner Edward Dent, a most able craftsman; and when he eventually died, in 1843, the firm was bought up by Charles Frodsham, so that the continuity of its reputation for high-grade work was assured. In its own day – and despite the acrimonious, even malicious, criticisms of Earnshaw – there is no doubt that the Arnold establishment, whether under the supervision of father or son, was generally considered to be the chronometermakers of choice.

The second of the two great English chronometermakers of this period, as has just been hinted, was Thomas Earnshaw. He was a very different person indeed from John Arnold: jealous, very deprived as a young man and often forced, because of his comparative poverty, to work for other people, whom he always suspected were out

opposite page, above
The final development of the marine chronometer into a form in which it would be recognisable today was carried out by John Arnold and Thomas Earnshaw. This early Arnold chronometer in its octagonal kingwood case dates from about 1795. The use of gimbals to maintain the chronometer in a consistently horizontal position was by no means universal yet. Museum of the Worshipful Company of Clockmakers, Guildhall, London.

opposite page, below
As competition sharpened to produce a functional chronometer that could be made in quantity, various consortia of craftsmen joined in. Paul Philip Barraud and George Jamison made this deck watch in 1798.

above
Inevitably many believed chronometer design went too far. Ulrich's special constant-force escapement as shown in this marine chronometer of about 1830, by Joseph Croucher, evoked from one expert the remark, 'There is a quality of suspended animation about it suggestive of catalepsy'. Museum of the Worshipful Company of Clockmakers, Guildhall, London.

above right
Thomas Mudge's son engaged various combinations of craftsmen to make copies of his father's design of chronometer in the late 1790s. One such combination consisted of William Howells together with Barraud and Jamison who made the deck watch (opposite). Other combinations included 'Pennington, Pendleton and others' and 'Howells and Pennington'.

to steal his inventions. He was born in 1749, and his influence stretches well into the nineteenth century, as he did not die until 1829. He, like his competitor Arnold – and there was always much rivalry between them – invented a form of spring detent escapement but, being unable to afford to patent it, arranged with a craftsman in rather better circumstances than himself, one Thomas Wright of the Poultry, in the City of London, to do it for him. However, Wright left it rather late, by which time Arnold had already produced his arrangement, which was very similar indeed to Earnshaw's. Much acrimony followed. Earnshaw accused another maker called John Brockbank, for whom he had once worked and to whom he had shown his invention, of having betrayed him to Arnold. It is clear that the two inventions must have been arrived at almost simultaneously, but whether this was coincidental or there was some element of treachery or collusion will probably never be known.

The technical differences between Arnold's and Earnshaw's escapements are perhaps best summed up by saying that Arnold's has the theoretical edge, but Earnshaw's works out best in practice. Both makers solved the problem of quantity production, at a reasonable price, of a technically more than adequate marine timekeeper; and where Arnold contributed in the design of balances and balance springs, Earnshaw solved the difficult technical problem of making bi-metallic elements by fusion – previously the brass and steel strips were just riveted together. Thus honours must be about equal.

above
Chronometermakers at the end of the eighteenth century seem to have made a practice of modernising their past manufactures if and when the opportunity arose. Among other things, Barraud always took any chance to remove his former partner Jamison's name from both dial and movement. This example was made by them in 1797 and is interesting because its regulator dial numbers seconds in fours instead of the conventional fives.

above right
The dial of this pocket chronometer by John Barwise, made in 1800, shows a different version of the regulator dial incorporating three subsidiaries for hours, minutes and seconds respectively. The sector at the top is an up-and-down indicator. Museum of the Worshipful Company of Clockmakers, Guildhall, London.

left
This early example of a marine chronometer by Thomas Earnshaw dates from about 1795. It is numbered 245 although Earnshaw's numbering has not so far been properly rationalised. British Museum, London.

England was not, of course, the only country to try to solve the longitude problem. France, in particular, had its pioneers, notably Pierre Le Roy. Son of a famous horologist father, and born in 1717, he started to experiment with timekeeping at sea in the 1740s; by 1766 he was demonstrating to Louis XV his fully developed timekeeper. It was a superb machine with a number of original features: temperature compensation, for instance, was achieved by using on the balance a thermome-ter filled partly with mercury and partly with alcohol. As the surrounding temperature dropped, the mercury moved towards the rim of the balance, slowing it down, and vice versa. Le Roy's timekeeper, in sea trials, just about equalled H.4 in performance.

Le Roy died in 1785, but another French pioneer, Ferdinand Berthoud, survived him by twenty years. Berthoud arrived at the design of a spring detent escapement at much the same time as Arnold and Earnshaw in England, but his principal claim to fame rests upon his experimental machines. He hardly ever seems to have made two alike; and his accompanying technical writing is of value.

In England, by the death of Earnshaw, chronometers had become commonplace; and, what is more, they eventually settled into a pattern, which has remained largely unaltered to the present day, based upon his design. Arnold and Earnshaw had among their contemporaries craftsmen of high calibre: men like Barraud and Brockbank, Jamison, Margetts, Pennington, and, of course, Emery, together with a few others. These were succeeded in the nineteenth century by even more skilled people, for the Victorian era was nothing if not the peak period for mechanical excellence. It is sad indeed that very little of this special expertise still exists today, where radio time signals and beacons as well as electronic gadgetry has largely superseded the handmade precision timekeeper that first solved the longitude problem.

The Industrial Revolution – The Nineteenth Century and Beyond

As a social and technological phenomenon, the Industrial Revolution had no very clear beginning or ending. Some people regard it wholly as a spin-off from the development of steam power, in which case it is entirely technological; others see it solely in terms of the progression from an agricultural base to an industrial one, and the enormous re-education programme that that must have involved. However it is seen, in human terms it represents one of the greatest upheavals mankind has experienced – on the small scale if one considers only Britain, but gradually spreading to affect much of the world.

Most will agree, however, that this evolutionary process – or whatever one may choose to call it – started in the eighteenth century and extended well towards the middle of the nineteenth. Some even argue that it is still going on. It wrought change throughout the whole of society, for nobody was entirely immune or insulated from its effects.

In the horological field, as the eighteenth century drew to a close, there had not yet arisen the nationwide demand for cheap timekeepers that

right
Turkey was one of the principal export markets for English watches at the turn of the eighteenth and nineteenth centuries. The example shown is by Isaac Rogers and has no fewer than four cases. The two innermost are of plain silver, hallmarked 1780. Next comes a case covered in tortoiseshell, and finally a protective wooden outer case shaped like a cone. The watch is complete with its original carrying cord, ornamented with silver wire.

opposite page
A good example of the clocks that were made in small batches for such markets as China and India, this musical table clock was made for Barraud of London, whose name it bears, by the firm of Thwaites & Reed about 1767. There are Chinese characters on the back plate and those presumably of a repairer under the dial. Museum of the Worshipful Company of Clockmakers, Guildhall, London.

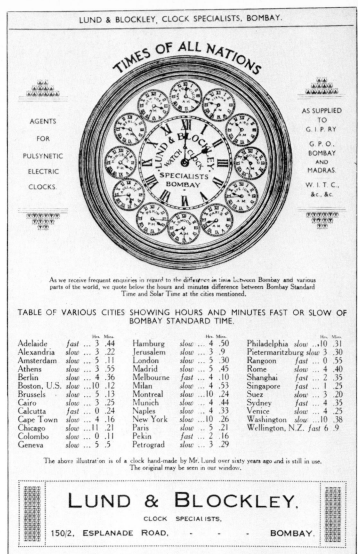

was rapidly to follow in the wake of the railways. The clockmakers, however, were quite content – those that were not engaged in the chronometry competition, that is – to cater for the needs, such as they were, that existed nationally while busily developing their extensive and highly lucrative export market.

It is difficult to say how and when Britain's huge turnover in hand-finished clocks and watches for foreign markets started. It undoubtedly sprang from the enormous reputation for workmanship of the highest quality that followed the technological gains achieved in the seventeenth and early eighteenth centuries. By 1800 the principal markets seem to have been the continent of Europe – where, for decades, English and especially London-made products had been the subject of massive local forgery, so revered were the genuine articles – the Near East, especially Turkey, and, in the Far East, India and China. In those days the exporting craftsman went to enormous lengths to ascertain exactly what his customers required, and then to meet it in every minute detail, a factor allegedly ignored by many modern British exporters. The result has been an extensive heritage of English-made export watches and clocks which embrace features imposed upon them by their foreign buyers.

It is often said that the products the English exported were only those that were not good enough for the home market. It seems more likely that, being realists, they adjusted the quality of such goods according to the price they could obtain and the variety demanded; for it is certainly not true to say that no pieces of the best kind were exported – far from it. Looking first at the Far Eastern markets, the Chinese seem to have had an insatiable appetite for clocks of the most elaborately decorated kind, which had also to possess novelty or entertainment value. Thus, automata – often not in any human image, but using revolving jewelled spirals, glass water-simulating spouts and falls, rotating finials and cupolas that are made in segments and splay out as they fly round – were all-important, as was the provision of music to accompany them. The casework also had to be embellished in what, to the English taste at that time, must have seemed a most vulgar manner; it is quite customary to find the nominal maker of such clocks has built into his structure imported Swiss

This is probably the oldest surviving *perpetuelle* or self-winding watch since it came from the workshop of A.-L. Breguet, the supreme craftsman, in 1783. On the back of the gold case is the initial 'N' surmounted by a crown, and although its earliest history is by no means certain, it is said to have belonged originally to Czar Nicholas I of Russia. Museum of the Worshipful Company of Clockmakers, Guildhall, London.

right
The back of the movement of the Breguet *perpetuelle* reveals noticeably the heartshaped counterpoised weight which operates the self-winding mechanism and also the tuned steel gongs on which the quarter-repeating action sounds. Museum of the Worshipful Company of Clockmakers, Guildhall, London.

opposite page, left
Inscribed 'Vulliamy London Clock and Watchmaker to the King of the British Empire', this large mahogany organ clock was made about 1820, and from the Turkish numerals on the dial its intended market is self-evident. Vulliamy was, of course, watchmaker to George III. British Museum, London.

opposite page, right
An ephemeral fragment from the early twentieth century, this leaflet advertises the Bombay office of a well-known firm of London clockmakers, Messrs Lund & Blockley.

enamels, usually from Geneva, as well as sundry other components not generally used in products for the home market. At the end of the eighteenth century, these highly decorated – or perhaps grossly over-decorated – but beautifully constructed pieces, whose functional qualities left nothing to be desired, were not only purchased direct by the Chinese; it was taken for granted that any British ambassador to the Chinese court who wished to make his mark with the Emperor would present such a clock as a gift. The Honourable East India Company did likewise in order, no doubt, to sweeten relations. Yet is is clear that the Chinese valued such devices wholly as sophisticated toys of the time, not as timekeepers; and indeed, many far more ordinary kinds of timepiece were delivered to the Chinese market for much of the eighteenth century, from both Britain and other European countries. There is a detailed account of the intricacies of the Chinese market for timekeepers in Professor Cipolla's *Clocks and Culture: 1300–1700*.

India was, of course, particularly susceptible to the absorption of large quantities of English-made timekeepers as simply another manifestation of its Empire status. The East India Company handled clocks and watches until it was finally wound up just after the mid nineteenth century. By that time, most English manufacturers of any repute had either opened their own offices in the subcontinent or had appointed local agents. Even though clock- and watchmaking in England was still a craft-based manufacture – as will be seen, it did not finally abandon this method in favour of mass-production until the twentieth century – there were firms operating in the Clerkenwell area of London who made clock movements in quantity for the trade, probably from late in the eighteenth.

From the fragmentary records of such firms that have survived, it is not uncommon to find orders received for dozens or half-dozens of movements 'to suit the India market' or 'according to the Chinese taste'.

Coming nearer home, it is curious to note that, whether or not the Islamic peoples were instrumental in transmitting any original knowledge of clockwork to Western cultures, by the eighteenth century English craftsmen were supplying a large number of fine timepieces to the Near East, and particularly to Turkey. It is not at all uncommon, therefore, to find good London-made clocks and watches with dials inscribed with numerals in Turkish characters, and sometimes the maker even went to the trouble of having his signature translated into the vernacular as well. Watches made for the Turkish market left this country with at least three cases, instead of the customary pair, and were often fitted with yet a fourth on arrival at their final destination. This extraordinary protection may have been simply to exclude dust and dirt in a country where such inconveniences were part of the way of life to a larger extent than in Europe. The generality of Turkish watches are cased in silver, the two inner ones being plain, the third usually covered with tortoiseshell having a row of decorative pins bordering the edge. When, outside all this, the Turks added another case, it was completely in their own tradition, so that it is as unlike the rest of the watch as can be imagined.

Finally, a word about British exports to Europe. The popularity of English clocks and watches stemmed from their reliability, which in turn derived from the traditional English interest in performance rather than appearance; so they were extensively copied, but they were also bought in quantity and much sought after. One of the most thriving European markets was Holland; timepieces intended for that country will always be found to have the arcaded minute band which was so much favoured there. The forgeries of English work, incidentally – and they are likely to be encountered from time to time – are almost invariably very easy to detect. It never seemed to occur to those that produced them that they might study what they were attempting to emulate in order at least to attempt a facsimile. Mis-spellings of makers' names, styles wholly out of keeping with English practice, forged hallmarks on cases that will withstand only a cursory glance before they are detected – such is the common trend among these articles. For the very reason that they are usually so unlike what they purport to be, although

188

often of good quality in their own right, they make an interesting subject for specialised study.

This was the commercial export situation in the English clock and watch industry, then, as the nineteenth century commenced. It was not to remain for very much longer in such an obviously healthy state.

Technologically, as has been seen, the development of precise time-measurement as a navigational aid spanned the second half of the eighteenth century and much of the first half of the nineteenth, and in the midst of this period there flourished a remarkable French craftsman-designer, whom many consider to have been the greatest genius in this field ever to have lived. Abraham-Louis Breguet was born at Neuchâtel in Switzerland in 1747 and died in 1823, and during his working life produced some of the most elegant, as well as the most superbly designed and constructed, timepieces the world has ever known. He made a substantial contribution, by way of original invention, to the progress of accurate time-measurement, but more particularly, perhaps, he seemed to have at his disposal a never-ending supply of creative designs for his work, so that virtually every object that left his atelier was unique. This is not strictly true, of course: his 'Souscription'

watches, for which clients subscribed in advance just as one might do for a luxury edition of some special book, were made in series. But otherwise his capacity to please his richer patrons with special productions seems to have been inexhaustible. Today, as might be expected, his watches and clocks are highly sought after by collectors, and fetch very large sums of money. The majority of them doubtless perform every bit as well as when they were first made and, as his epitaph, can thus stand comparison with that accorded to any other great man.

The nineteenth century saw the emergence and development of mass-production methods for the manufacture of clocks and watches, which in turn generated the greatest tensions in the trade in Britain that had ever been known. Rightly or wrongly, the craftsmen who had been nurtured all their lives in a tradition of quality and pride in workmanship, coupled with a small batch-production system and hand-finishing, could not bring themselves to change the habits of a lifetime which, in the process, would inevitably have meant surrendering something of the individuality which they could impart to their product. The trade maintained outwardly that mass-produced timepieces could never compete with the quality article either in

performance, reliability, finish or in any other important characteristic and steadfastly refused to move from that entrenched position. In so doing, they were deliberately swimming against the stream that was being followed by most of the other manufacturing nations, or the ones, at any rate, who were significant in the world horological scene. Principal among these were to be the Americans, the French, the Germans, especially the Black Forest cottage industry, and eventually the Swiss. The result of this inflexibility was that, by 1842, England had become the world's largest market for cheap imported clocks, and eight years later the annual figure for such imports had reached a record peak of 228,000. The home trade, needless to say, was in complete chaos, and unemployment rife.

So it is a sad fact that the typical household clock in Britain in the last century was foreign. From the 1840s onwards, cheap American-manufactured brass clocks, derived from a design that had originated in Germany, were selling at ridiculously low prices, while the Black Forest product – of rudimentary construction, with wood used for as many components as possible in place of the much more expensive brass – also rapidly gained acceptance. The most popular version of this last type, known as the postman's alarm, had a mainly wooden movement behind a circular painted dial, which was encircled by a hinged and polished hardwood bezel holding the protective convex glass. Centrally positioned on this dial was a small

top
The work of London watchmakers was extensively forged on the continent throughout the eighteenth century, but it is not difficult to detect. Purporting to be a watch by John Ellicott, this movement is signed 'Ecklicot, London' and is of late eighteenth-century vintage. Museum of the Worshipful Company of Clockmakers, Guildhall, London.

centre
This Breguet watch incorporates his device, the tourbillon, which is intended to counteract position errors. The escapement is a lever, and the tourbillon rotates in one minute. Museum of the Worshipful Company of Clockmakers, Guildhall, London.

left
Probably Swiss and of the early nineteenth century, this watch is falsely signed 'Breguet', but it is a fine watch in its own right, incorporating a pin-wheel lever escapement. Museum of the Worshipful Company of Clockmakers, Guildhall, London.

right
Very much more elegant than the average English skeleton clock, this mid nineteenth-century specimen is unsigned, of eight-day duration and notable for the two large spring barrels on the same arbor which drive the two-train movement. Museum of the Worshipful Company of Clockmakers, Guildhall, London.

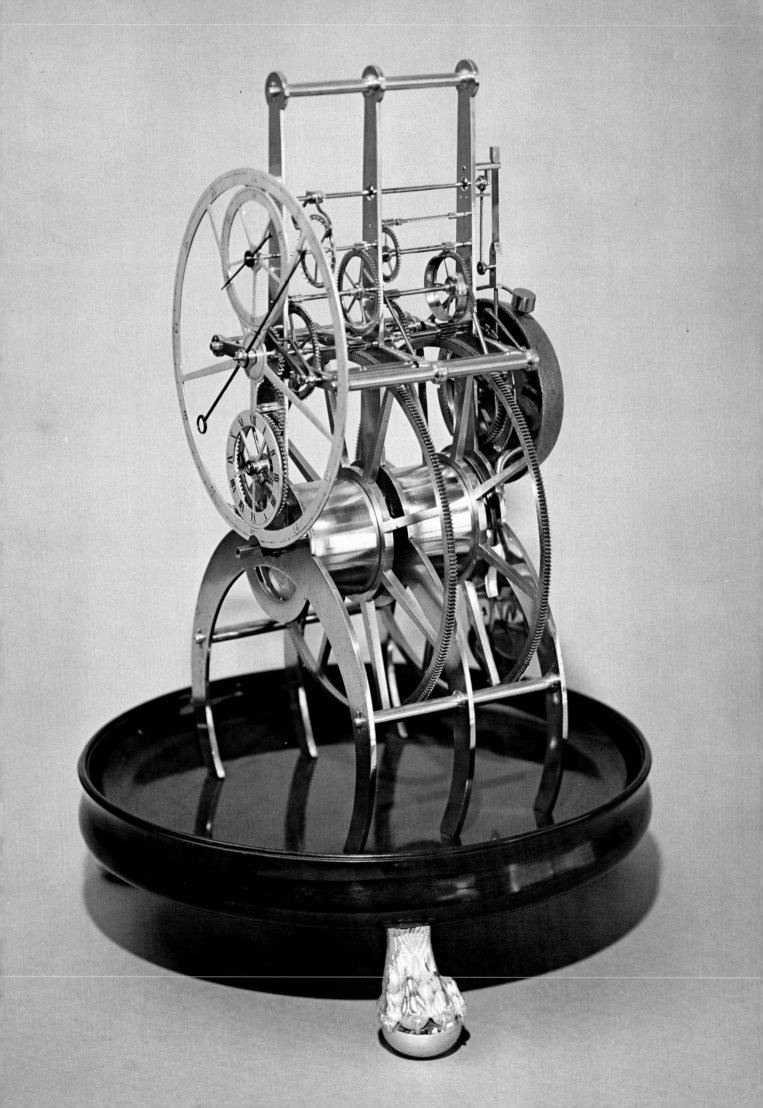

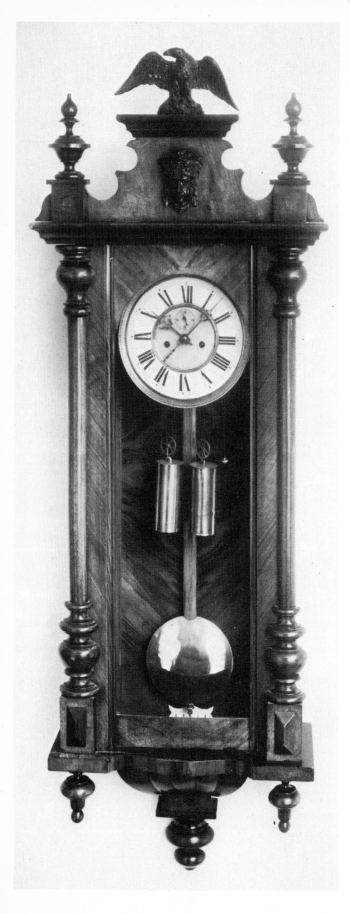

alarm dial, and the whole mechanism was weight-driven, elementary and trouble-free. Other versions of the Black Forest clocks included the ubiquitous cuckoo clock, often – incorrectly – attributed to the Swiss.

Another foreign import was the French clock. Their standard factory-made product, a clock mechanism contained within small circular plates, had been so perfected that, even with such seemingly outdated features as locking-plate striking, it must have been the most accurate mass-produced clock made anywhere in the world. The other popular clock for which the French must take credit – even though it, too, was made elsewhere – the carriage clock, or *pendule de voyage*, became very popular in a range of qualities from the cheapest to the best, and was often sold through agents whose very English names contrast quaintly with a place of origin such as 'Paris'. The very few – mainly London – craftsmen who made a wholly English carriage clock, reserved the style for their best quality and most sophisticated mechanisms, so that such a clock emanating from the firm of, say, McCabe, Frodsham, Dent or Vulliamy will be a timekeeper of excellence. Towards the end of the century, Victor Kullberg (1824–1890), a Swedish craftsman who settled in London, produced some eight-day chronometer carriage clocks of unrivalled elegance and performance.

Finally, by the last quarter of the century, there had come into circulation a clock known always as a 'Vienna regulator', although at various times it was copied outside Austria by, among others, the Germans and Americans. These clocks contained certain anachronisms: for example, because of the shortened pendulums in some models, their seconds hands rotate once in forty-five instead of sixty seconds, and are therefore solely for decoration. Yet, despite such idiosyncrasies, there is usually built-in maintaining power, to keep the clock going while the weights are being wound up, and both pendulum crutch and escapement pallets can generally be adjusted. Vienna regulators are capable of a most impressive performance, given good conditions, and the best of them embrace far higher standards of quality than their detractors will ever give them credit for. Indeed, one well-known firm in this field, Lenzkirch, are said to have finally closed down when they felt that, for various reasons, they could not maintain the superior performance of which their clocks had been capable. Nevertheless, the term 'regulator' applied to such clocks was, strictly speaking, a misnomer.

So, apart from the specially produced London-made carriage clocks just mentioned, what was the native English clock style during the nineteenth century? Indeed, was there one at all?

For a start, the traditional longcase clock of London quality seems to have met a sudden end in popularity and virtually to have become extinct

Dating from about 1890, this Vienna regulator clock has the name of the maker, 'Lenzkirch', stamped across the back of the wings of the eagle which surmounts it.

about 1820, although there are provincial examples from later than this. It was not resurrected again until about 1900. The craft did, however, continue to turn out sufficient hand-finished movements to keep things ticking over. It was correctly thought that there would always be a demand for such work, from the wealthier members of the community and from institutions of various sorts, and many such movements went into three-quarter-length clocks which hung from, or rested upon, a bracket fixed to the wall. These often looked like a longcase clock without its base, and the cases tended to be ornately carved and pretentious, claiming to follow such revived styles as Egyptian, Gothic, Jacobean, Louis Quatorze or Quinze, and others. It can honestly be said of such clocks that they were made superbly well: like so much other nineteenth-century craftsmanship, an enormous fount of skill and knowledge was applied to products that, artistically, were unworthy of it. Thus many, if not most, survive to the present time and function supremely well: it is virtually impossible to wear them out.

The same strictures apply equally to the mantel, bracket or table equivalents of the three-quarter wall clock; they were usually designed in 'improved' versions of earlier styles, with more elaborate decoration incorporating caryatid figures, frets, mounts and finials of every sort and

An attractive carriage clock made about 1840 and signed 'J. B. Beguin à Paris 5', it strikes the hours and half-hours and also repeats on a bell. The club-tooth lever escapement has jewelled pallets. Museum of the Worshipful Company of Clockmakers, Guildhall, London.

The most commonly encountered Black Forest clock in England is the so-called postman's alarm of which this is a typical example. It was imported into Britain by the firm of Camerer Cuss & Co. who are still in existence.

kind, the whole on a robust and indestructible scale. The largest of these were an inescapable feature of the library, hall or dining-room of any large house, or the directors' quarters of an institution; the more imposing the environment, the larger and more ornate the clock. Alongside such ostentatious English styles, there was also a resurgence of interest in materials like buhl and papier-mâché, and these found favour in revived versions of usually French designs from the previous century.

If there was a typically nineteenth-century native clock design then it was that known as the English dial clock. This is the spring-driven clock, so familiar on railway stations and other public places, but also seen in smaller versions in kitchens and offices but not generally in living-rooms, of which the outstanding feature is simply a painted iron dial, normally not bigger than fourteen inches in diameter, protected by a convex glass set into a hinged brass bezel and all within a turned mahogany surround. These clocks had substantial movements with heavy pendulums, and perform universally well. Sometimes they are fitted with longer pendulums, necessitating an extended

left
Spherical skeleton clocks were made by a handful of London makers around 1800. They are found in a variety of sizes, and this example signed 'Henricus Gratte, invenit et fecit Londini' is small, standing only 10⅝in high. It has a verge escapement and strikes the hours on a bell. Museum of the Worshipful Company of Clockmakers, Guildhall, London.

right
The finest English makers sometimes used the carriage clock module for their best work. This eight-day chronometer carriage clock, completed in 1896, is by the famous expatriate Swedish maker Victor Kullberg, who passed his working life in London. Museum of the Worshipful Company of Clockmakers, Guildhall, London.

trunk below the otherwise round profile of the clock, and this variety is known as a 'drop dial'. The English dial has quite a long history, certainly back into the eighteenth century when the dials were silvered on brass, rather than painted iron, and the escapement was a verge, often planted with the rest of the movement between triangular-shaped plates.

Another variety of nineteenth-century English clock is that form known as a skeleton clock, so called because the whole movement is positioned between skeletonised plates and everything is clearly visible through its protecting glass dome. The early history of this form is not clear: it may have derived simply from 'skeletonising' some other kind of clock in order, for the sake of novelty, to display the movement. But it is certain that skeleton clocks are not the masterpieces of apprentices to the craft, as was once thought. The lace-like plates are sometimes just patterns in symmetry, but often deliberately made to represent a building, usually a cathedral. There is a French style called a skeleton clock, much less solid and plebian and obviously a different design altogether, so that the English version, in fashion from about 1860, can be considered a distinctive type.

Although the domestic longcase clock went into eclipse at this time, the scientific equivalent, the regulator clock, continued to be produced by the best firms, in small quantities but to the highest standards. Such clocks went either to observatories and similar scientific institutions, or were installed by clock- and watchmakers to regulate their stock as well as, perhaps, to time those clocks and watches temporarily in their care while undergoing overhaul. The cases of regulator clocks have always been strictly utilitarian and devoid of any kind of decoration whatsoever; so, even if they had been widely available, they would not have appealed to the average Victorian household.

Mention of that remarkable Queen brings to mind that the most famous tower clock in the world, Big Ben, which looks down upon the Houses of Parliament at Westminster, was constructed and erected during her reign. The designer of the clock, Edmund Beckett Denison, was born in 1816, succeeded to his father's baronetcy as Sir Edmund Beckett in 1874, was given a peerage under the title of Baron Grimthorpe in 1886, and died in 1905. His was perhaps one of the last minds that could range, with equal success, over several completely unrelated fields and reach the top in every one; nowadays, progress has made it difficult enough for any man to aspire to succeed in one field, let alone several. Beckett was a very successful lawyer – a Queen's Counsel, no less – as well as an architect of no mean pretensions, an astronomer and a horologist of great ability and inventive capacity. The Westminster clock was built by Frederick Dent to Beckett's designs in 1854, bench-tested for five years, and finally installed at the top of its tower in 1859; and there is much excellent literature available about it, including Beckett's own work on the subject, in which is included his detailed description of the double three-legged gravity escapement he developed especially for the clock. The title 'Big Ben', although it is generally applied nowadays to

This French clock in its alabaster and gilt case was presented to the author's grandfather in 1875 by the surface men of the colliery of which he was manager. It is typical of the factory-made but good quality clock of the period.

the clock as such, is strictly the name of the great hour-bell, weighing nearly thirteen and a half tons, and so called after Sir Benjamin Hall, the Commissioner of Works who placed the order for its casting.

Big Ben has been subjected to most of the minor irritants that plague large public clocks from time to time – invasions of birds and accumulations of snow, among others. Over the 117 years that it has occupied the tower at Westminster, there have been about thirty stoppages from such causes, none of long duration. However, in the early hours of 5th August 1976 Big Ben suffered a major breakdown, far and away its most serious to date. The rates of chiming and striking of the great clock are controlled by giant fly-governors, whose vanes rotate against the resistance of the air. On this occasion the fly-shaft on the quarter-chiming train fractured. Effectively this released the train to run out of control under the power provided by a

Charles MacDowall, who was born in Wakefield and died aged 82 in London in 1872, was a clever horologist with a taste for the novel approach. He made skeleton clocks with oblique-toothed gearing and invented the 'helix lever'. Museum of the Worshipful Company of Clockmakers, Guildhall, London.

weight of 1¼ tons. Total disintegration of the train followed, as the weight plunged to the bottom of the tower, and the remainder of the clock did not escape unharmed. The main frame was fractured in several places and had to be bolted together with steel plates and supported by lifting jacks. The damage to the clock room itself caused by large fragments of flying metal resembled the effects of a bomb explosion – indeed, this was the first thought of those who entered therein immediately after the accident. It has been possible, thanks to the great skill and ingenuity of those responsible for the clock, to restart Big Ben and to restore the hour-striking action, which was also damaged quite severely, but it is likely to be many months before its famous quarter chimes will be heard again. If, as seems likely, the causative factor was metal fatigue, then conceivably the whole future of the original mechanism may be at a stake. Certainly radiographic and magnetic flaw investigations

The movement of the French presentation clock represents the stage of development reached by the factory-made round French clock movement towards the end of the nineteenth century. Notable features are locking plate striking, long considered obsolete in other countries, and the particular type of pendulum adjustment attributed to Brocot.

Large and elaborate bracket clocks of this kind which was made by Barraud & Lund about 1885, were considered essential in boardrooms, libraries and similar institutions.

have revealed serious invisible faults in at least two of the remaining wheels. How fascinating it would be if Beckett himself were still alive to apply his inventive mind to the many problems involved.

Although Beckett devoted a great deal of time to horology, being an accomplished theorist and an author of technical and literary stature, he cannot really rank as a professional horologist, since he can only have derived a very small part of his income, if indeed any, from such activities. His work on clocks is usually held up as a prime example of the great contribution that the gifted amateur has to offer in this field. He was elected President of the British Horological Institute in 1868 – an honorary post, of course – and, with his architect's aspect now to the fore, designed their headquarters building in Northampton Square, Clerkenwell, which the Institute continued to occupy until very recently. Although they were not attributable solely to Beckett's influence in the trade, it is interesting to note that Victoria's reign saw the construction of some fine large public clocks, mainly in churches; and although these may not always exhibit the individual characteris-

tics possessed by tower clocks from earlier periods, nevertheless they are exceptionally reliable timekeepers and possess much of merit in their various parts.

Big Ben was, of course, a unique clock – and despite its all-pervading aroma of impending standardisation and mass-production, the nineteenth century did see some other outstanding custom-built clocks produced, both in England and elsewhere. Mention has been made earlier of the third Strasbourg cathedral clock, built by Schwilgué and opened in 1842. The great French clockmakers like Breguet, already recognised as outstanding by 1800, and others such as Berthoud and Janvier, were exerting an international influence in Europe, so that countries like Austria produced one or two superb craftsmen making clocks of astonishing individuality. Mathias Ratzenhofer, for instance, made a series of three remarkable productions in the form of a vase of flowers, a wheelbarrow full of flowers and a sunflower clock. They were all exquisite in concept as well as in execution. In Britain, pride of place for horological novelty in the nineteenth century probably belongs to William Congreve, an artillery officer at Woolwich whose principal claim to fame is perhaps his invention of a military rocket. Congreve almost certainly never knew of previous attempts in Europe to use a rolling ball as a time standard; if he did, he clearly thought it worthwhile to try the system again. Thus, in 1808, he completed and patented his rolling ball clock, of the tipping platform type, which has been studiously copied by various firms subsequently, though on a very small scale. He seems only to have made one clock of this kind himself, and it appears to be the only one that is weight-driven. There is little doubt that, even if the basic principle was not original, the finished product was a great improvement on anything of the same kind that had gone before, although it needed the most delicate adjustment to make it give of its best.

What was happening in clockmaking elsewhere in Europe? The Black Forest is perhaps a good starting point. A cottage industry adopted by peasants in the middle of the seventeenth century, it progressed very slowly throughout the eighteenth, the thrifty craftsmen continuing to use wood as far as possible for every component, at least until the second half of that century, when at last brass wheels started to become usual. These were mounted upon wooden arbors, however; brass arbors and plates were not to appear until well after 1800. The cuckoo clock first appeared probably between 1730 and 1740, at about the time that the foliot balance was replaced by the pendulum; but very few such clocks that date prior to 1840 have survived, and the familiar 'chalet' style did not appear before 1850. The craft product that had started in such a modest and rudimentary

right

A watchman's 'telltale' clock originally located in one of the big banks in the City of London. The dial bears the signature 'Barrauds, Cornhill, London', and it is possible to place its date at 1816. The dial revolves against a fixed pointer which can be seen above 12 o'clock, and the pins to be depressed by the watchman are clearly visible around its edge.

below

The cuckoo attachment to Black Forest clocks at first was incorporated into the painted shield-shaped dials of their wall clocks, and the chalet type of cuckoo clock does not appear before about 1850.

ted. This basic system, even using much of the original control equipment, was in use until destroyed by bombing during the Second World War; even then, it was partially rebuilt and continued to give a similar service, albeit on a more restricted scale, until economic considerations finally forced it to close down only as recently as 1964.

It will be obvious that, from considerations of scale alone, the watch presents a multitude of different – and generally more difficult – problems in its manufacture than the clock. Manual dexterity, when hand-working watch parts as opposed to those for a clock has to be much more sensitive and highly developed to avoid a disaster that can, in extreme cases, negate several days' work. By the nineteenth century, however, the evolution of the watch was being adequately paced by development of the quite sophisticated technology needed to manufacture it. Mass-production aside – and this was an essentially American phenomenon which will be dealt with in the next chapter – skilled craftsmen in Victorian England had brought the mechanical arts to a zenith, and were able to use hand tools, often of their own making, as well as a variety of hand- or foot-powered machine tools, to fashion complex multi-component assemblies to a degree of precision and to smaller tolerances than at any previous time in history. In a sense, this remarkable progress towards precision workmanship was just a logical further step in what was already a long heritage. Seventeenth-century invention produced a timekeeper that kept going, even though haphazardly; in the eighteenth, the target was reliability coupled with ever more precision in performance, and this spilled over into the nineteenth and even the twentieth centuries. Once the main principles of precision mechanical timekeeping had been established, however, there was at last time to devote to the convenience of the user, in such matters as winding mechanisms – the ubiquitous key-winding system was so unwieldy by comparison with the nowadays commonplace button-wind or, in watchmakers' parlance, 'keyless' system – as well as in the method of activating ancillary motions such as chronographs and

repeatingwork. Such were the preoccupations of makers towards the end of the nineteenth century.

At the beginning, however – by 1800 – the verge was probably still the most common design of watch escapement, followed closely by the cylinder. The duplex was just coming into favour, for those who wanted a quality watch but could not, perhaps, afford a pocket chronometer. The lever, which was eventually to assert itself as the finest escapement for watches, was still something of an anachronism; invented, abandoned, reinvented in the 1780s and 1790s, and abandoned again apart from its close cousin, the rack lever, it was ripe for yet a further appearance. The rack lever had many attributes comparable with the eventual form that the escapement was to assume; yet, because of its rack and pinion, it was not in the technical sense a 'detached' escapement, being always in contact with the train throughout its cycle of operation. In the second decade of the century two intermediate forms of detached lever, known respectively as Massey's crank-roller and Savage's two-pin lever, appeared and continued to be made for some time, although very shortly thereafter the first true version of the English lever, called the table-roller lever, made its appearance. This would have been about 1825, and it very quickly established itself, undergoing only one other modification, in the latter half of the century, to incorporate a double roller, which did not affect the action of the escapement. By mid century or shortly thereafter, then, the lever watch had superseded the duplex and the detent – the pocket chronometer was always a fragile machine to carry on the person – while the cylinder was obsolescent except in its cheap imported version. The only other escapement still being made was the verge, and this continued until about 1900, although principally in the provinces. It seems curiously appropriate that the oldest mechanical escapement known to mankind should have had such an incredibly long life, yet, for those who did not need the most precise timekeeping, it was a robust device, reliable in service and easy of maintenance.

The first attempts to devise an easier system of winding up the watch and to dispense with the inconvenient watch key, were made in 1820 by Thomas Prest, foreman at Arnolds, the chronometermakers at Chigwell in Essex, although the celebrated John Arnold senior, the founder, was long since dead by this time. Although it employed a button on the pendant similar to the modern system, Prest's design possessed certain technical disadvantages and was never popular during his lifetime. Other approaches to the problem involved what is usu-

ally called 'pump-winding', that is, a push-pull action applied to the pendant knob. A certain A. Burdess, a Coventry maker, devised a system by which a lever, pivoted to the back plate, engages with a ratchet arrangement acting upon the fusee arbor. The lever projects through the watch case, and can be pumped up and down, the ratchet engaging – and therefore turning the fusee – on the downward stroke, and then free-wheeling on the upward. His watches also possessed an unusual system for hand-setting, having a wheel with a milled edge projecting outside the rim of the movement, yet being in constant engagement with the minute wheel. The additional friction caused to the motionwork thereby must surely have made the arrangement most unserviceable. A number of other winding systems were tried out, especially towards the end of the nineteenth century; many of

George Littlewort patented a special type of lockable three-day duration watch for use by the guards on mail coaches. Museum of the Worshipful Company of Clockmakers, Guildhall, London.

these employed a button, but often it had to be wound while pressure was applied simultaneously to a push-piece located beside the pendant on the band of the case. Failure to do this meant that the winding train was not engaged, and the button just turned freely between the fingers. A variation of this system utilised two push-pieces, one each side of the pendant. Pressure on one together with operation of the winding button, wound the watch; pressure upon the other gave the facility to set the hands, just as in the system which was eventually universally adopted. The height of absurdity in attempts by the watch trade to dispense with the

Another version of the watchman's clock was carried by the watchman himself. This one is called 'Hahn's Patent Time Detector'. The working of this clock is described in the text on page 200.

key-wind system was probably reached as late as 1870, when the firm of Barraud & Lund marketed watches whose pendants were topped by buttons looking exactly like those fitted to keyless watches. However, when the button was pulled, it came free of the pendant, only to reveal that attached underneath it – and concealed within the pendant when not in use – was a key!

It may sound, from the foregoing, as if the English watch trade had been somewhat obstinate as well as stupid in their development of keyless winding. They had their problems, though, not the least of which was their long-established belief – almost a creed, one might say – that one prerequisite for accuracy in watches was a fusee. Although many fusee keyless watches were made, and suc-

cessfully – these are held in high esteem by collectors today – it is in general much more difficult to adapt the fusee watch for keyless winding than the going barrel watch. Eventually, this consideration was to seal the fate of the fusee, which was abandoned towards the end of the century. Foreign manufacturers had by then been using the going barrel successfully for a long time, and it must have been hard for the English trade to have to yield on such a basic principle; yet force of circumstances gave them little choice.

There were other technical advances going on alongside those mentioned, so that it was almost a case of consolidating the fundamental inventions in watchmaking to produce the article that was perfect in all respects – appearance, reliability, performance and convenience of use. Thus, although the table-roller lever watch, once established, became the standard good-quality watch, there were still those makers – James Ferguson Cole, for example – who sought to improve the

204

escapement even further. Yet another ingenious maker, Thomas Cummins – until recently, relatively unappreciated – was not only one of the first to use the lever escapement in quantity after its revival, but also employed it in special watches of the very highest quality, starting about 1822. Yet inventiveness did not always produce the results expected. For example, Breguet, although not first in the field, had adapted the principle of the pedometer to produce an automatic watch – he called them '*montres perpetuelles*' – but this fashion, even by such a master, had only a relatively short life. Next, Harwood suited the same principle to the wristwatch in 1923. Even then, the fashion was short-lived, and automatic watches have not become really popular until recent times.

In the latter half of the nineteenth century, apart from standardising, in the end, a functional keyless winding system, a rather better arrangement was devised for operating additional motions on watches – chronographwork, for example, or repetition actions. This took the form of slides, as they are called, built into the band of the case and operated by a thumbnail. Such action was more positive, as well as more suitable for the thinner plainer designs of late nineteenth-century watches, than anything that had been tried before, especially now that the elongated pendant, reminiscent of the old pair-case watch, had disappeared. As to additional complexities, the minute repeater became fairly commonplace – musical watches had had a short vogue earlier in the century, but again the fashion did not last – as well as various types of stopwatch and chronograph mechanisms. Much complicated repeating, musical, chronograph and similar work was made in Switzerland and imported into Britain where it was fitted quite happily to English-made watches.

But how did the appearance of the watch change in the period under review? The pair-cased watch was still the norm in 1800 and was to continue for some decades still in the provinces, even if London usage was changing. The first real hunter and half-hunter watch cases – even these often have a pair-case *en suite* – have the thick profile of the styles that preceded them and, for some reason, were mostly made in Birmingham around 1802–04. The first single-cased watches – these are often called 'consular' cases – looked like pair-cases; the glazed bezel opened and the hinged movement swung outwards, as if one were opening the inner of pair-cases. Behind the movement but integral with the rest, the case is double-backed, the outer one hinged and opening to permit winding through the inner, which is, of course, fixed. This type of single case gradually evolved into that which prevailed throughout most of Victoria's reign; in this the pendant had shrunk to become a mere knob on the case, with the bow pivoted in it. The band of such cases, and sometimes a border

The Scotsman Alexander Bain was the first to apply electricity to drive the pendulum of a clock, an invention which he patented in 1840. Museum of the Worshipful Company of Clockmakers, Guildhall, London.

205

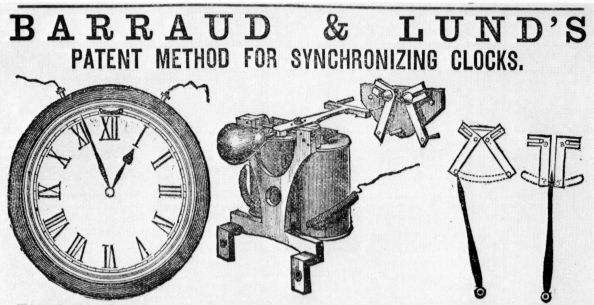
round the back as well, were knurled, and later engine-turned designs became customary. For a while around the mid century, cases with cast decoration, usually with a floral motif, became common, and these coincided with a sudden return for a time to metal dials instead of the enamel ones which had been in use since the previous century. Where gold was the metal involved, it was not unusual to find applied decoration in different coloured alloys, the whole usually being described as in 'four-colour gold'. Metal dials were soon discarded in favour of enamel ones, however, and, as the century continued, the heavy gold open-faced ('O.F.') watch, as well as the hunter and half-hunter, became popular. Of the latter styles, of course, the hunter has a solid cover over the dial which has to be opened before the time can be read, while in the half-hunter a hole is cut in the centre of the cover, of sufficient size to allow the directions of the hands to be ascertained, these being read against a ring of hour numerals engraved around the edge of this aperture. Initially there was some tendency to overdecorate these handsome watches: either the cases were cast to provide relief all over, or sometimes just an elaborated monogram or at least an ugly cartouche waiting to contain one, were provided. But by the

last two decades of the century such watches had evolved into the plain, functional and generally high-grade timekeepers which our grandparents and their parents were accustomed to wear.

The other radical change which took place in the pocket watch during the last century was the gradual disappearance of any decoration on the movement. The original purpose of decorating movements, presumably, was to make them a focus for the admiration of both their owners and those who were allowed to examine them, while at the same time, perhaps, drawing attention away from their indifferent capabilities as timekeepers: it will be remembered that such decoration was applied from a very early stage in the evolution of the watch, long before it could realistically be considered as anything more than an ingenious toy for the rich. By 1800, such decoration had already become degenerate by comparison with what had gone before, but there was still plenty of it: the watch cock, for instance, was still likely to be the site of all-over engraving of a kind, even though piercing, as an added attraction, had been discarded. The shape of the cock, too, remained as it had been – a round 'table' above the balance, joined to a splayed 'foot', which was screwed to the movement. However, two influences seemed to be

left

The firm of Barraud & Lund were among the first to use electricity to synchronise 'slave' clocks with a regulator, and this advertisement for their process appeared in the *Horological Journal* in January 1878. This method was in use on the railways by 1892.

right

This small watch, presumably intended for a lady, originated from a famous London watchmaking firm, James McCabe. It incorporates a duplex escapement and dates from 1835, that is, during the last decade in which this form of controller continued to be made.

The common English watch in 1800 was still the ubiquitous verge. This example by Barraud, which has a subsidiary calendar dial, is typical of the best quality practice at that time, this particular one having been made in 1797.

This watch by John Roger Arnold, son of the famous chronometermaker, is fitted with the early system of keyless winding developed in 1820 by Thomas Prest, Arnold's foreman. Museum of the Worshipful Company of Clockmakers, Guildhall, London.

at work during the first three decades of the century. The high-precision watch movement – the pocket chronometer, that is – was quickly to become completely plain, as well as needing modification to the shape of its watch cock to suit the helical balance spring.

It was almost as if the makers mutually decided that precision and decoration did not mix: in fact, they do not, in the sense that the last thing a proud craftsman in this field wants is for some nosey busybody to be constantly prying into his precision machine, and doubtless affecting its performance by letting in dust and moisture. Thomas Earnshaw, in fact, was so adamant on this point that many of his pocket chronometer movements are screwed into their cases and need special tools to extract them. Breguet took a like view.

Another influence, which in a sense seemed to be going in the opposing direction, was experimentation in the shape of the watch cock probably as part of the general trend towards a much thinner watch. The traditional English hand-finished watch was robust, heavy and thick, all characteristics which supported its good and reliable performance. However, the demand was for a change, sparked off, no doubt, by the French, who were making watches of a thinness and elegance which

The movement of the Arnold watch also reveals the particular type of 'sugar-tongs' compensation curb, favoured by the younger Arnold. The escapement is a ruby cylinder. Museum of the Worshipful Company of Clockmakers, Guildhall, London.

left
Made by Henry Borell of London, this elaborate enamelled and gem-set automaton clock was a present from George III to the Emperor Ch'ien-lung of China in about 1790. At the hour a small door opens below the dial, and ships move about on simulated waves. Jürg Stuker Gallery, Berne.

must have been much envied by their cousins across the Channel. The full-plate watch – in which the train is planted between two solid plates with the balance mounted outside them, pivoting in its cock which is screwed to the back of the movement – had, perforce, to give way to something thinner and therefore more sophisticated, but without detracting from any of its finer advantages, such as performance. The eventual solution, of course, was to cut away part of the back plate and drop the balance into the cavity so formed. It still required its own cock, but this time screwed to the underside of the front plate. Experiments in this direction were going forward among London

left

A transition stage in the evolution of the half-hunter watch is illustrated in this specimen by Thomas Glase of Bridgnorth. It is essentially a silver pair-cased verge watch, and the inner case has been fitted with a half-hunter cover. The cases are hallmarked 1794. Museum of the Worshipful Company of Clockmakers, Guildhall, London.

below

This varied collection of lever watch movements includes a rack lever with compensation curb by Robert Roskell, a Massey's crank-roller lever by Yeates & Sons and a somewhat later example, showing a form of pump-winding patented by Adam Burdess of Coventry in 1869.

opposite page

This heavy decorated gold watch with its four-colour gold dial was made by Alexander Watkins of London for the Great Exhibition of 1851. It has an eight-day movement and a spring detent escapement and is a quarter-striking and repeating clock-watch. Museum of the Worshipful Company of Clockmakers, Guildhall, London.

makers as early as the 1820s, so that three-quarter plate movements became commonplace and the so-called half-plate rather less so, although the full-plate movement continued in country practice for the rest of the century and even beyond. As to decoration, this continued throughout the short period of trial to find a new watch cock shape, and for some time after the rounded-wedge-shaped cock table had been adopted. Finally, decoration became completely perfunctory and haphazard – there was even one short period in which a circular raised area on the back plate immediately above the spring barrel became the site of engraved decoration – before eventually disappearing altogether.

The only other European watchmaking countries of any consequence in the last century were France and Switzerland. The French, led by such style-setters as Breguet, Motel and others, set their sights on high-quality thin watches of the greatest elegance and, certainly at the beginning of the century, placed themselves alongside the English in their insistence upon the best standards. The Swiss, curiously enough, had made little impression on the world horological scene before 1800, having managed to 'export' only some of their finest craftsmen to other countries so that it almost seems that, for the first quarter of the century, they still marked time while waiting for the advent of mass-production. In the end, the French and the Swiss took the same road, while the English clung obstinately to their illusions about the hand-finished watch, even though in this sphere too they had been largely overtaken by the French. The Swiss meanwhile made something of a speciality of novelty during the early decades of the century: musical and repeating watches, with automata ranging from simple *jaquemarts* simulating the striking of bells beside a cut-away dial to other very much more complicated actions. Soon, however, the pace was to be set by pioneers like Frédéric Japy, whose engineering skill provided so many of the first machine tools in Switzerland, and Favre-Jacot who opened the first watch factory. One of the side effects of this fundamental change in methods of production was the gradual replacement of the former common Swiss full-plate verge movement with the much more readily quantity-produced Lepine calibre – in which there is really only one plate, all the train wheels and other components being pivoted in cocks screwed to it – together with the cylinder escapement. The Swiss maintained this style for the remainder of the century, and the French also adopted it.

When the Great Exhibition opened in London in 1851, the Swiss made a great impression with their display; sadly, there was only one English firm, Rotherhams of Coventry, who had employed steam-powered machinery in making their exhibits. This followed a lone attempt, a few years previously, by a Swiss called P. F. Ingold to make

watches in England using machine tools. It was instantly and vociferously opposed by the trade in Clerkenwell and Coventry, who successfully crushed it. In fact, Ingold had had contacts with America, the fount of mass-production methods, and nobody will ever be able to assess accurately how much damage must have been done by the English craft to its own future livelihood by this inward-looking unprogressive attitude. The extraordinary thing is that, rather than admit the error of its ways, the craft continued to hold to its hidebound attitude which it did not finally abandon until the late 1920s, when the economic depression made life on the former system impossible. Fine watches, at such times, are made to be broken up for the intrinsic value of their precious-metal cases, not bought new over the counter!

In terms of horological achievement, how can one sum up the nineteenth and twentieth centuries? Certain it is that nothing very new was discovered, for there was little of fundamental significance still awaiting invention in the respective arts, if one ignores the ordinary mains electric clock working synchronously with the alternating current, which after all is only an electric motor with gearing. All-embracing fashions in art – such as Art Nouveau and Art Deco – were reflected, certainly, in clocks; but although other objects in these styles have made their mark, the horological applications seem mostly to have failed to survive. However it may be presented or disguised, there has already been a precedent for almost every complexity or additional action; thus automatic watches were an eighteenth-century development, calendar watches even earlier, alarm watches earlier still. Stopwatches, chronographs, timers, call them what you will, there is nothing even comparatively recent about them: they have been around for centuries! The only peculiarly twentieth-century feature, or fashion if you prefer it, has been the wristwatch, attributed to the First World War period when it was much more convenient than a pocket watch; since some early examples seem to have been made up by fitting ladies' fob watches with lugs either side to take a silk or leather strap it may even have preceded that great human débâcle by a few years. But it hardly rates as an epoch-making discovery such as, for example, the first successful application of the pendulum.

There were important fringe inventions, nevertheless – not of a mechanical nature them-

212

left
James Ferguson Cole experimented towards the middle of the nineteenth century in an effort to improve the already well-established lever escapement. This watch was made in 1848. Museum of the Worshipful Company of Clockmakers, Guildhall, London.

below left
These three lever movements dating from late in the nineteenth century, include an example by W. D. Pidduck of Manchester, which obtained an 'A' rating at Kew Observatory, another by Donne & Son which has an up-and-down indicator, and a 'machine-made lever' from the well-known Liverpool firm of Thomas Russell.

selves, but of the greatest use in mechanical devices. In 1920, for instance, the Nobel Prize was awarded to Charles-Edouard Guillaume (1861–1938), who was at that time Director of the International Bureau of Weights and Measures in Paris, for discovering certain nickel-steel alloys that were virtually impervious to changes in temperature. Called by their inventor 'Invar' and 'Elinvar', they replaced almost overnight all previous systems for temperature compensation. The two other major developments in the last seventy years have been the free-pendulum clock perfected by W. H. Shortt in 1921 – an electro-mechanical device of astonishing accuracy, and only overtaken by the electronics-based quartz crystal clock, invented in America in 1929.

Even though the English craft of the fine watch might appear to have presided over its own funeral, there is one consolation to be derived from such seeming obstinacy. Those directly involved sadly reaped no benefit, for it is only now just starting to pay off. Because the tradition of the hand-finished watch lasted so much longer in England than elsewhere – for it was still possible to have one made to suit one's taste less than fifty years ago – many such fine watches must still be in circulation, and certainly some are eminently fit for collection. Such quality pieces help to offset the dearth of any other interesting twentieth-century developments. Wristwatches, *per se*, are not very attractive objects, but doubtless they also will become collector's items in the end; and it is amusing to speculate how long it is going to take, in view of the speed with which at the present time fashions in collecting are catching up with history!

below left
This early leather wristwatch strap, believed to date from about 1908, is designed to contain a small pocket watch, thus converting it for wearing on the wrist. Museum of the Worshipful Company of Clockmakers, Guildhall, London.

below
The first application of the self-winding principle to wristwatches, this specimen by John Harwood, who made his prototype six years before, dates from about 1928. The Depression forced the firm into liquidation shortly afterwards. Museum of the Worshipful Company of Clockmakers, Guildhall, London.

East Meets West

Anybody taking up the study of horology seriously reads certain standard works of reference, visits museum collections, joins appropriate organisations and perhaps, if his means will allow, starts to collect items which particularly appeal to him. There is a very dangerous tendency, once this stage has been reached – and it may take five months or fifteen years, depending upon individual circumstances – to lapse into a state of euphoria based on the wholly erroneous belief that all the basic knowledge necessary to enjoy and appreciate every aspect of the art, craft and science of the subject has now been carefully explored and assimilated. In fact, the student has become an expert, or so he thinks.

The only real expert in horology is the one who recognises that there is no such animal, since it is not possible to become one within the capacity of one mind and one human life-span. The infinite ingenuity of man in things mechanical has made it absolutely certain that no one person will ever be able to locate, let alone examine, every permutation of mechanical components in the form of a timepiece that has ever been constructed, to say nothing of the limitless combinations of complications that are frequently associated with such objects. Without doing that, nobody has any right to claim comprehensive knowledge of the subject. Even to the present time, the world's big auction houses, and even the most prominent specialist dealers in the field, continue to turn up from time to time horological objects the exact like of which have not been seen before by the majority, if not indeed by any, of those claiming expertise in such things. Naturally the degree of novelty varies from one item to another: it is rare for anything to come to light so exceptionally unique as materially to affect the recorded course of horological history, yet it does happen. Perhaps this is one of the characteristics that makes horology such an exciting subject for study.

The most convincing way to demonstrate the precept set out above is probably to consider in some detail two totally different horological cultures, at the same time recognising that, in dealing with such a universally experienced phenomenon as the passage and measurement of time, these are but two among many that possess marked differences one from another. Like time itself, there is a quality of the infinite about the range of instrumentation associated with it, not to mention such arbitrary characteristics as the periods into which time is divided.

Japan

For all its modern commercial and technical achievement, in the matter of time-measurement Japan presents an extraordinary paradox. It is only a little over a century – the exact year was 1873 – since she abandoned a method of time-measurement and a complicated calendar that had been long since outmoded, and changed to the European system. But the paradox extends even further. Once the change had been made, most of the obsolete timepieces were exported as novelties, so that they have now become extremely rare in their country of origin, although common enough in advanced Western countries. Finally, and as if this was not enough, Japanese clockmakers of the pre-1873 era were innately conservative, so that accurate dating of many of their wares within a span of two and a half centuries is an impossible task, even if one encounters them.

This Japanese 'lantern' striking clock on its lacquered stand has a steel movement with a single foliot. The hand revolves against the fixed lacquered dial, and the engraved panels enclosing the case are of silvered brass. British Museum, London.

There are a number of other problems connected with any proper study of old Japanese horology which it is as well to recognise from the beginning. It will be obvious that the flimsy construction – by Western standards – of Japanese houses, built without solid walls and with rooms divided by movable partitions, precludes the accommodation of heavy weight-driven wall timepieces or brackets of any kind. Furthermore, the Japanese, unlike other cultures, do not favour heavy items of furniture such as chests of drawers, cabinets or even mantelpieces. Indeed, normally their rooms – certainly those in which they entertain guests – are absolutely empty save for some special object, which will have been brought in temporarily for the occasion, to suit some particu-

Another version of the lantern clock encloses it within a wall-bracket and glazed hood. This example has a revolving dial with adjustable numerals. British Museum, London.

Another Japanese lantern clock, this one has more elaborate decoration than the previous example, indicating a somewhat later date. British Museum, London.

The aspiring student horologist from any Western culture who wants to learn about Japanese practice faces an enormous obstacle from the beginning. There is no work in his own language to guide his studies and provide the groundwork. Actually this is not entirely true, as will be seen from the Further Reading list on page 254; but, taking the English language as an example, the most authoritative work on Japanese horology forms part only of a general dissertation on clockwork that was published nearly fifty years ago, has long since gone out of print and is now, in fact, both scarce and expensive on the secondhand market. But, more important, it has never been updated in the light of recent research, if indeed any substantial corpus of such has so far been undertaken. It could be a prolific field for the right person to explore.

lar mood and which may be enhanced by other temporary features specially arranged in its vicinity. Finally, of course, clocks in long cases, so that their dials were six feet or more from the floor, would serve little purpose in surroundings in which people customarily sat on the ground.

It is clear from the foregoing that any clock which must, of its very nature, form a permanent part of the domestic scene, would be anathema to the Japanese who had no taste for permanence in their surroundings; and it will not be surprising, therefore, to discover that clocks were mainly confined to the temples and to the homes of nobles and the very rich, where it was customary to keep a clockmaker occupied with their continual adjustments, as the calendar demanded. It is certainly true that even educated Japanese have been largely ignorant of these relics of a bygone age, and a British diplomat writing early in the present century of his experiences in Japan in the third quarter of the previous one, mentioned that neither clocks nor punctuality were common, and it was always very difficult to be certain about the time of day.

So, strangely, the best evidence as to the antecedents of Japanese clocks must perforce come from the instruments themselves, and from the occasional references in the literature of that land. Of the latter, one volume of a three-volume treatise on mechanical toys and clocks which was published towards the end of the eighteenth century is relevant; a more recent account devoted wholly to Japanese horology was published in 1924. Both will be found in the Further Reading list.

It is rather beyond the scope of this book to deal at any length with the history of Japan from the time when it first accepted mechanical timekeeping devices, even if this were known with any accuracy. Did clocks arrive with the Portuguese, when they first reached Japan about 1542? Or did they emanate from the Spanish, or possibly the Dutch, who, of all the European merchant countries, seem to have devised the most effective, albeit short-lived, trading arrangements with Japan? Even Britain's East India Company traded with Japan for ten years early in the seventeenth century but, being uncompetitive, finally abandoned the market. However this may be, there is evidence that Japanese craftsmen, who were very skilled indeed in the working of metals, slavishly copied the crude sixteenth-century domestic clock that was current in Europe and almost certainly did so under the supervision of European masters.

This, however, at once focussed attention on a key problem. The Japanese divided the day according to a method which had its origins in China, not into twice twelve hours, each of equal length, as customary in the West. The Chinese system reckoned time according to the 'natural' day, starting at dusk. Each period from dusk to

Features of this lantern clock include double foliot, striking and alarm. The hand revolves against a lacquered chapter ring. British Museum, London.

dawn and from dawn to dusk was divided into six equal divisions; but, owing to the seasonal variation in the length of the periods, the length of such divisions varied according to the time of year. These divisions – which we may, for ease of expression, loosely call 'hours' henceforth, although it will be understood that they are of constantly varying length – were sounded in temples by strokes upon a bell, ranging in descending order from nine to four. To complicate the matter even further, each hour not only equated with a specific number of bell strokes but also with a sign of the Chinese zodiac. The hour was, in fact, designated by its zodiacal name, and since some of these signs were considered lucky and others not, it needed only a glance at the clock to see if the time was propitious for any special course of action. Although generally the divisions on clock dials incorporated both number and sign, there are examples which exhibit only the one or the other, while yet a third

right
This Japanese equivalent of the mantel or bracket clock has a brass and steel movement, a double foliot and a revolving hand. The movement is encased in engraved brass plates with turned columns, the whole being then enclosed in a wood case with glazed panels. British Museum, London.

opposite page, right
An elaborate mantel clock in a Shitân-wood case: the skeletonised movement has rack striking, a balance rather than a foliot, and a revolving dial with moveable numerals. In the base there is a musical box. British Museum, London.

opposite page, left
This musical mantel clock playing on six bells also incorporates a lunar dial. British Museum, London.

variety retains the signs for noon and midnight but numerals for the rest. As to this use of hour numbers, it is not out of keeping with Oriental tradition, which so often seems to organise things in a reverse order to that used in the West, that the Japanese should count their hours backwards. It is more difficult to say why the numbers 9 through to 4 should have been chosen. Several theories have been advanced, based on numerological considerations, but there is no evidence to support one against another. It does seem certain that the numbers 1, 2 and 3 were reserved for temple use in a different, probably liturgical context, while 9 possessed supposed magic properties and was therefore reserved to indicate the two invariable moments of each day, midday and midnight.

It has already been mentioned that clocks had to be continually adjusted as the calendar of the seasons influenced the precise lengths of the two periods of each day. But the Japanese calendar itself – the system for determining chronological dates – was excessively complicated; indeed, there were three different methods, all in use together. One consisted of counting by the years of the reigns of Emperors, in much the same manner as British Acts of Parliament are still dated. The second depended upon reckoning by a period of indeterminate length and dating from some important event after which the period was named. The third and final system is generally termed the 'sexage-

nary cycle', and utilised periods of sixty years. It could be adapted, however, to designate cycles of months and days, and was the system used for calendar indications by clockwork.

Clocks made by native craftsmen in Japan fell into three broad classes, two of which, although not strictly comparable with any Western counterpart, are frequently categorised by the same stylistic terms.

The first style, which is usually called a 'lantern' clock, covers any weight-driven clock supported on a stand on the floor or on a bracket, or suspended by a loop. Its sides are encased by plates, not unlike the European clock which is known by the same name, and it is surmounted by a bell. This is the oldest style of Japanese clock; it was made continuously from the early seventeenth century until the whole mode of timekeeping was changed in 1873, the only development of significance being from about 1830 when changes to the structure occurred as a result of the desire to increase the area available for decoration. The stands for such clocks varied from a truncated cone to a more table-like version with cabriole legs, in every case the weights hanging inside it and clearly visible.

Portable spring-driven clocks enclosed within a glazed wooden case, and resting either upon a bracket or a suitable piece of furniture, are sometimes designated 'bracket clocks'. Drummond

Robertson did not consider that any of those he had encountered had been made prior to about 1830. Much embellishment was lavished upon the visible plates of the movements of these clocks, and most of them have a wheel balance and a balance spring. The striking system is also peculiar, in that it is a compromise between locking-plate and rack striking, using elements of both.

Finally, there is the weight-driven 'pillar clock', to which no European clock even approximates, so called because it was long, narrow, very lightly constructed and could be attached to the main upright of a building in a wholly unobtrusive way which the Japanese, with their delight in unoccupied space, would not find offensive. This was the cheapest quality clock of the three styles, and also seems to have been introduced about 1830. It varies in length from one to four feet, with the movement contained in a glazed box at the top, and the pillar or column below the movement is hollow. The weight moves up and down inside this structure, and a pointer attached to it, which projects through a slit running the length of the front of the column, indicates the time against movable division marks, permitting adjustment as necessary for the variable periods of night and day. The remarkable feature of such clocks is that, at first sight, their construction could not conceivably permit of any striking mechanism. This deficiency was overcome by the ingenious expedient of using the striking train as the weight to drive the going train. It was then only necessary to fit each division mark with an internal pin which unlocks the train as the weight reaches it. There were, nevertheless, certain drawbacks to the system, the solutions to which are regrettably much clumsier than the original concept.

The necessity for frequent alteration of the calibrations of the clock in Japan produced some interesting devices which will not be found on any Western timekeepers. Several of these depended upon the special characteristics of the foliot balance, which was retained for at least two centuries after it had been abandoned elsewhere in the world. Thus one early form of clock had no provision for maintaining Japanese time other than by the unsubtle and inconvenient method of moving the weights on the foliot arms every sunrise and sunset.

The obvious system for coping with a situation like this was by movable hour divisions, and further to facilitate additional complications like striking, these were usually located upon a rotating hour circle which indicated the time against a fixed pointer. The hour markers themselves were planted friction-tight in a groove running around the circle so that their relative positions could be adjusted at will. Each had a pin projecting from its back, so that as the divisions were moved, the pins inevitably moved with them. Then, when the hour

circle rotated, the pins as they passed the fixed pointer would release the striking train, and the hour would sound.

Towards the end of the seventeenth century probably the most ingenious approach to this problem was evolved. This required two entirely separate verges and foliots, one for the day and one for the night; each verge was linked to its own escape wheel, but these were mounted back to back upon a common arbor, and effectively each escapement was capable of being engaged with or disengaged from the going train by means of a flexible mounting for the lower pivots of the verges. The change-over was performed automatically twice a day by the clock itself, simply by means of a cam actuated by the locking-plate. All that was necessary then was to set up the weights on each foliot to reproduce the rate required for the day and night hours of the current half-month – that was the period during which they remained constant. The clock did the rest.

Although it sounds cumbersome, so was the time-measuring system employed by the Japanese – and despite the clear advantages, if only in terms of convenience of operation, of the double foliot arrangement, single foliot clocks were still being made in Japan well into the nineteenth century. The Japanese, as a result, probably developed the foliot controller to as great a degree of proficiency as it was inherently capable of attaining; the arms, for example, generally have between thirty and thirty-five notches, often with engraved gradations for ease of adjustment. Such clocks, even so, usually required winding twice a day.

The striking trains of Japanese clocks indicated the six primary divisions of day and night – counting backwards from nine to four – and occasionally there will be found provision for striking a half-division. The locking-plate system adapted quite easily to this, remembering that it could only be unlocked when the movable hour divisions on their rotating dial reached their correct position oppo-

left
Described by Drummond Robertson as a 'fancy' clock, this Japanese timepiece is a combination of the lantern and pillar clock, and reading the time by either method is possible. British Museum, London.

above
Another so-called 'fancy' clock, this example might better be described as a sword clock. The principle is much the same as a pillar clock. British Museum, London.

right
This clock has a double foliot, a steel striking movement and a brass case engraved with flower sprays. The wooden stand is decorated with lacquer. British Museum, London.

A hexagonal travelling clock with wood outer case, this timepiece is only 3in wide. British Museum, London.

below
Described as a 'doctor's clock', this timekeeper is one of the nearest Japanese equivalents to a watch. The extreme outer measurements including the protective Shitân-wood case, are about 5½ in x 1in. The movement is spring-driven with a balance. British Museum, London.

site the fixed pointer. Alarm trains and calendar-work were sometimes added, but not until after about 1700. The former utilised that primitive but nonetheless effective means by which a peg is inserted in the appropriate hour division at which the alarm is required to go off, and when the correct moment is reached the peg trips the alarm train.

Japanese timepieces are hardly ever signed or dated; and the use of specific materials in the construction is of little help as a guide to dating. The national garment, the kimono, provided no receptacle capable of housing anything like a pocket watch as it is known in the Western world, although small portable clocks disguised to resemble the inro, or medicine box, and attached to the girdle are known. There are other versions of tiny clocks, spring-driven naturally, which may have been carried similarly; and indeed, although attention has been principally focussed upon the three common categories of Japanese domestic clock, other styles – which Drummond Robertson refers to as 'fancy clocks' – will occasionally be found. Similarly, the Japanese seemingly made some large astronomical and other complicated and specialised clocks, but they must be so rare that it is unlikely one will ever be encountered.

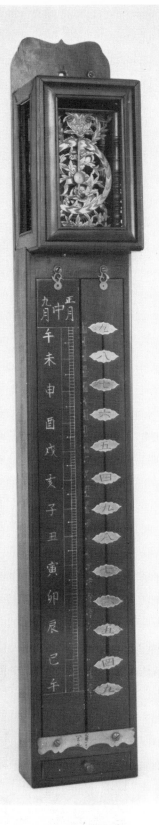

An elaborate example of the pillar clock with two time scales, one fixed and one moveable. At the top, the skeletonised movement is enclosed in a glazed Shitân-wood hood. British Museum, London.

right
In another development of the Japanese lantern clock, the weights are enclosed within a pedestal case such as this one in red lacquer. British Museum, London.

America

The most important single feature of the American horological heritage must be its single-handed pioneering development of mass-production methods, which were subsequently and so successfully adopted by the Swiss. Nevertheless, there was a craft tradition in America long before quantity and standardisation became important criteria in the field of horological manufacture.

The dividing line, very roughly, is the year 1800. Before that time, isolated craftsmen working very much in the English tradition, made some remarkably fine clocks, mainly longcases, and generally employing wood for both case and movement since brass was a scarce and expensive commodity. Among the earliest clockmakers working in America may be mentioned Abel Cottey, who set up in Philadelphia in 1682 and developed a considerable business making clocks that, with their flat-topped hoods, were indistinguishable from their English predecessors. In fact, Philadelphia and surrounding areas became well-known for clocks throughout the eighteenth century, as production gradually expanded. The second quarter of that century saw the introduction of break-arch dials and shallow domed tops, the cases themselves remaining largely undecorated. Then, from about 1760, the English provincial style of hood surmounted by curling 'horns' became popular

and remained in vogue throughout the rest of the century. Towards the end of that time, however, a kind of cresting of irregular outline was introduced, known colloquially as 'whale's-tails'. As brass became more readily available, the custom arose for thirty-hour duration movements still to be made of wood, but eight-day and longer-running mechanisms were fashioned in the more expensive material.

While the War of Independence (1775–83) was being fought, clockmaking in America came to a sudden halt, the craftsmen presumably being better occupied in other ways. However, when life returned to normal again, the longcase clock was now thought something of an extravagance – it was certainly expensive by the standards of those times – and a number of makers occupied themselves with the problem of producing a smaller and less costly timekeeper for ordinary domestic use. Hitherto American clockmaking had very much followed the English pattern, but now for the first time the Americans were on the point of creating a wholly native style, which in various manifestations was to remain popular for a long time to come.

There are four major types of American clocks, and at this point it will be useful to list them. The tower clock takes precedence, as being the earliest type of clock of which there are records, apart from a few domestic clocks that had been imported. There are any number of seventeenth- and eighteenth-century references to tower clocks, and as the years rolled by various famous names in American clockmaking history added such clocks to the repertoire of their manufactures. These included such giants as Simon Willard, Eli and Samuel Terry, and Seth Thomas.

Next come tall clocks, the American terminology for the English longcase. As has been mentioned Pennsylvania predominated in this particular manufacture, although such clocks were made all over the eastern seaboard. The earliest had metal dials about ten and a half inches square; lack of decoration throughout can probably be attributed to Quaker influence. Later, the dials became even larger. A derivation of the tall clock, often called the dwarf tall clock despite the apparent contradiction in terms, attained a height of not more than four feet. Very few seem to have been made, mainly in the early nineteenth century.

The third type of American clock is the wall clock. This came in a number of different shapes and styles, the earliest being the so-called 'wagon-wall'; such clocks are, to all intents and purposes, tall clock movements without any casing. Then came the 'banjo' clock, a style which, at its best, is both graceful and functional; many connoisseurs hold this to be the greatest artistic achievement by the Americans in the field of horology. The 'lyre' clock is much like the style just

mentioned except that its trunk is shaped like a lyre, while the 'girandole' has a circular base where the 'banjo' has a rectangular one.

Lastly, the American shelf clock derived directly from the early American producers' desire to find a more convenient and less expensive substitute for the tall clock. The earliest were made by the Willards and others after the War of Independence, while perhaps the finest development of this style was that introduced by Eli Terry in 1817 and known as the 'pillar and scroll' clock. Another clock style which, at its best, has an unsophisticated, even naive, attractiveness that is completely

opposite page
Made by Birge & Fuller of Bristol, Connecticut, about 1835, this style is known as the 'steeple on steeple'. The eight-day movement is driven by a wagon spring. British Museum, London.

above
This view of the movement of the steeple clock shows the wagon spring, which is flexed when the clock is wound up. British Museum, London.

Lyre clock, a variant of the banjo clock, made in the first quarter of the nineteenth century.

unique, the 'pillar and scroll' was as subject to the transience of fashion as any other artefact, and from a peak of popularity in 1825 it went into a decline, being replaced in the 1830s by the so-called 'bronze looking-glass clock' for the invention of which Chauncey Jerome claimed credit. At about this time, too, there appeared the OG clock, the name deriving from the wavelike moulding ('ogee') of its rectangular case; this continued to be made until 1914. It was the largest-selling product of the Connecticut branch of the industry.

It is a curious reflection on the state of the industry in America during the last century that even shelf clocks had to be weight-driven until 1845, when springs became available as a power source at reasonable cost. From that moment on, individual makers marketed a stream of different styles dictated by their own whims and, doubtless, by local demand. There are far too many of these for

anything like a comprehensive list to be given in the space available, but among the more popular may be mentioned the steeple clock, the beehive, and the acorn. Finally, there came the age of novelty – 'gimmickry' might be the best description to use – during the last two decades of the century. Negro automata figures with blinking eyes, and rejoicing in such titles as 'Topsey' and 'Sambo', clocks with conical pendulums, clocks in which the escapement causes a piece of weighted thread to wind and rewind itself continuously round a post, clocks in 'Marblized' cases somewhat resembling the Victorian attachment to polished slate – these and a host of others heralded the aesthetic decline of the American clock business, although doubtless it continued to be profitable.

Before turning to American watches, mention must be made of the phenomenon of mass-production and the key American figures in the clock industry concerned with it. Eli Terry (1772–1852), already referred to in connection with the 'pillar and scroll' clock, was the first man to produce cheap clocks in quantity, at first with wood but later with brass movements. In 1806, he took upon himself the production of a single order for four thousand clocks and devised not only the factory to make them in, but also the sales techniques for distributing and retailing them. In fact, he changed the whole system of clock purveying of those days in which, first, the clock was ordered and only then was it made by hand and sold to the client. Henceforth, clocks were to be made first, then ordered and sold subsequently. This was an important milestone in the commercial development of America.

The secret was that machines making identical parts could produce a hundred in the time it would take a craftsman to make one. At the peak of Terry's production of his 1806 order, clocks were being made at the rate of about sixty a day. Not only did Terry continue to develop his own quantity production and aggressive selling methods, but other inventive craftsmen were not slow to follow in his wake. Hydraulic power was used extensively to drive machinery, and by the 1820s clockmaking was at the peak of its boom, so much so that clocks were used in place of money as a form of currency. Even houses could be bought for sufficient clock movements. But inevitably the tide turned; by 1837, depression conditions brought clockmaking to a complete standstill and terminated for ever the demand for the wooden clock movement.

Boom conditions returned again the following year, however, after the introduction of yet another low-priced model, and by 1845 Connecticut clocks

A product of the Forestville Manufacturing Company is this 'acorn' clock of about 1850. British Museum, London.

226

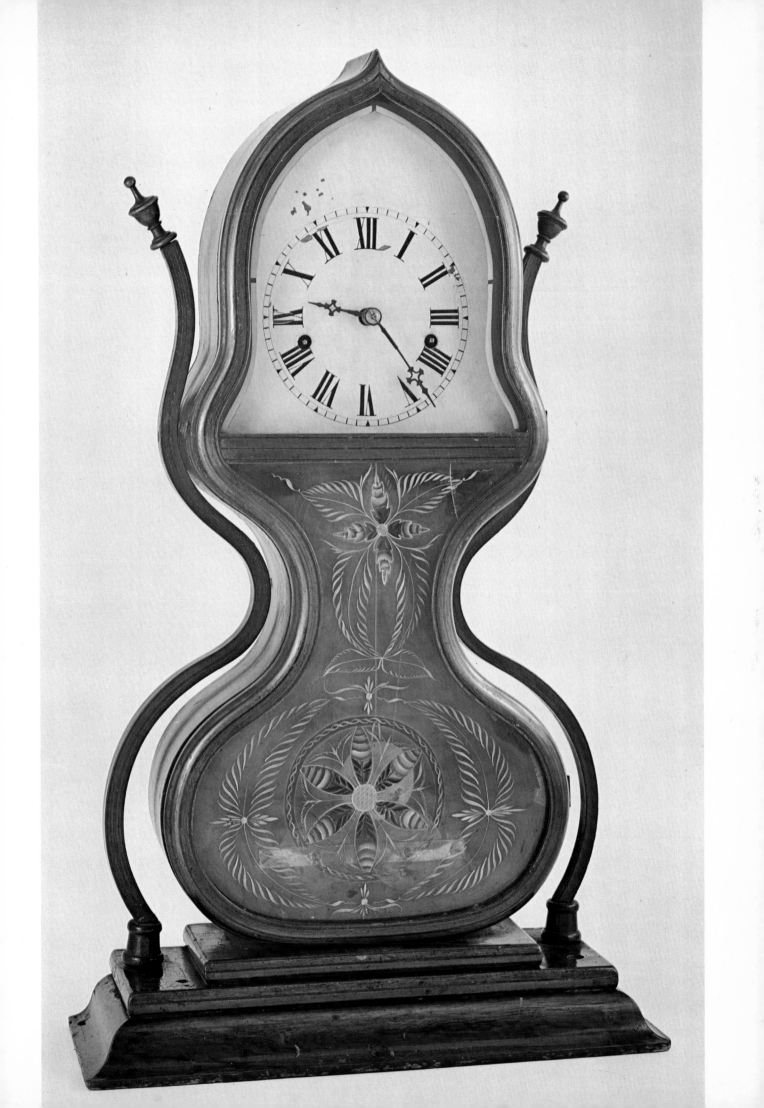

had cornered the market with an output of nearly one million clocks a year. This period saw the introduction into England of cheap brass weight-driven shelf clocks from the factories of one Chauncey Jerome, a leading Connecticut maker. This very prosperous period continued until 1857 when financial panic brought about another well-known manifestation of American commercial and industrial enterprise, consolidation. Clockmaking started to become concentrated within fewer and larger units, a trend that has continued to the present time. There are many illustrious names in

Shelf clock made by Seth Thomas about 1840 in Thomaston, Conn.

right
A fine banjo clock of about 1840 by A. Willard jr. American Museum in Britain, Claverton Manor, Bath.

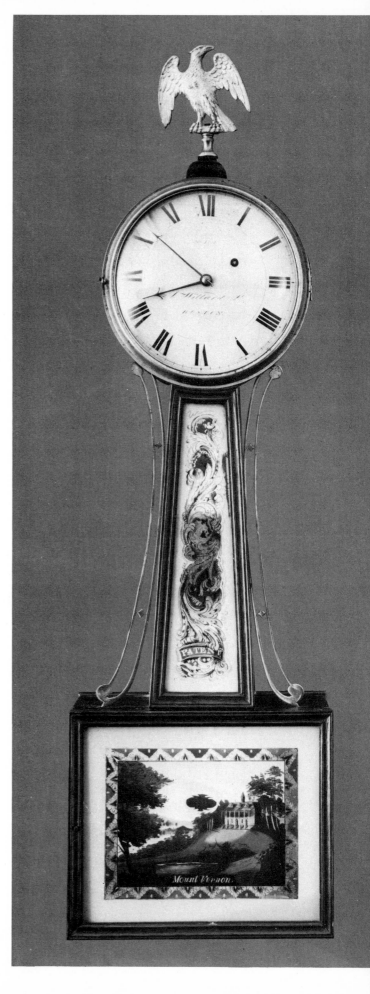

American clockmaking from both before and after the introduction of quantity production on factory lines. The Willards, Simon and Aaron, made many fine clocks of various styles, of which their 'banjo' is perhaps the most revered. Simon is said to have produced some four thousand of this model between 1802 and 1840. Gideon Roberts made another kind of wall clock, the 'wag-on-wall', in quantity and owned an assembly plant in Richmond, Virginia, after 1800; but it is not yet determined whether he used mass-production principles for his manufactures. Seth Thomas brought even greater commercialism to bear in the industry by buying the rights to certain patented designs of clocks from such as Eli Terry and producing them in quantity. He founded the Seth Thomas Clock Company in Plymouth, Connecticut, in 1853 employing some nine hundred operatives; the firm exists to this day.

The story of watchmaking in America is shorter – if no less dynamic – than that of clock manufacture. Although precise evidence is somewhat lacking, it would appear that, prior to about 1850, there was little native production in America, and those watches that survive are nearly always European imports even if they may have American names on the dials and movements. It is possible, too, that parts were brought into the country, and the assembly and finishing carried out locally. There is a record of a factory in Norwich, Connecticut, belonging to Thomas Harland, that is said to have produced two hundred watches and forty clocks annually, around 1800, but none of them is now known to exist. Luther Goddard is the first big name in American watchmaking. He began making watches in Shrewsbury, Massachusetts, in 1809 to counteract a shortage produced by tariff restrictions on the imported product and continued until a couple of years after the embargo was lifted in 1815, when he found himself no longer able to compete with the excessively low prices, whereupon he returned to gospel preaching. Even so, it has never been discovered whether his business – in which he certainly employed other watchmakers – was mainly that of assembling foreign-made parts, or whether the whole manufacture took place on American soil. A second attempt to quantity-produce watches – they only made between eight hundred and one thousand altogether – was started by the brothers Henry and J. F. Pitkin between 1837 and 1841. They started in East Hartford and finished in New York City. Jacob Custer of Norristown, Pennsylvania, is also reputed to have made a number of watches in 1843.

But the real start of the American mass-production watch came in 1850 with the founding of the Waltham Watch Company by Edward Howard and Aaron Dennison. They designed special machinery for volume production and laid the

The 'OG' clock is so named because of the ogee configuration of the wooden moulding in which it is framed. This eight-day example was made by E. N. Welch Manufacturing Company of Forestville, Connecticut. It was clearly made with export to Britain in mind, since it attempts to portray the royal arms in its lower panel.

basis of a business which survived successfully for exactly one hundred years, closing down in 1950. Another famous watch 'name', Elgin, started life in 1864 as the National Watch Company (of Elgin, Illinois), but pressure from the consuming public is said to have caused the incorporation of the location into the firm's name in 1874. It continued to make fine watches until the early 1960s.

Such watches as these were by no means cheap, however, and American brilliance next applied itself to the design and mass-production of the really inexpensive commodity. The Auburndale

229

Watch Company, first in the field in 1875, made a watch to sell for about fifty cents, but this attempt failed. Then in 1880 the Waterbury Watch Company started to produce watches well-known by that name to every collector; by the time that that design was discontinued, in 1891, total production had exceeded one million. Finally, of course, R. H. Ingersoll and his brother initiated the famous 'dollar watch' in 1892. There were many other adventurous attempts to mass-manufacture watches during the last quarter of the nineteenth century, and most met with inevitable failure. One famous maker that survives to the present time but which started in 1892 is the Hamilton Watch Company.

The story of horology in America is one of development and exploitation of the mass market immediately that this became a profitable expedient. It may be significant, in this context, that America had no real craft tradition to withstand – had it so chosen – this course of events, as happened in England. Also, of course, it followed exactly the same pattern as occurred in other industries, even though clocks were the first peacetime product to be so affected; there is a marginally earlier American mass-production contract for war material. If the self-evident contrast with the course of events in Japan may seem to be extreme, it is no more than a clear demonstration of the proposition with which this chapter commenced – that is to say, that the bands of the horological spectrum, on a global view, take such an infinity of shapes and forms, and the concepts range over such a variety of ingenious inventions, as to make the mastery of the entire field, in all its minutest detail, both a physical and an intellectual impossibility. Within that one limitation, the interest generated by this subject can be enormous and exceptionally enjoyable.

above
Early attempts to mass-produce cheap watches are represented by these examples of the series E and F produced by the Waterbury Watch Company in the last two decades of the nineteenth century. Series E (top) has the famous 'longwind' 9ft spring, requiring 140 half-turns of the button to wind the watch fully. Series F (below) was the first series using a spring of normal length.

right
The 'Yankee' was a very early model designed by R. H. Ingersoll, and it was made by the Waterbury Watch Company to be sold for $1. Museum of the Worshipful Company of Clockmakers, Guildhall, London.

left
Widely known as a 'Sambo' clock, this replica of an American 'nigger minstrel' is in a painted cast iron case with eyes that move in time with the escapement. It dates from about 1875. British Museum, London.

Collectors and Collecting

Now, in the mid 1970s, antiquarian horology as a hobby and pastime, and involving varying degrees of serious study on the part of its proponents, is big business. The world's great auction houses, but perhaps especially those in London, New York and Geneva, handle many thousands of pounds' worth of artefacts and related literature in this category each year, and membership of learned societies devoted to the subject continues to grow by leaps and bounds.

But it has not always been so. Until about twenty years ago, the number of serious collectors in England – to give one example – could almost be counted on the fingers of two hands. Many people believe that a significant side effect of the Second World War was a speeding-up in the steady decline of the hand-made article, and that one aspect of horology that gives it such a wide appeal today is that it can put back into appreciative hands objects that have been made individually, with great care and craftsmanship, and which consequently possess some indefinable but nonetheless recognisable characteristics not to be found in the wholly machine-made commodity. Such a phenomenon – a widespread hunger for the craftsman-made as opposed to the mass-produced article – manifests itself in many other directions at the present time and, when related to new goods, has of necessity become increasingly expensive to assuage.

In England, at different times, horology has been the fashionable recreation of kings. Charles II concentrated his attention upon Edward East's watches and the establishment of Greenwich Observatory, as we have seen, while George III built his own Royal Observatory at Kew, on the outskirts of London, in 1769, and there has survived to the present day notes written in his own hand on the correct method of disassembling a watch. Apparently he was given instruction in

such things when a young man, as part of his education; and he retained the great interest he thus acquired into later life, for not only did he commission the first watch with a lever escapement from Thomas Mudge, but he was also intimately concerned with John Harrison's chronometer experiments and himself tested H.5 at his observatory at Kew.

There were in the eighteenth century, too, a number of wealthy collectors and patrons of the arts who included clocks and watches incidentally in the 'cabinets' of curiosities and bygones which they assembled with such loving care: prominent among these was, of course, Sir Hans Sloane whose library and collections formed the nucleus from which the British Museum was established. This kind of general collecting has carried on, among the wealthiest of families, right to the present century with such remarkable accumulations as that assembled by John Pierpoint Morgan, the American financier and merchant banker, whose tastes embraced not only pictures, but ceramics, books, watches and other items of artistic value and interest. He was in his time – he died in 1913 – the greatest art collector in the world, and, in the field of horology, one of the great rarities among the literature on the subject is the *Catalogue* of the Morgan watch collection, which was sumptuously printed in a tiny edition in 1912. A mere forty-five copies of this *Catalogue* were produced on hand-made paper, and a handful more upon vellum, and they were all privately distributed to friends and to a few of the most important libraries. His watches are now in the Metropolitan Museum in New York.

It was probably not until the years between the two World Wars that the specialist horological collector really came into his own. To the older generation of collectors today, the magic names of Wetherfield, Iden, Prestige and others still conjure

The heart of Old Greenwich Observatory is Flamsteed House, named after the first Astronomer Royal, appointed by Charles II in 1675. It contains the famous Octagon Room, on the roof of which is the Time Ball, a visual time signal installed in 1833. Royal Greenwich Observatory, as it is now called, moved to Herstmonceux Castle, in the heart of the Sussex countryside, in the early 1950s, since London's 'smog' made observational astronomy virtually impossible.

The Octagon Room, the focal point of the old Observatory, was fitted out with equipment by the best makers, including the pair of clocks with two-seconds pendulums by Thomas Tompion.

Founded by George III as his private observatory – for he was keenly interested in horology and allied sciences – Kew Observatory, in the Old Deer Park at Richmond, on the outskirts of London, has been used to rate timekeepers and issue performance certificates for them since 1885, a duty taken over by the National Physical Laboratory in 1912. More recently it has been a Meteorological Office.

up a stream of anecdotes and recollections of specific clocks and watches associated with their collections. These, too, are inevitably linked with the names of the great dealers of those days – Malcolm Gardner, the Websters father and son, James Oakes and others, not to mention the famous 'old school' of craftsmen restorers. Nowadays, however, the sheer weight of numbers of people fascinated by the subject, each striving to follow that particular one of its multitudinous threads which especially appeals to him, makes the emergence of any one personality as a subject for admiration, respect, envy, speculation or any of the other passions or emotions associated with ardent collecting, that much more unlikely. Many would feel some slight loss as a result; it is almost as if the craftsman-orientated collector had been converted into some kind of movement representing 'horology for the masses'.

Much is to be learnt, nevertheless, from any study of these single-minded student-collectors of the 1920s and the 1930s since, being so early in the field, they had a much wider spectrum of choice – especially if they had only limited means – than will ever be available again. Sometimes, too, their collections became so important as entities that it was obvious that they should be preserved in their entirety when their owners died. Such a collection was, of course, that formed by Courtenay Ilbert and now in the British Museum. Another that has been preserved complete and is located at his home town of Bury St Edmunds is that formed by the late

Gershom Parkington, the famous cellist. Existing photographs of famous collectors of international status in their own surroundings are usually revealing, and it is important that they be preserved. Here we shall examine two such photographs, of a British and an American collector respectively.

Courtenay Adrian Ilbert has been mentioned sufficiently frequently to need little introduction. Born in 1888, he was educated at Eton and Cambridge, taking an honours degree in engineering, and then became professionally associated with a firm specialising in railways in India. During the Second World War he was engaged with the Ministry of Supply in that division dealing with the control of timber supplies. But principally, throughout his life from schooldays onwards, he was fascinated by horology and collected avidly. He was a man of retiring disposition, gentle and quiet but shrewd and, in his own way, both friendly and generous. His encyclopedic knowledge of horology became legendary in his own lifetime, as did his collection and supporting library, both without doubt the finest of their kind in the world of his day. He was generous in helping others of like interests with explanations illustrated by examples from among his own acquisitions, and frequently lent his greatest treasures for public exhibition, losing thereby on occasion when they came back from some overseas commitment deranged or damaged; yet he never grumbled. He lived in a large double-fronted Georgian house in Chelsea, in central London, which had been in his family for several hundred years. The clock room, which led off on the left of a large hallway, ran the full depth of the house, of which it had once clearly been the drawing-room. Although it was a large room by any standards, one had to pick one's way with the greatest care between the enormous number of 'exhibits' – of all shapes and sizes – which included a double line of clocks, placed back to back, and running the length of the room, all available wall-space being already occupied by others of the same species. The carillon clock by Nicholas Vallin of 1598, mentioned elsewhere in this book, was elevated upon a scaffolding in order to obtain a reasonable drop for the weights, and anyone wishing to inspect it closely had to do so by ladder. Yet another famous feature of Ilbert's clockroom was the huge chest of drawers – the type is generally described as a Wellington chest – in which he kept his working 'library' of watches. Its twenty-four drawers contained over one thousand specimens spanning three hundred years of watchmaking, and it was in constant use as a reference source when enquirers brought watches

right
One of the greatest collectors of this century, the American financier John Pierpoint Morgan published this catalogue of his watches which has become a great rarity on its own account.

Major Paul Chamberlain, seen in his workroom. His bench has a brass plate upon its facing end bearing the name of Jules Jurgensen, a very celebrated Danish craftsman, and its original owner.

An outstanding feature of Courtenay Ilbert's famous collection of clocks and watches, now in the British Museum, was this giant chest of drawers, in which he kept his 'reference library' of over 1,000 watches and watch movements. As shown here, he used this constantly to identify timepieces brought to him.

to show him or dealers to sell to him. Ilbert enjoyed the friendliest relations with the trade at large, since he never tried to purchase behind their backs or outdo them at auctions. The result was that he was always given first refusal of anything of special interest that came on the market, and one dealer in particular – whom Ilbert had helped to establish himself – acted virtually as his agent. The two used to go on protracted purchasing expeditions abroad, especially in Europe where Ilbert made some remarkable discoveries.

Ilbert died in 1956 after a lengthy illness which, towards its climax, was both painful and excessively disabling. Yet his indomitable spirit enabled him to continue the work he loved right to the very end, even after he had to a substantial extent lost the power of speech. He had concerned himself with the production of a fresh edition of the clock and watch collector's 'bible' – Britten's *Old Clocks and Watches and their Makers* – as co-editor with two other eminent horologists, one of whom had already predeceased him. The finishing touches were put to the text only while he was confined to his bed in hospital, and it is a fitting memorial to such a man that at least some part of his enormous knowledge did find its way on to the printed page

for the benefit of many who will always try, however unsuccessfully, to emulate him.

Major Paul Chamberlain, an American born in Three Oaks, a small town in the state of Michigan, in 1865 was, like Courtenay Ilbert, an engineer by profession. Educated at Michigan State College and Cornell University, he had established himself as a successful structural engineer by the advent of the First World War. He had also amassed a collection of some three hundred watches which, now that he had to turn his attention from his hobby to the exacting task of producing the much needed 75mm gun, he presented to the Chamberlain Memorial Museum in his home town. He subsequently prepared a detailed catalogue in which every item of this collection was described and classified.

When Chamberlain was finally demobilised from the army with distinction, his engineering practice had virtually disappeared, and his health was impaired sufficiently as to discourage him from attempting to rebuild it. He therefore turned the full force of his intellect and enthusiasm upon antiquarian horology, starting a second collection of watches which, when he died in 1940, numbered some twelve hundred specimens.

Thus, for a substantial number of years, Chamberlain lived in and for that special ambience of antiquarian horology which he constructed in his home in the Adirondacks and which became the staff of life not only to him but also to the many students in the field who visited him and came to regard his workroom almost as a shrine. There appeared in 1941 – sadly, he never lived to see it in print – what most horologists regard as a fitting epitaph, his book *It's About Time* which, without any shadow of doubt, is the most original and competent book on any aspect of antiquarian horology ever to emanate from the American continent. It reflects the travels far and wide of the author in search of material – in this respect, too, he resembled Ilbert – and also his interest in people, for he was able to cultivate the friendship and, inevitably, command the respect of leading craftsmen in many countries. He had a formidable memory which was well stocked with a bank of historical, technical and biographical detail, any minutest part of which he could instantly recall and from which, over some twenty-five years, he was able to formulate the many articles, certainly over one hundred, which he contributed to domestic and foreign trade and technical journals. In America, Chamberlain was regarded as just as great a horological guru as Ilbert was in Britain, yet both were modest, retiring men who would have been horrified at the thought of themselves as anything other than mere students and researchers, more experienced perhaps than the great majority of those who came to sit at their feet, but 'experts' never!

This small device – a mere 2½in in diameter and just over 1in thick – is an alarm mechanism of French origin, known as a 'reveille-matin' and made in enormous quantities by Antoine Redier in the mid nineteenth century. The pointer is turned to a figure corresponding with the difference in hours between the hour of setting and the alarm going off. A spring-driven train drives a tiny pendulum, gradually turning the hand back to zero – twelve o'clock – when the alarm sounds.

William Gossage, who died in 1877, became a famous industrial chemist, and his only horological patent, taken out in 1823, was for an alarm device which he is said to have needed to awake him at five o'clock in the morning to pursue his studies. His alarm is used in conjunction with a pocket watch, placed on top with its winding square fitted into a similarly squared pipe, connected to the mechanism. As the watch runs down, the pipe is turned and this, correspondingly, turns back the alarm dial to zero, when the bell sounds.

The environment with which such a man as Chamberlain surrounds himself and in which he can work best is well demonstrated by the photograph of him in his workroom – always, seemingly, called the Schoolroom, because it was constructed from the remains of a demolished schoolhouse and added, as an extension, on to his home. His workbench – he is facing away from it in the photograph – was originally the property of Jules Jurgensen, a nineteenth-century member of a very famous Danish family of craftsmen, who were based in Copenhagen and much respected by collectors everywhere. The brass nameplate on the side is just visible. At the left, clearly discernible under its glass shade, is his astronomical clock by an early nineteenth-century Paris maker who became famous for the handful of such clocks he made. His name was Raingo – nobody ever seems to have recorded any Christian name for him – and his surviving planetary clocks, a more appropriate description than just astronomical clocks, include specimens in the possession of the Queen and located at Windsor Castle, in the Sir John Soane Museum in London, and in the Musée des Arts et Métiers in Paris. The last-mentioned was incomplete when Raingo died, and it was finished by Paul Garnier, another famous French craftsman of the day.

Other elements which contribute to the sheer atmosphere of this photograph include the portraits of clockmakers on the walls, and even on this small scale, the faces of Ellicott, Graham, Tompion and Mudge can be clearly identified. Cham-

While hardly in the mass-produced range, this small clock by Payne, South Molton Street, London, is a delightful relic of Regency London which, because it is a timepiece only, will be somewhat less expensive than a clock with additional trains.

berlain possessed many books on horology in a variety of languages – some of which can be seen – and also collected old clock- and watchmaking tools, which, of course, he used. The lights, adjustable if in somewhat primitive manner, reflect precisely that air of disregard for everything but the mechanically important which so many of the old school of craftsmen adopted. Their workshops customarily dusty and, to the lay eye, untidy to the point of chaos, they yet knew where everything was and, in the tiny space upon their benches in which they actually worked – for the remainder of the work-top would be teeming with hand tools and other paraphernalia, in total disarray – they could turn out the most immaculate results, achieving fit and finish such as would never be believed possible simply by viewing their working conditions. Yet this is the way they liked it.

This photograph of Chamberlain's workroom acts as a good starting point for anybody surveying the horological scene today with, perhaps, a view to starting up a collection, even if only on modest lines. The Raingo clock is but one example of the many classes of antique clocks that have priced themselves out of the market so far as anyone but the wealthy is concerned – the figure fetched by one of his clocks when it was sold in Zürich in 1970,

Seen from the back, the Payne clock shows obvious signs of
quality, from the style of the pendulum to the provision of a
capability to anchor it, when the clock is to be carried about.
The movement is spring-driven, with a fusee and a duration
of eight days.

when the peak of the market had by no means been
reached, was 27,500 Swiss francs, and this was just
for a *pendule de cheminée* – so that it can be disre-
garded for all practical purposes. Those who are
sufficiently fortunate as to be able to muster the
funds needed to acquire horological articles in the
top flight of artistic and technical achievement for
their collections have no need of advice from this
book: they will without doubt be able to afford the
professional advice of dealers and others who are
active in the marketplace for such objects. Here it
is the intention to deal with more moderately
priced yet collectable items such as can still be
found from time to time in the average antique
shop or auction room. Some of the fringe items –
that is to say, ephemera associated with clocks and
watches rather than the timekeepers themselves –
come up regularly in the bigger auction rooms, too,
but as yet have not become popular enough to
force up the price beyond the reach of the average
small collector's purse.

So what clocks can such a novice collector of
meagre means aspire to? It has to be recognised
that, except for the magical exception that proves
the rule, the seventeenth century is wholly out of
court. So, too, is most of the eighteenth century
except possibly for the odd and inevitably rather
coarse provincial item.

The nineteenth century, however, offers some
scope provided the collector does not aspire too
high. English clocks of this period were, of course,
still craft-made, and the Victorian over-
elaboration of case that so many exhibit – although
restraint in such details is by no means unknown –
has taken on, in the appreciation of many connoisseurs, a kind of 'folksy' quaintness which makes
them now far more widely accepted than ever
before. Looking at Europe, the commonplace and,
from the collector's point of view, once universally
despised Vienna regulator nowadays fetches anything between one and two hundred pounds, but is
an interesting and relatively unresearched subject
for study, as is, too, the round French factory-
made clock movement fitted into so many different
kinds of case. Both are admirably functional as
well as collectable. Black Forest clocks are not yet
popular among collectors although they certainly
merit attention, if only on account of the ingenuity
of their wooden movements; but the early specimens are rather unlikely to be encountered and
would probably make a good price if they were.
The postman's alarm is a perfectly serviceable
clock, simple though it is. Cuckoo clocks and similar extravagances – the other well-known style is
the trumpeter clock – have a novelty value that
perhaps serves to inflate their intrinsic worth for
the average collector, especially if they can also be
construed as 'antique'.

None of the clock styles mentioned so far has
derived wholly from the true mass-production systems pioneered in the last century – even the

The plates of antique watch movements have customarily been separated by pillars which, at first comparatively plain, soon became the subject of embellishment. The potance, which is riveted to the underside of the plate and forms part of the fusee stop work, was also the subject of decoration, often elaborate, but not so varied in style as the pillars. Some of the many different designs of pillars are shown here (left to right, top to bottom): Tulip, Roman, Elaborated Roman; Ellicott, Decorated baluster (English provincial usage), Roman (Dutch version); Decorated baluster (Dutch version), Square baluster, Bombé baluster.

factory-made French round movement has its roots in the eighteenth century – so at some point a collector will start a fashion in this area. It could be profitable; mass-produced items are consumable and instantly replaced once they become even moderately unserviceable. Fashion, too, plays a large part. It is likely, therefore, that far fewer still survive than superficial consideration might suggest. The same thing applies as our survey of the field advances into the present century. The period before, during and for a few years after the First World War saw interesting things happening horologically: the folding travelling clock came into its own, often based on the so-called Goliath watch, and the wristwatch was in its initial stages of development. But it is very much an unexplored field up to now.

The 'golden age' of the watch cock is generally considered to be around the turn of the seventeenth and eighteenth centuries when the cock had reached both its largest size and the peak of its decorative style. As time passed, the cock tended to get smaller, and its decoration to degenerate, until eventually, following an experimental period in which various random shapes were employed for the table, it gradually settled into the plain wedge-shape which is common to the present time.

Clocks have hardly ever suffered that sad fate of so many thousands of watches, of being uncased for the sake of the melting value of the precious metal involved. However, their movements are sometimes found to have been rehoused in cases which the discriminating collector recognises as being so unrelated in period and anachronistic as to render them undesirable, and he may then impose an arbitrary divorce upon such an unhappy 'marriage'. If he cannot afford a reproduction case in the correct style, he may still run the movement on show, as an exhibition piece. The best practice does not accept the philosophy, therefore, that any case is better than none at all: if the case is blatantly inappropriate it will detract so very substantially from any merit the movement may possess. In this the pure layman might very well disagree, being possibly concerned more with the clock's function than with its original appearance.

So what about the multitude of watch movements, long since separated from their cases – the biggest melting-down of precious metal watch cases of all time took place in the great British Depression of the 1930s – which appear on the market with fair regularity? They make marvellously collectable objects, from all sorts of points of view. The mainly mechanically minded collector will want them, perhaps, to demonstrate the workings of various kinds of escapements, some common and not too expensive, others rare and rather costly, or to show the lay-out of different trains or the idiosyncrasies of particular makers. If a principal interest is in the decoration of the watch movement through the ages, then the watch cock and slide plate – the latter houses the balance spring regulator – and also the pillars separating the plates of older movements will be the main focus of attention. Most such decorated movements might very well be relatively uninteresting mechanically: the verge escapement in watches went on for so many centuries that it is most unlikely to be collected on its own account, yet from the decorative viewpoint many such movements are highly desirable, displaying an enormous variety of styles and qualities of craftsmanship. National styles, too, can be well defined in this kind of collection.

Mention of the watch cock brings to mind the collector who specialises in this single component, on account of its intrinsic beauty or perhaps because of the huge variety of designs with which it has been decorated, or yet again because certain designs are very rare and therefore desirable. But how has it happened that so very many watch cocks have come to be separated from their movements – for they appear in large quantities from time to time in the sale rooms?

The answer is again to be found in the dreadful economic crisis of the 1930s. Watch cases were destroyed wholesale for their metal value, but antique watch movements had intrinsic value too. Although the basic structural materials were common metals like brass and steel, all visible brasswork, the plates, the wheels and decorative elements already mentioned like the pillars, cock and slide plate were gilded, and the gold thus deposited upon these surfaces could be recovered. The gilding process used, incidentally, bears no relationship to the electro-deposition commonplace today; it was variously called mercurial gilding, fire gilding or water gilding and consisted essentially of brushing on to the preheated brass surface a sponge-like amalgam of gold and mercury which had previously been prepared. When the amalgam had taken hold and a good surface obtained, the mercury was driven off as vapour by the application of more heat, leaving the gold

ASTRONOMICAL CLOCK.

'fired' on to the brass. The finish that can be obtained by this process cannot be duplicated by any other, according to enthusiasts; but it is a very hazardous one to carry out, since mercury vapour is an accumulative and highly toxic gas, and those who operated the process risked an abnormally high death rate.

So when bullion dealers melted watch cases nearly fifty years ago, they were also on the lookout for movements that would be worth scrapping for their gold content. The watch cock, however, being very highly decorated, was often separated from the rest of the movement and put aside, to be mounted up subsequently as a piece of jewellery. In consequence, many watch cocks reappeared as necklaces, brooches and the like, and collectors today will frequently go to some trouble to have such items reconstituted and all traces of mounting-up removed, so that the cocks can take their rightful places again as intricate and often beautiful examples of handiwork, upon which the

left
This hand-coloured print from the *Repository of the Arts*, published by R. Ackermann in 1824, illustrates one of Raingo's famous astronomical clocks. A similar one can be identified under its glass dome to the left of the picture of Chamberlain's workshop.

below
The keys forming the main feature of this illustration are mounted upon a gold 'Albert' chain, which is now intended for use as a bracelet, an example of the tendency to make items of jewellery out of such objects. Styles to be found in this circle include the plain crank key – said to be one of the earliest forms – the folding crank, the continental decorated crank key, and a variety of other later forms. In the centre are male and female versions of the Breguet or 'tipsy' key, while on the other side, and bordering the picture, are eight steel Victorian keys in virtually mint condition, all found together in the same old-established London jeweller's shop, where they may well have stayed since first being taken into stock.

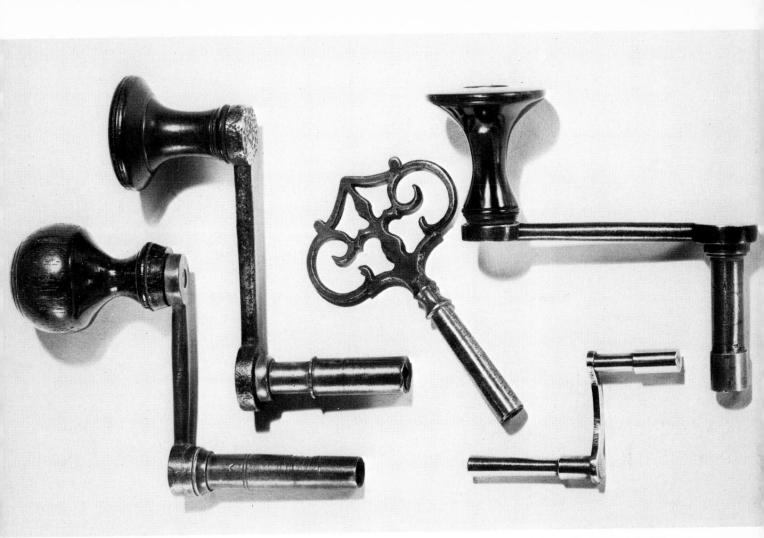

Cranked keys for clocks are customary for the conventional longcase and bracket designs, and these usually have a turned wooden handle. The wholly brass cranked key comes from a Vienna regulator, while the steel cast key with pierced plate is a mass-produced late nineteenth-century key.

greatest skill has been lavished. Much of this work, it is thought, was done by women; and, even in Tompion's day, the specialist watch cock maker charged substantial sums for the finest examples of his work.

Much speculation has focussed upon the source of the designs incorporated into watch cock decoration. No two cocks will ever be found to be identical, but the differences are often so slight that they can only be attributed to individual handworking, and one celebrated collector in this field, a few years ago, reckoned to have amassed over forty cocks which were clearly based on the same original design. This suggests that watch cock makers may have had pattern books – in the same way as decorative engravers did – from which to work, but although a few such items have survived in other European countries, evidence of an equivalent English practice is so far rather limited.

A separate book could easily be based upon watch cock decoration: the motifs, ranging from

geometric to pictorial, from 'inhabited foliage', as the auctioneers describe it, to all kinds of arabesques, from grotesque masks to mythical birds and beasts, reflects a vast gamut of invention. Then there is the matter of symmetry on either side of an imaginary line through the centre of the cock table; at certain periods this is popular, at others not. In the later stages of the development of the watch cock, all sorts of strange shapes of cock table were tried out. The conventional circular table gave place to squares, rectangles, stars, crowns and a host of others that defy easy description. By contrast, in the earlier stages, around the turn of the seventeenth century, strangely shaped features, generally described as 'wings', projected from the neck of the cock. Cocks can be found into which the balance spring regulator has been integrated, so that, to operate it, the whole centre of the cock table must be rotated. The index, or pointer, is fixed to this table and indicates the degree of regulation against a scale engraved upon the wide neck of the cock. Most watch cocks are made of brass that has been fire-gilt. The use of silver as a decorative metal for watch movements is found, but has never been common; silver cocks, as a result, are scarce and sought after. The decorative content of a watch cock is sometimes important. On either side of the year 1700, for instance, watch cocks

above

above
It is not uncommon for the outer case of a pair-cased watch to have become separated from the rest and, especially if it is decorative, for it to have survived as a separate entity. The four such outer cases shown here are clad in leather, reverse-painted horn (a cheaper alternative to enamelled work), tortoiseshell inlaid with silver, and shagreen. An interesting collection can be formed from items such as these.

above left
These verge watch movements display a variety of decoration ranging over the period from about 1680 to the end of the eighteenth century. Features of significance include regular or irregular borders to the cock feet, which also may be either pierced or solid according to the period, and the size and complexity of decoration of the slide plate housing the balance spring regulator.

left
Most watch movements are enriched with fire-gilding on the base metal, which is generally brass. Silver has been used only very sparingly in this context, but is found in the heritage of several European countries. This illustration includes British, French and Dutch movements of the eighteenth century.

decorated with the royal coat of arms seem, for some reason which is not at present understood, to have been confined to a particular type of watch, the so-called 'wandering-hour dial' watch, which has been described on page 128. It is inconceivable that all such watches, and there must have been plenty of them since a fair number have survived intact, can have had royal connections; yet there is almost always either a portrait of the monarch on dial or movement, or a coat of arms, or both. Other rare and desirable forms of decoration on watch cocks include the monogrammed cock, in which initials, generally those of the watchmaker, are woven into the decoration of the cock table; the masonic cock, which features the emblems and symbols of Freemasonry, such symbolism often being repeated upon the watch dial; cocks with signatures and dates, displayed on an otherwise blank area around the edge of the cock foot, a fashion which seems to have lasted a few years only around 1750 and which also seems confined to a type of cock generally described as having a 'lace edge' to the cock table; and finally the only wholly pictorial watch cock, which features a farmyard

245

Short fob chains can be found in an enormous variety of styles and materials, from the elegance of enamelled and gem-set gold to the more simple cut steel versions shown here. The double fob chain is steel inlaid with multicoloured gold, and is most probably of Italian origin or made by immigrant craftsmen from that country. The folding bed-hook shown attached to the right-hand chain was used to suspend the watch from the drapes of the bed when retiring for the night. An alternative to this procedure was to use a watch stand (see page 247).

above right
Watch chains emerged in their final form during the second half of the nineteenth century, and many different linkages are to be found. Among those shown here are a Queen's chain, distinguished by its metal tassel, and an Albert made of plaited elephant's hair reminiscent of the Indian Empire.

scene, and of which several closely related but nonetheless different arrangements survive.

The watch, as such, has many more ancillaries associated with its operation than has the clock. There have been, and perhaps still are, collectors specialising in clock keys, but the range of these is very limited. The normal type of crank-shaped key will have a turned wood – or, very exceptionally, ivory – handle, and they come in sizes varying from the normal domestic bracket and longcase key to the very much larger type needed for a turret clock. Later types of keys for such as carriage clocks and the Vienna regulator are normally made entirely of brass, sometimes cranked and sometimes straight. Many of the mass-produced clocks had cheap cast steel keys, sometimes with flat pierced and shaped plates by which to turn them. That more or less covers the whole range.

Watch keys, on the other hand, come in as many varieties as do watch cocks, and a far wider range of materials was used in their construction. The cranked key, usually in gilt metal, is considered to be the earliest style devised, but it is also believed to have had a very long life. Apart from this it is exceedingly difficult to be specific about dates or the currency of styles. Watch keys are often so elaborate and have been worked in such unfamiliar materials that they must have been the product of jewellers or perhaps specialists; watch key makers are almost unknown as a branch of any craft, however. There is hardly any literature on this subject, which never seems to have attracted the attention of researchers, perhaps because watch keys so often appeal to ladies as an item of adornment – they are frequently worn mounted as charms on bracelets – and have not yet come into their own as objects for serious study. Mechanically they comprise very few types: firstly the crank key with its near relation the folding crank which has its two joints hinged so that, when not in the functional Z-shape as used for winding, it lies completely flat, and secondly the resilient type are the only departures from the conventional straight one-piece key. The resilient key – sometimes called the Breguet or 'tipsy' key – has a ratchet arrangement built into it to prevent the key, and therefore the watch, being wound up the wrong way. Rotated in the right direction the key winds up normally; in the reverse direction the handle of the key simply freewheels, accompanied by the sound of the click riding over the tops of the ratchet wheel teeth. Both 'male' and 'female' keys are known – the latter is the conventional kind which fits over the winding square, while the former is the reverse, that is to say, the key itself terminates in a solid square which fits into a corresponding aperture on the watch, generally not for winding up but for such functions as altering the hands or setting an

The alternative to using the folding bed-hook for securing the watch at night was to place it in a watch stand, and it may be that hooks were used only when travelling. Watch stands, like the other watch ancillaries, come in a profusion of designs and materials, the latter ranging from wood and metal to papier-mâché and pottery. The Rococo example showing Father Time with putto and hourglass is of eighteenth-century German origin, and the inside of the watch compartment has been carved in a quilted effect. The turned mahogany stand surmounted by ivory finials is a relic of Georgian England, while the third, made of fruitwood edged in box, is a nineteenth-century provincial piece.

The most famous workshop print is the Stradanus version of about 1578. This print, which appeared in the *Universal Magazine* in 1748, lacks perspective but is interesting on account of the octagonally dialled 'Act of Parliament' clock hanging on the wall, especially since it predates the Act itself by half a century.

alarm dial. Breguet, the famous French craftsman, not only favoured the resilient key, which is sometimes called after him, but also used male keys for various purposes. There are several large collections of watch keys in museums throughout the world. In London one of the best is that in possession of the Worshipful Company of Clockmakers and exhibited with the rest of its collection at Guildhall Library. In America a large privately owned collection was presented some years back to the Rollins College Art Museum in Winter Park, Florida, and must be one of the best collections in that country.

Keys are but one of several kinds of ancillary to the watch, and the others, being often decorative as well as functional and therefore popularly collected for themselves, will bear brief scrutiny. The watch key was generally carried with the watch,

and attached to the same fixing, usually some form of watch-chain, that connected it to the wearer. When pockets were first introduced, about 1625, they were confined to the breeches and remained thus until the long waistcoat made its appearance about 1675. The fob, as it came to be known, was the pocket in the waistband of the trousers in which the valuables might well come to be carried, hence the highwayman's cry of 'Turn out your fobs!' The short chains called fob-chains, on one end of which would be attached the watch, had one or more swivel hooks at the other end which would be allowed to hang out of the top of the fob pocket and from which dangled watch key, seal and other small accessories. When waistcoats came into fashion, the short fob-chain continued in use but was allowed to hang out of the waistcoat pocket instead. The long chain, extending across the front of the wearer and terminating in opposite pockets of the waistcoat is a relatively modern development, certainly not earlier than mid nineteenth century. Indeed, various styles of long watch-chain are often referred to as 'Alberts', after the Prince Consort, while a particular style of chain which incorporates metal tassels is always known as a 'Queen's chain'. Such tassels were a commonplace decorative addition to certain ladies' accoutrements, such as muff and skirt guards – the latter used to hoist the hem of the skirt out of reach of mud and puddles in the streets, without any necessity for bending down – and might well have

been a fashion originated by Queen Victoria. This would explain the extension of the term 'Queen's' to a watch-chain, since it hardly seems likely that the monarch would have sported one herself.

The ladies' version of the fob-chain is called the chatelaine. An ornamental arrangement of chains and swivel hooks, the whole device hangs from the belt or waistband by a large hook located behind the main boss from which the rest is suspended. The chatelaine was originally used by the mistress of a medieval castle, as a means of carrying about the various keys she needed; in its later forms, it not only accommodated the watch, with its key and odd seals, but also such other small but useful accessories as scissors, thimbles and trinkets of various kinds. In some chatelaines – especially those very decorative and nowadays enormously expensive versions enriched with costly enamelling and pearls, and in which watch, chatelaine and all associated items are decorated *en suite* – the suspension hook has disappeared, and it would seem that such are really just highly elaborate fob-chains.

Fob seals, interesting study though they are, cannot be defined as part of the horological lineage and are therefore outside the scope of the present work. One accessory that will often be found both on fob-chain and on chatelaine, and which can be included, however, is the folding bed hook. Whether at home or *en voyage*, the owner of a watch did not necessarily leave it in his dressing-table

drawer when he retired at night; if it was a repeater, he could discover the time at will and without any need of a light by setting off the repeating action. He therefore hung it from the drapes of the bedstead by a bed hook, or placed it in a watch stand. Bed hooks were generally made retractable, like the blade of a pocket knife, because they were of necessity sharp and could not be carried about except with some kind of protection for the wearer. Sometimes the hook forms part of the watch key, and pivots into the body of it when not in use. Others were made as entities in their own right, and purely on stylistic grounds – for, like the watch key, the history of the bed hook remains largely a mystery to the present day – it would seem that they may have been used for several centuries, certainly well into Victorian times.

Mention of the watch stand brings to mind again the photograph of Chamberlain's workshop, for two of these can be seen on top of the bookcase at the back of the room. Left of centre is a very handsome type, in which the watch is framed in an arch supported by two pillars. From a black and white photograph it is difficult to be certain, but it looks as if this stand is surfaced in tortoiseshell. On the same level but right of centre, is a smaller rectangular watch stand of a well-established type, with the main panels in a finely figured wood and the edges banded with box. Such stands as this were essentially country-made pieces, but the graining and colour contrast between the woods

Portrait prints of clockmakers, usually copied from original paintings which, in many cases, no longer exist, cover a wide range of periods and personalities.

far left
This portrait of George Graham is of interest as being a nineteenth-century reproduction of an eighteenth-century mezzotint by J. Fabre, after a painting by T. Hudson.

centre left
William James Frodsham, F.R.S., one of the few clockmakers to have achieved this distinction, is here seen in a lithograph by Ada Cole from a painting by an unknown artist. Printed by Day & Son.

centre right
Abraham-Louis Breguet, probably the most famous horologist of all time, is known from several portraits as well as a sculptured bust. This lithograph by Langlumé is taken from a painting by A. Chazal.

above
One of the rarer portrait mezzotints of clockmakers of the later eighteenth century, this representation of John Ellicott, F.R.S., was executed by Robert Dunkarton after a painting by Nathaniel Dance. Like so many of these prints, it incorporates a wealth of period detail in the clothes and furniture, making it a fascinating social document.

One kind of watch paper is the hand-worked type, employing one or more of quite a range of techniques, which serves a purely decorative and possibly sentimental function. Apart from colouring, these can include cut paper, drawn thread, embroidery and the like.

opposite page
The second kind of watch paper is the one placed within the watch case by the repairer to advertise his wares and services. Occasionally such repairers noted upon the back of the paper the work done on the watch, the amount charged, and other useful information.

left
The third category of horological print of which examples might be sought concerns the illustration of some complex clock, such as this astronomical clock by Jos. Naylor of Nantwich, Cheshire. Britten mentions two clocks by this maker, one in the Cluny Museum, Paris. The print is dated 1751, and Naylor died the following year. Museum of the Worshipful Company of Clockmakers, Guildhall, London.

give them great appeal. They are unlikely to be earlier than of nineteenth-century provenance, but examples of eighteenth-century watch stands do survive, often in exuberant styles involving allegorical figures of Time with putti in Rococo settings, or with Atlas supporting the watch as though it were the world. There are innumerable varieties of this useful adjunct to the watch, mainly in wood but sometimes in metal, while there are versions in porcelain and pottery, as well as in less obvious materials like ivory, which was also used for turned finials surmounting wooden stands, especially those in more typically architectural styles. Museum collections do not seem to embrace this kind of artefact in any organised way, and one of the finest collections was formed privately at the beginning of the present century by Sir Gerald Ryan. This collection was extensively illustrated in the December 1919 issue of *The Connoisseur*, which even now forms almost the total corpus of literature on the subject. The styles and qualities of watch stands included in the Ryan collection seem almost entirely to have disappeared, and examples that do appear from time to time in the auction rooms are generally of much lesser merit. It would be interesting to know where some of the finer of these objects are now located.

There is just one more somewhat ephemeral ancillary to the pocket watch, and that is the watch paper. Essentially this takes the form of a liner placed between the inner and outer cases of a pair-cased watch to ensure a good tight fit, and since many such watches will still be found to have a rose silk liner rather than a paper one, and often obviously antique silk at that, it may be that this was the original form of the watch 'paper', placed between the cases by the maker of the watch himself.

In its generally understood and most frequently encountered form, however, the watch paper takes the shape of a printed advertisement for a watchmaker, who when traceable, usually turns out to be a craftsman who has repaired or overhauled the watch at some time in its career. Sometimes he will be found to have written on the back of the watch paper a note of the exact work he has carried out as well as the charge made for it, while his printed inscription will certainly contain useful information about his business address and the type of work or wares which he offers. It is not unusual to find several such papers compressed into the outer case of a watch – even occasionally to the extent of nine or ten – and where they have been annotated by the craftsmen concerned they provide an interesting chronological record of the performance of the watch often over quite a span of years. There is a fine collection amounting to some twelve hundred such papers, arranged in three volumes, in the Library of the Worshipful Company of Clockmakers of the City of London.

There are other varietes of watch papers, however, whose provenance is not quite so well understood. It was once believed, for instance, that the embroidered fabric 'papers', often with entwined initials or a heart motif, were worked by the lovelorn maiden for her betrothed, and indeed such is probably the case. But certain versions of these, notably the one portraying a sailor with his sweetheart which is usually both painted and stitched, recur frequently in nearly identical form and so must have been worked from some kind of pattern. Quite a range of techniques was used in making these decorative papers of the non-advertising sort, such as drawn thread, cut paper – often in the most intricate and minute patterns, so that one wonders not only at the patience needed but at the size of the scissors used – and painting upon paper or silk, not to mention the hand-colouring of printed decorative motifs such as maps and marine scenes. Another form used was the calendar, while equation tables are commonly found as watch papers, but usually with a watchmaker's name and address in the central space. Very occasionally a watch paper will be found to advertise some kind of business other than watchmaking, but these are combined with a calendar and were obviously given away as a gimmick with the commodity concerned.

Although advertising had not reached the advanced state that prevails today, it was quite normal during the last century for craftsmen to solicit custom by taking space in street directories to display what they could offer. This typical page comes from Wrightson & Webb's *Directory* of Birmingham for 1835.

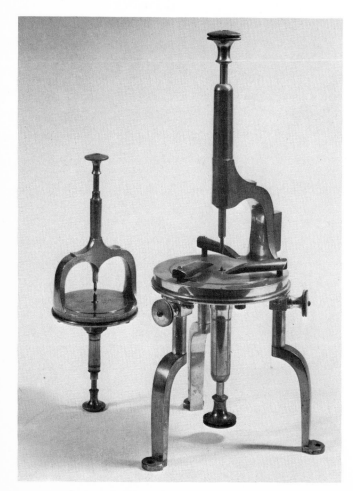

Before leaving printing in its association with things horological, the field of prints connected with clock- and watchmaking is an enormous one and makes a very interesting study. It can, for convenience, be divided up into categories according to the subject matter, and such a classification might have one section devoted to clockmakers' workshop scenes, another to portraits of the craftsmen themselves, a third to specific clocks, usually of the monumental kind, and finally a miscellaneous category for the oddments that do not fit easily into any of the first three. In the first of these classes there is a wide range of prints to be collected, from the famous Stradanus version of 1578, the earliest record of such an establishment, through various English and European depictions in the eighteenth century, and finishing perhaps with nineteenth-century photographs illustrating factory working in its early stages. In the second category, probably the best-known are the mezzotints made in the eighteenth century, usually copied from painted portraits, the originals of which have only in very few cases survived. There are about a dozen or so of these, including all the most eminent English craftsmen from Tompion and Graham to Arnold and Mudge.

The prints of monumental clocks are of great importance since they can show any changes that have been made superficially to the appearance of a surviving example. Mention has been made previously of prints of Richard Greene's Lichfield clock and Jacob Lovelace's Exeter clock, both being important in this respect. There are innumerable representations of the Strasbourg cathedral clock, and these may still be found for a reasonable price; but most horological prints of any substance in all categories have become rare and expensive of recent years, and they are perhaps best sought in places off the beaten track where the existence of a horological plate as one illustration, say, in a book about crafts and trades, would not be recognised as significant.

These are nineteenth-century chronometermakers' uprighting tools, which allow the craftsman to translate accurately the marking out of the pivot holes of his z movement from one plate to the other. The smaller tool bears the name of Charles Mill Frodsham.
right
A few of the commoner hand tools used by the craftsman at the bench, including pin tongs and vices, calipers of various designs, gauges, screw plates, and a Birch universal bench key, which will fit any size of a watch winding square. At the top is a fusee testing rod for watches, a stake for riveting verge balance wheels on to their arbors, and a special kind of small lathe for turning verge balance wheels.

252

Horological literature must play an ancillary role in any type of collecting in the field of clocks and watches; but the older works, long out of print, will be found only with difficulty, even from booksellers specialising in the subject, and they will be very expensive. There are plenty of modern works, however, which are useful to the student if not yet collectable for themselves, and some attempt has been made to outline these in the Further Reading lists (page 254). The bibliography on clocks and watches is vast, and now grows apace from year to year as a direct result of the growing enthusiasm for horological knowledge shown by ever-increasing numbers of people throughout the developed world. In the last year or two, there has been a movement by certain specialist publishers to produce facsimile reproductions of some of the rarest and most famous works on horology and, if it serves to bring such works to the hands of those who otherwise would never be able to aspire to the originals, then such action can only be applauded.

Finally, there remains one obvious field for the horological collector to consider, that of the tools of the trade. The first difficulty here is for the uninitiated collector to recognise a clock- or watchmaking tool if he meets one, unless he has first familiarised himself by spending time in a suitable workshop with the right kind of guidance at hand. Very many old tools, as they have been superseded, have been broken up for their brass content and, even to the present time, the occasional tool will turn up whose purpose puzzles the experts. The aspiring collector will keep a watchful eye open for any clockmaking or similar business that is being dispersed, in the hope of acquiring an old lathe, perhaps, or some useful hand tools; and he will clearly recognise that the best way to acclimatise himself to what such objects look like and are used for is to learn to handle them himself. Many tools were made, as part of their apprenticeship, by the craftsmen who subsequently used them. They will be found to have been beautifully worked, so that not only are they a joy to handle but also they are a pleasure simply to look at. Their shapes and intricacies often reflect the sheer excellence of the horological craft at its prime, and the student who formulates his approach to the subject only after a careful contemplation of the make-up and purpose of such objects as these is unlikely to go very far wrong in recognising the best in craft standards and thus eventually acquiring an intuitive appreciation for the quality of a piece which is so essential to the forming of any worthwhile collection.

Bibliography

FURTHER READING

General Books
Baillie, G. H., *Watches, their history, decoration and mechanism*, London, 1929.
Baillie, G. H., Cecil Clutton and Courtney A. Ilbert, *Britten's Old Clocks and Watches and their Makers*, 7th edition, London, 1956 (8th edition revised and enlarged by Clutton, London, 1973).
Bassermann-Jordan and Hans V. Bertelet, *Uhren*, Braunschweig, 1961.
Beckett, Sir Edmund, *A Rudimentary Treatise on Clocks and Watches and Bells*, London, various editions to 1903.
Bruton, Eric, *Clocks and Watches*, London, 1968.
Camerer Cuss, T. P., and T. A. Camerer Cuss, *The Camerer Cuss Book of Antique Watches*, Woodbridge, 1976.
Chamberlain, Paul, *It's About Time*, New York, 1941.
Cipolla, Carlo M., *Clocks and Culture: 1300–1700*, London, 1967.
Clutton, C., and George Daniels, *Watches*, London, 1965.
Defossez, L., *Les Savants du XVIIe Siècle et la Mesure du Temps*, Lausanne, 1946.
Gelif, Edouard, *L'Horlogerie Ancienne*, Paris, 1949.
Jagger, Cedric, *Clocks*, London, 1973. Revised edition, 1975.
Joy, Edward T., *The Country Life Book of Clocks*, London, 1967.
Lloyd, H. Alan, *Some Outstanding Clocks over Seven Hundred Years*, London, 1958.
Milham, Willis, *Time and Timekeepers*, New York, various editions from 1923.
Moore, N. Hudson, *The Old Clock Book*, 2nd edition, New York, 1936.
Pioneers of Precision Time-Keeping, a symposium by the Antiquarian Horological Society, London, n.d. (about 1962).
Robertson, J. Drummond, *The Evolution of Clockwork*, London, 1931.
Tallquist, Prof. H., *Uhren och Urteknikens Historia*, Helsinki, 1939.
Tyler, E. J., *European Clocks*, London, 1968.

Dictionaries, General and Technical
Britten, F. J., *Watch and Clockmakers' Handbook, Dictionary and Guide*, London, various editions from 1881.
Carle, D. de, *Watch and Clock Encyclopedia*, London, 1976.
Lloyd, H. Alan, *The Collector's Dictionary of Clocks*, London, 1964.

Technical Books
Carle, D. de, *Clock and Watch Repairing, including Complicated Watches*, London, 1974. This author has written a number of other technical books of value.
Gazeley, W. J., *Clock and Watch Escapements*, London, 1956.
Gazeley, W. J., *Clock and Watch Making and Repairing*, London, 1956.
Haswell, Eric, *Horology*, London, various editions from 1928.
Holtzapffel's Turning and Mechanical Manipulation, London, various editions to 1894.
Rawlings, A. L., *The Science of Clocks and Watches*, London, 1944.
Reid, Thomas, *Treatise on Clock and Watchmaking*, Edinburgh; 7 editions, 1826–1859.
Saunier, Claude, *Treatise on Modern Horology in Theory and Practice*, London, various editions from 1867.

Lists of Makers
In England there are already in print a number of lists by counties or large towns, and more appear every year. Neither Switzerland nor Germany has yet produced national lists of craftsmen though there are some local studies in the former and on Augsburg in the latter. America is well served, with representative lists of makers in most of the authoritative works, as well as a number of specialist studies, in particular covering the early manufacturers.
Baillie, G. H., *Watchmakers and Clockmakers of the World*, London, various editions to 1972.
Campos, J. L. Basanta, *Relojeros de España: Diccionario Bio-bibliográfico*, 1972.
Chenakal, V. L., *Watchmakers and Clockmakers in Russia: 1400 1850*, London, 1972.
Loomes, B. *Watchmakers and Clockmakers of the World*, vol. 2, London, 1976. (For vol. 1 see under G. H. Baillie above.)
Morpurgo, E., *Dizionario degli Orologiai Italiani 1300–1800*, 1950.
Morpurgo, E., *Nederlandse Klokken en Horlogemakers*, 1970.
Peate, I. C. *Clock and Watchmakers in Wales*, Cardiff, 1960.
Smith, J., *Old Scottish Clockmakers from 1453 to 1850*, Wakefield, 197 .
Sidenbladh, Elis, *Urmakare i Sverige*, Stockholm, 1947.
Tardy, *Dictionnaire des Horologers Français*, Paris, 1972.

INDIVIDUAL MAKERS
Daniels, George, *The Art of Breguet*, London, 1975.
Ditisheim, Lallier, Reverchon and Vivielle, *Pierre Le Roy et la Chronométre*, Paris, 1940.
Hawkins, J. B., *Thomas Cole and Victorian Clockmaking*, Sydney, 1975.
Jagger, Cedric, *Paul Philip Barraud*, London, 1968.
Lee, R. A., The Knibb Family – Clockmakers, London, 1964.
Mercer, Vaudrey, *John Arnold & Son*, London, 1972
Quill, Humphrey, *John Harrison – The Man Who Found Longitude*, London, 1966.
Salomons, David, *Breguet*, London, 1921 (French edition 1923).
Shenton, Rita, *Christopher Pinchbeck*, Ashford, 1976.
Symonds, R. W., *Thomas Tompion, His Life and Work*, London, 1951.

INDIVIDUAL COUNTRIES
England
Beeson, C. F. C., *English Church Clocks 1280–1850*, London, 1971.
Goamen, Muriel, *English Clocks*, London, 1967.
France
Tardy, *La Pendule Française des origines à nos jours*, Paris, various editions to the present time.
Edey, Winthrop. *French Clocks*, London, 1967.
Japan
Hyoe Takabayashi, *Tokei Hattatsu-shi* ('Development of Clocks'), 1927.
Mody, N. H. N., *Japanese Clocks*, original limited edition of 200 copies, London, 1932 (facsimile reprint, London, 1968).
Rambaut, A. A., *Notes on Some Japanese Clocks*, Dublin, 1889.
Switzerland
Jaquet, E., and Alfred Chapuis, *Histoire et Technique de la Montre Suisse*, Basle, 1945 (English edition, London, 1970).
United States of America
Daniels, G., *English and American Watches*, London, 1967.
Palmer, Brooks, *A Treasury of American Clocks*, New York, 1967.
Palmer, Brooks, *The Book of American Clocks*, New York, 1974.

Types of Clock and Watch
Allix, Charles, and Peter Bonnert, *Carriage Clocks – Their History and Development*, Woodbridge, 1974.
Bain, Alexander, *A Short History of the Electric Clock, With Explanations*, London, 1852.
Bruton, Eric, *The Grandfather Clock*, London. 2nd Edit.
Chapuis, A., and Eugène Jaquet, *The History of the Self-Winding Watch 1770–1931*, Geneva, 1956.
Coole, P. G., and E. Neumann, *The Orpheus Clock*, London, 1972.
Edwardes, Ernest L., *The Grandfather Clock*, Altrincham, 1971.
Edwardes, Ernest L., *Weight-driven Chamber Clocks of the Middle Ages and Renaissance*, Altrincham, 1965.
Gould, Lt-Cdr R. T., *The Marine Chronometer*, London, 1923.
Hope-Jones, F., *Electrical Timekeeping*, London, 1940 (recently reproduced in facsimile).
Mortensen, Otto, *Jens Olsen's Clock*, Copenhagen, 1957.
Needham, Joseph, Derek Price and Wang Ling, *Heavenly Clockwork*, Cambridge, 1960.
Royer-Collard, F. B., *Skeleton Clocks*, London, 1969.

Exhibition and Collection Catalogues
This is only a tiny selection of English catalogues. Many museums round the world have published literature on their own collections.
Art-Journal Illustrated Catalogue to the Industry of All Nations, The, Great Exhibition catalogue, London, 1851.
Britten, F. J., *Old English Clocks – The Wetherfield Collection*, London, 1907.
Clutton, C., and George Daniels, *Clocks and Watches in the Collection of the Worshipful Company of Clockmakers*, London, 1975.
Ilbert Collection of Clocks, Catalogue of the, London, 1958: printed by Christie's as a sale catalogue, but not issued as the collection was bought privately for the British Museum.
Lee, Ronald, A., *The First Twelve Years of the English Pendulum Clock*, exhibition catalogue, London, 1969.
Tait, Hugh, *Clocks in the British Museum*, London, 1968.

Bibliographies
Baillie, G. H., *Clocks and Watches – An Historical Bibliography*, London, 1951.
Tardy, *Bibliographie Générale de la Mesure du Temps*, Paris, 1943.

Related Subjects
Chapuis, A., and Edmond Droz, *Automata – a Historical and Technological Study*, Neuchatel, 1958.
Cousins, Frank W., *Sundials*, London, 1969.
Goodison, N., *English Barometers 1680–1860*, London, 1969.
Gunther, R. T., *Early Science in Oxford*, Oxford, 1923.
Michel, Henri, *Scientific Instruments*, London, 1967.
Smith, G. H., and E. R. Smith, *Watch Keys as Jewelry*, New York, 1967.
Tardy, *Les Coqs de Montre*, Paris, n.d.

Horological Societies
Antiquarian Horological Society, New House, High Street, Ticehurst, Wadhurst, Sussex TN5 7AL, England.
Freunde Alter Uhren (President: Prof. Dr Richard Mühe), 7743 Furtwangen, Ilbenstrasse 54, Germany.
National Association of Clock and Watch Collectors, P.O. Box 33, Columbia (Pa) 17512, USA.

There are also comparable bodies in France and Switzerland. The American organisation is both the oldest and the largest: 30,000 members at the last count, and it has been in existence well over thirty years. The British society, next in order of seniority and with the more serious-minded approach to the subject, to judge by its literary output, was founded in 1953 and has something over 4000 members. It is also the most cosmopolitan, having a membership spread throughout the world, while the other organisations in the field tend to be more local. Each of the three bodies listed arrange foreign horological tours for their members from time to time, to take in museums and private collections outside their own countries. These and other events add a social dimension, to leaven what is fundamentally an academic and research-orientated interest.

Index

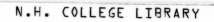